MEN IN REBELLION

MEN IN REBELLION

Higher Governmental Leaders and the Coming of the American Revolution

---

JAMES KIRBY MARTIN

RUTGERS UNIVERSITY PRESS

NEW BRUNSWICK · NEW JERSEY

Copyright © 1973 by Rutgers University, the State University of New Jersey

Library of Congress Cataloging in Publication Data

Martin, James Kirby, 1943–
  Men in rebellion.

  Bibliography: p.
  1. United States—Politics and government—
Colonial period.   I. Title.
E188.M37   973.3'11   72-14142
ISBN 0-8135-0750-2

Manufactured in the United States of America

Portions of this book appeared in "A Model for the Coming American Revolution: The Birth and Death of the Wentworth Oligarchy in New Hampshire, 1741–
1776," Vol. IV, No. 1, *Journal of Social History,* and in "Men of Family Wealth
and Personal Merit: The Changing Social Basis of Executive Leadership in the
American Revolution," *Societas—A Review of Social History* 2 (1972).

For Karen

Contents

Tables

Charts

Preface

HISTORIANS have debated and argued about the causes of the American Revolution for nearly two centuries. More properly, perhaps, students of the Revolution have sought to identify and explain (among other problems) the reasons why provincial Americans, nurtured for over a century and a half under the seemingly benevolent guidance of Great Britain, threw off attachments to British sovereignty during the mid-1770s. It is the main purpose of this study to offer another, and, it is hoped, *complementary* set of reasons as to why that split occurred. My conclusion is that the coming of the American Revolution resulted from a structural crisis in power and political placement among leaders in the colonies making up the late provincial political elite. My statements grow out of a collective biographical analysis of the lives and political careers of high officials resident in late colonial and early revolutionary governments. It is not my purpose to argue that mine is the only correct interpretation. As a historian my goal has been to supplement rather than to supplant what other treatments have concluded.

One cry from younger scholars today is that older historians have been negligent in investigating America's "inarticulate," those common and less than common people who left no verbal or written record of their thoughts and actions. Yet the same statement must be made about the study of socioeconomic and political elites. It is my opinion that historians of the American Revolution have brushed over leadership elites. The tacit assumption in so many studies has been that elites simply did not exist. But the assumption here, based on the data that follow, is that elites did exist and greatly influenced the process of revolution. It is time, then, that we come to grips with the needs, wants, and expectations of those few individuals who most enjoyed power, privilege, prestige, and community standing in the early American political arena. Such men were in the position to make decisions and to lead the general populace in rebellion. There was no malicious plot or conspiracy on their part to bring about revolution and a declaration of independence. Such sentiment developed very slowly and only after it became clear that the mother country would continue to frustrate the expectations of men in the political elite. Accordingly, we need to consider what factors moved some within the political elite to open rebellion, that is in relation to other elite leaders who found it difficult if not impossible to sever all ties with Great Britain. The drive to satisfy the wants and expectations of elite leaders gave the first stages of revolution its true form and character.

In another vein, academicians are fortunate in that they exist in a community of scholarship which supports rather than suppresses full and ample discussion of divergent viewpoints. Moreover, professors are fortunate in that they have friends and colleagues with whom they may exchange ideas freely. This manuscript has benefited immensely from such interchange. Knowledgeable and thoughtful individuals have met with the author at various stages of the manuscript's development, offering not just criticisms but suggestions which vastly improved the content of this study. To each of those listed here I owe a real debt, not only for their thoughts but also for their willingness to take time from busy schedules to assist the author. If this manuscript has merit, it is the product of the efforts of Professors Merrill Jensen, Norman K. Risjord, Morton Rothstein, Stanley I. Kutler, Robert F. Berkhofer, Jr., Carl E. Prince, Peter N. Stearns, Richard P. McCormick, Lloyd Gardner, Gerald N. Grob, Philip J. Greven, Jr., and J. William Gillette. The author must accept responsibility for faults. I too must acknowledge the efforts of Professor Lawrence Landweber of the University of Wisconsin Computer Sciences department who programmed the data. The tables appearing in the text represent a sampling of the some twelve hundred tables from which Professor Landweber's program allowed me to select.

At the same time I willingly thank many other individuals and organizations: students Denis Girard and Mark E. Lender who suggested more in conversations than perhaps they realized; librarians at the University of Wisconsin, the Wisconsin State Historical Society, and Rutgers University who aided the author by searching out and obtaining sources containing biographical information about long-forgotten leaders; individuals on the Wisconsin Alumni Research Council who provided funding for computer costs; colleagues on the Rutgers University Faculty Research Council who not only supported the author during a summer when further research was necessary but who also awarded a grant to cover the costs of typing the final manuscript; editors of the *Journal of Social History* and *Societas—A Review of Social History* who granted permission to reprint materials here that originally appeared in somewhat different form in the pages of their journals; Mrs. Harold Meinkoth who carefully typed various manuscript drafts; and my wife Karen who offered comfort, aid, editorial assistance, and tolerance.

JAMES KIRBY MARTIN

New Brunswick, New Jersey
October 1972

"Last Thursday Morning March 3d. [1774] died Andrew Oliver Esquire Lieutenant Governor. This is but the second death which has happened among the Conspirators, the original Conspirators against the Public Liberty, since the Conspiracy was first regularly formed, and begun to be executed, in 1763 or 4."

—JOHN ADAMS, Diary entry of March 6, 1774. A prominent lesser official in Massachusetts commenting on the deeds and death of a well-known higher official.

MEN IN REBELLION

CHAPTER ONE

Introduction: Who Ruled in Late Colonial America?

I

SINCE THOSE years when the American Revolution drew to a close, historians—both professionally trained scholars and interested laymen—have pondered, reflected, and written about the causes and consequences of that momentous sequence of events. Most commentators have tried to escape from the miasma of myth surrounding the colonists' liberation from England; rather they have focused on more fundamental questions than those of purely antiquarian and patriotic interest. Several basic questions have been debated: What caused the American Revolution? Was the Revolution the product of conflicting principles or conflicting interests between Great Britain and her upstart colonies? What is the proper point of departure in understanding the causal pattern? What about the effects of the Revolution? Did the movement produce drastic changes in social and political relationships among the former colonists? Did common people emerge from the Revolution with more power and authority than they had known under British sovereignty? Or did the Revolution refine and institutionalize previous patterns of middle-class equalitarianism in eighteenth-century America? Such questions seem relatively uncomplicated, but answers have become increasingly convoluted. Scholars have constructed elaborate arguments, have begun historiographical controversies, and have even resorted to slurs and name-calling, all in the pursuit of the elusive goddess of finality and truth. The consequence of so many conflicting interpretations has been that the original point of scholarly exegesis (the concern with assessing the nature and the significance of the American Revolution) more than once has been lost in the shuffle of facts, opinions, and hypotheses.

Perhaps the problem is that the American Revolution has been overstudied. Having stated that, it would seem contradictory to argue that interpretations of the causes and immediate consequences of the American Revolution were incomplete. (In fact, the likelihood is that interpretations will never be complete.) Yet the primary purpose of this study is to explore a heretofore neglected dimension of the causal pattern of the Revolution with the hope that it will shed light for the ongoing scholarly quest to understand all aspects of that movement. My purpose is to make explanations more complete.

The materials that follow favor no one historiographical camp, but they seek to build upon the insights of the well-known schools of thought. Thus my concern is with the *process* of rebellion as it related to the consequences of revolution for the national period of United States history. Three fundamental questions dominate in the text: Why did some men rebel against the authority of Great Britain when others did not? What motivated the insurgents? What were the effects of their actions in terms of political and social developments growing out of the revolutionary process?

Issues, events, and ideologies do not represent the point of departure in research design. Rather my decision was to analyze (using standard methods of collective biography) the characteristics of the lives and the political careers of a large number of major political figures involved in the process of coming revolution. Having discovered common patterns in the lives and political fortunes of such men, patterns relating to the needs, expectations, aspirations, and frustrations of specific groups within the late colonial political elite, my contention is that the question of who ruled in late colonial America is central to deciphering the nature and the course of the revolutionary experience in America.

II

One standard assumption of scholars of early American history has been that the organization of prerevolutionary socioeconomic and political relationships affected the causal tone of revolution. Historians writing in different historiographical traditions have viewed colonial society in contradictory terms, and interpretations of the coming Revolution have changed as research about the nature of prerevolutionary America alters conceptions of that society. Thus it is necessary to look at historiographical patterns so as to gain an accurate perception of the importance of leadership elite analysis for a more complete comprehension of the causal chain of rebellion.

The beginnings of interpretive polarization about the nature of prerevolutionary society date to the early years of the twentieth century when a young and brilliant scholar, Carl Lotus Becker, published his study of *The History of Political Parties in the Province of New York, 1760–1776.* Becker may be credited with founding the "Progressive" or "conflict" tradition in revolutionary historiography. He claimed that the split between England and the American colonies gained momentum just as much from the desires of those common citizens who wanted to democratize American society as from the desires of those who wanted to sever ties with Great Britain. The Revolution thus emerged as two problems: "The first was whether essential colonial rights should be maintained; the second was by whom and by what methods they should be maintained. The first was the question of home rule; the second was the question, if we may so put it, of who should rule at home." [1] To Becker the impetus toward revolution came from an internal contest between the upper and lower classes in colonial society, between those having political authority and those having none, between an aristocracy controlling politics and an increasingly conscious class of democratic citizens demanding a larger voice in the affairs of state. The latter were carrying the day by 1776 and were setting a new democratic tone in American political development.

For Becker and those other historians stressing the role of a rising commonalty of citizens insisting upon greater political rights, the working assumption was that of upper-class control of the agencies of political decision-making. Moreover, the upper classes remained insensitive as well as unresponsive to the needs of the lower orders in society. The pattern could not have been otherwise if the Revolution had overtones of internal class conflict. [2]

When Becker analyzed political factionalism and related it to individual and group behavior, he predicated his findings on the assumption that New York was anything but an equalitarian and fluid middle-class society. He divided New York's citizenry into three highly stratified classes. The great landholding families—the Livingstons, Schuylers, Morrises, De Lanceys, Van Cortlandts, Philipses, and others—were at the top of the socioeconomic structure. They owned vast manorial estates numbering in the thousands of acres, and many of their progeny controlled internal and external commerce as wealthy merchant princes. The middle class of citizens were freemen in towns and freeholders in the countryside (those with franchise rights). Certainly more numerous than members of the great families, the middle class of voting citizens represented less than one half of New York's population. The third and lowest class of inhabitants were individuals who as freehold farmers did not own enough property to qualify for enfranchisement, who as tenants on the great manors lived meagerly and eked out existences with all the overtones of serfdom, and who as drifters and unskilled laborers resided in the towns but did not have enough money at any one time to purchase freemanship status (the mark of the enfranchised).[3]

Becker did not deal with the problem of fluidity or mobility in the class structure. His concern had to do with the effects that inequitable property distribution and stratified classes had upon the operation of New York politics. His conclusion was that the great families, represented by the names De Lancey and Livingston, dominated the political structure and offices in prerevolutionary New York. The mass of citizens, by comparison, were not enfranchised and had few outlets for political expression. The Livingstons and the De Lanceys fought as family-oriented factions in the lower house of the Assembly seeking to control the distribution of socioeconomic and political rewards for the dominant clan. Average citizens, lacking fundamental political rights, rarely had their needs verbalized or represented in political decision-making.[4]

But the nature of New York politics changed dramatically after the end of the Seven Years' War when Great Britain sought to implement its "new" imperial programs. The mass of heretofore "inarticulate," unheard, and politically deprived inhabitants turned to mass meetings, mob violence, and group suppression in thwarting ministerial schemes like the Stamp Act and the Townshend duties. Originally, political leaders from the great families who opposed ministerial plans stirred the masses. Ironically though, the citizenry, once moved to action, did not retreat into its original state of political impotence. Popular leaders emerged who turned the threat of mob activity against the great families themselves and led inhabitants in their demands for broader political rights. The great families had hatched a monster that was now returning to haunt them. Becker summarized the process as follows: The Revolution turned out to be much more than a "contest for home-rule and independence"; it speeded up the process leading toward "democratization of American politics and society." [5]

It was Becker's analysis of what he thought to be the highly stratified New York social structure that led to the formulation of his classic thesis. It was a society in which a wide chasm existed between the favored families on top and the mass of unenfranchised citizens on the bottom. It was a society in which less than half of the free white adult males had the right to vote, or so Becker estimated.[6] It was a society, given the imbalance in property distribution, that was ripe for class conflict. When Great Britain introduced its new imperial plans after 1763, the ministry injected the catalytic agent leading to conflict among the classes and eventually to a greater degree of democracy than had previously been known in New York. Becker stated the question simply: "Who should rule at home?" Was it to be the favored few from the great families, or was it to be the commonalty of citizens? Ending his study with collapsing British authority, Becker concluded (but did not demonstrate) that the common inhabitants were on the verge of overwhelming the upper class and taking control of New York's political machinery.[7]

The "Progressive" internal class conflict approach to rising revolutionary fervor served as a model for historians until after the end of World War II when a younger generation of historians asserted that middle-class democracy was the norm in prerevolutionary America. The "consensus" or "Neo-Whig" historiographical mood relied heavily on the assumption that landholding opportunities were widespread and that surprisingly high numbers of free white adult males had franchise rights (a function of property distribution). The relationship between the less stratified vision of late colonial society and the causal pattern of revolution perhaps received its most thorough treatment in Robert E. Brown's *Middle-Class Democracy and the Revolution in Massachusetts, 1691–1780*.[8] Brown constructed his assumptions upon the general availability of virgin land in Massachusetts and the other American provinces. Abundant land produced an open and egalitarian socioeconomic structure with little potential for class consciousness or class conflict. Hardy and industrious individuals migrating to Massachusetts had no trouble in acquiring titles to land—its availability held prices down. Determined individuals went to work, cleared off timber, and within a short number of years produced enough foodstuffs to pay off any outstanding debts contracted in acquiring property titles. Soon the average freehold farmer accrued enough acreage and personal wealth to meet requirements for voting. Thus individual economic opportunity resulting in political rights, as Becker implied, was not lacking for the majority of citizens. The unlimited supply of land in the New World served as the formative agent in the creation of a large middle class. As Brown put it: "It makes a tremendous difference in our understanding of colonial society whether 95 per cent of the men were disfranchised or only 5 per cent." [9]

Difference, indeed, it did make in Brown's hypothesis about the coming Revolution. If the mass of citizens worked freehold farms, if they belonged to a broad-scale middle class, and if the free white adult men had political rights, then why, Brown reasoned, would internal class tensions have occurred in the dynamics of revolution? Why would anyone assert the importance of a rising democracy when socioeconomic and political democracy already had risen across the land? There had to be some alternative explanation, then, to internal class conflict in delineating the process of revolution.

Brown argued that his archetype citizen, the middle-class democrat, saw new ministerial policies after the Seven Years' War as a threat to the open reality of colonial society. When the Crown after 1763 attempted to cut into the known rights of American citizens, approving such acts as fixing the number of districts to be represented in the lower house of the General Court, thereby barring new frontier communities from having representatives in the Assembly, colonists perceived that the Crown was corrupting what Americans held most dear—their open and democratic socioeconomic and political environment. Massachusetts men would not stand idly by and let the London ministers strip them of the good society. Eventually embattled farmers took up muskets, went to war, and fought "a revolution to preserve a social order rather than to change it." [10] According to Brown and other "consensus" historians, Americans were united, not torn by class tensions, in the common cause to protect their rights, liberties, and way of life. What the pattern specifically meant to Brown was that the coming Revolution had not been a problem "of attaining a democratic society but of keeping the democracy they [American colonists] had, a democracy threatened by British imperialism." [11]

III

Several other scholars joined Brown in the search through local records in attempting to determine how many individuals could vote in eighteenth-century America. Chilton Williamson combined many such research efforts and estimated that between 50 and 75 per cent of all white adult males had voting rights before the Revolution.[12] Since citizens had to fulfill a variety of colony-wide requirements based on wealth and landholding, the logical conclusion was that large numbers of male colonists had accumulated at least a minimal degree of economic stature in the New World. Economic opportunity, therefore, was relatively widespread. But the misleading tendency has been to conclude from this progression of information that Americans had achieved political democracy based upon economic opportunity and franchise privileges. Any equation among these three variables is much too simplistic to demonstrate with finality that American politics operated democratically before, during, or after the Revolution.

The range of significant variables in the contemporary paradigm of political democracy does much more than treat voting rights as the critical factor in measuring levels of democracy in political systems. The paradigm implies some citizen voice in candidate nomination as well as choice in candidate type; it presumes that elected officials are sensitive to public opinion (if the public has any sense of issues and thought is not being manipulated by political leaders); it suggests that politicians know that their tenure in office will be short unless they work to fulfill verbalized constituency wishes; it means that citizens are highly politicized, understand the real difference between candidates and between issues, and that citizens use their franchise rights rationally as the final arbiter in the process of political decision-making. Few, if any, of these ramifications of political democracy are completely operative in today's political world, let alone were they operative in the eighteenth century when "democracy" conjured up entirely different images in the minds of politically informed and educated citizens.[13]

Recently many historians of various historiographical persuasions have emphasized that the eighteenth-century definition of "democracy" referred to one of three general socioeconomic orders (or classes of citizens) in functioning societies. The *demos* was the general order of common citizens; they needed to have their interests represented in at least one branch of government to give balance in decision-making and to act as a check upon the potential excesses of the two higher socioeconomic orders—the monarchy and the aristocracy. According to the most enlightened (though still medieval in overtone) political science of the times, the English constitution embodied the quintessence of mixed government, blending and balancing the three social orders of the monarchy, the aristocracy, and the democracy into the three working branches of government, represented in the King, the House of Lords, and the House of Commons. Students of politics feared an imbalance in authority among the orders. Men argued that too much monarchical domination without proper aristocratic and democratic checks in the other functioning branches of government had the dangerous potential to destroy liberties and to lead the body politic in tyrannical directions. The will of an uncontrolled and arbitrary monarch would eventually subvert the basic political rights and liberties of the aristocracy and the democracy. Yet too much power in the hands of the democracy had the equally disrupting effect of forcing the body politic in anarchical directions. An imbalance in favor of the democracy would result in "riots and tumults" as citizens fought with one another to control scarce socioeconomic rewards, such as property, social position, or even raw power itself. Too much democracy, furthermore, would produce in inexorable fashion a swing of the pendulum back toward aristocratic and/or monarchical domination so as to end popular excesses and to once again give peace and order to the political realm. In clocklike, rhythmic fashion, then, the most stable governments carefully balanced the social orders of democracy, aristocracy, and monarchy to avoid the extremes of tyranny or anarchy and to guarantee that the rights and liberties of all citizens would be protected.[14]

Thus the hierarchical conception of balanced government circumscribed the political authority of common citizens by limiting them to direct representation in only one of the three accepted branches of government. So long as conceptions of balanced government persisted, the democracy, even if it had the right to vote and to elect representatives, had a strictly confined voice in political decision-making. It was either proscription or anarchy.[15]

By the early part of the eighteenth century, moreover, well-read and politically sophisticated American colonists were discussing the similarities between the working parts of their provincial governments and the English model. Using somewhat faulty and tenuous logic, some American leaders claimed that governors represented and substituted for the monarchy; councilors forming the upper houses in Assemblies and serving as advisers to governors represented and substituted for the aristocracy; delegates to the lower houses in Assemblies represented the general citizenry (the democracy).[16] The analogy was far from perfect. There was no resident titled nobility in the provinces, yet individual and family wealth did serve as the basis of distinction between the "lower sort" and the higher orders in the colonial social structure. Prospering provincials, those forming the upper class, came to believe that it was their inherited right (in the absence of titled aristocrats) to control upper-hierarchy offices (referring to governors, councilors, and other high administrative, legislative, and judicial positions). If lesser citizens with little means gained too many upper-hierarchy offices, then there would be too much popular participation and the threat of anarchy. Ultimately all citizens would lose the known liberties of Englishmen as poorer men turned the interests of the political community to their private ends. Hence the upper class needed to control high political offices if balance was to be maintained and the political liberties of all men were to be protected and preserved.

The theory of mixed government, assuming an indivisible relationship between leadership in state and society, had the effect of weakening the overall efficacy of voting rights as the real arbiter in leadership selection and political decision-making. If the democracy of common citizens, for example, had a direct voice in the selection of upper-hierarchy officials, then the citizenry might attempt to take control of the branches reserved for upper-class gentlemen. Conveniently, most upper-hierarchy offices in most colonies were appointive, and therefore out of the domain of citizen control. When British home officials instructed their royal governors that "in the choice and nomination of the members of our said council as also of the chief officers, judges, assistants, justices and sheriffs, you are always to take care that they be men of good life and well affected to our government and of good estates and abilities and not necessitous persons or much in debt," the ministry wanted the "better sort" of men in high offices, not those of the democracy.[17] The purpose of the standing instruction was to weld men of wealth and social prominence to the interests of imperial administration. The immediate effect of the instruction, however, was to guarantee upper-hierarchy colonial offices to those men who substituted for the titled nobility in America, men of great wealth and high standing. The better sort of citizens were to give balance to colonial governments by making their presence felt in high provincial offices.[18] Such men had an independent hand, given the appointive nature of upper-hierarchy offices, and would not have to grovel to the masses and subvert the liberties of many for particular interests.

Not only did the eighteenth-century definition and meaning of democracy circumscribe the role of common citizens in politics, but so did commonly held "deferential" attitudes. Historian J.R. Pole emphasized that common citizens deferred to the better sort of gentlemen (measured by wealth, occupation, birth, and social standing) in political leadership. Citizens assumed that such men should hold provincial offices, if not all offices.[19] Wealthy and prominent men were less likely to be *corrupted* by power and to turn the public trust to private advantage. Like wise parents, the upper class had the breadth of knowledge and experience to guide and direct decision-making for their children. Like obedient children, the lower classes dutifully needed to follow the advice of their elders. Citizens were to be seen, but they were not necessarily to take an active part in the political process. Their betters already knew how to apply their wisdom in making reasonable decisions affecting the whole body politic. One colonial Virginian pungently summarized deferential assumptions relating to leadership in state and society: "It is right that men of *birth and fortune,* in every government that is free, should be invested with power, and enjoy higher honors than the people. If it were otherwise, their privileges would be less, and they would not enjoy an equal degree of liberty with the people." [20]

Suffrage rights had little impact on the colonial political process, then, when even elective Assembly "contests were almost invariably between members of the gentry," as J.R. Pole observed.[21] Even when citizens could vote for candidates, such as for assemblymen, their role in decision-making was constricted by the deferential norm. Common people were not supposed to represent themselves in office. The result was that upper-class citizens controlled Assembly seats in many provinces, besides dominating in upper-hierarchy appointive offices. Colonial political attitudes favored upper-class citizens and assigned to them the responsibilities of political leadership. Average citizens, even those with voting rights, stood on the perimeters of the political arena and let their socioeconomic superiors wield political authority.[22]

Thus the deferential norm contradicted (the democracy was to depend upon the stewardship of upper-class citizens in lower houses) but reinforced hierarchical assumptions. The better sort were to rule through innate wisdom and justice on all levels of government, given their superior qualities in personal wealth, education, and social standing.[23] It would be illogical to conclude that elected representatives in Assemblies felt compelled to put all constituency demands into law, given notions about the greater wisdom of the better sort and the anarchical potential of grasping common citizens. It also would be illogical to conclude that the provinces were open political environments in which citizens and leaders met freely to exchange ideas and to formulate policies. Historians need more evidence than percentages about widespread franchise rights and significant numbers of "middle-class" farmers to demonstrate that the colonies were little democracies. One would have to prove that political elites predicated upon socioeconomic standing neither existed nor believed in their right to rule, despite overwhelming evidence establishing the importance of deferential and hierarchical attitudes underpinning the acknowledged prerogative of the better sort to control offices and decision-making in prerevolutionary America.[24]

IV

Recent findings about deferential and hierarchical assumptions suggest that no meaningful equation may be drawn between economic opportunity, franchise rights, and popularly based political democracies. But such findings do indicate that systematic knowledge about the lives and characteristics of those who made up the provincial political elites would be of great value. General statements abound, but systematic analysis has been long in coming and now may be the product of the quantitative "revolution" in historical methodology. Several years ago, for instance, Professor Leonard W. Labaree stressed in reference to upper-hierarchy offices that "well-stabilized ruling groups" had emerged in each American colony in the eighteenth century, if not long before in particular cases. Committed to the proposition that they should rule, the political elites consisted of individuals "who by inheritance or acquisition owned the largest estates, had the best family connections, and most firmly supported the existing political system, be that system royal or proprietary province or self-governing Puritan colony." [25] Yet few have ventured to study political elites, or what is more important, to relate elite behavior to the process of revolution.[26]

The reasons for such reluctance are not hard to establish. Elite analysis lies beyond the concern of major historiographical schools. Historians writing in the "Progressive" tradition concentrated upon the process whereby the masses gained in political authority through the Revolution. Although certainly aware of the importance of elites in the distribution of political power, such historians sought to uncover the pattern by which the people overcame their generally oppressive rulers and established democracy in America. Such an emphasis, though with different ends than understanding the production of democracy, pervades even today in the writings of leftist historians who come to the Revolution with a vision of studying it "from the bottom up." [27] This is not meant to argue that the needs and wants of common citizens are unimportant or illegitimate historical interests. There is no doubt or question about that. But whether a rising commonalty was central to the revolutionary process is another question.

Those writing in the "consensus" historiographical tradition, on the other hand, have muted the presence or possible importance of socioeconomic and political elites by emphasizing the unity of American citizens on the eve of revolution. Rejecting "Progressive" propositions about a highly stratified and internally torn society, these historians have stressed harmony among provincials based upon what they see as the middle-class character of society. Middle-class citizens were unified in thwarting the British threat and in building the principles and ideals over which Americans went to war into their new political systems. Elites simply have no place in "consensus" historiography.[28]

Yet even middle-class societies may be dominated in the distribution of political authority by political elites consisting of the favored few. Given the importance of deferential and hierarchical attitudes in prerevolutionary America, it seems only logical to begin a more thorough examination of provincial political elites while studying the possibility that the needs and expectations of those in the elite played a crucial role in the process making for the American Revolution. Systematic inquiry about the political elite (what some might label as "history from the top down"), then, is the jumping-off point for the ensuing investigation of the causes and consequences of the coming revolution in America after the end of the Seven Years' War.

To facilitate the analysis of leaders confronting a state of political disequilibrium, the data below explore the lives and political careers of 487 men intimately involved with the destruction of old and the formation of new governments. Specifically, all those men who served as governors, lieutenant governors, secretaries, treasurers, attorneys general, chief justices and associate judges of superior or supreme courts, and councilors from the thirteen colonies who were in office just before the final disruption of old governments are compared to the new group of revolutionary leaders who took over these same offices when new state governments began to function in 1776 or 1777. In exact numbers 231 men filled the 267 offices listed above in the thirteen colonies during 1773 and/or 1774, depending upon the time of the collapse of particular provincial governments.[29] This group includes a hard core of governing officials who according to hierarchical conceptions represented the monarchy and the aristocracy (untitled men of wealth and stature) in colonial governments. For the sake of brevity and convenience, we may refer to these officeholders and their revolutionary counterparts as "executives," even though judges hardly qualify under that term.[30]

Of the 231 late colonial executives, only fifty-two of them survived the onslaught of revolution and managed to retain some executive political office. Thus there was an overall turnover rate in executive leadership of 77.5 per cent, an unusually high rate in such a short period of time given the general pattern of lengthy tenure in office during stable political times in eighteenth-century England and America.[31] The fifty-two men who retained some executive office joined 256 new executives in an expanded range of the same offices, specifically 308 men holding 337 positions from New Hampshire to South Carolina. (Georgia is not included in the collection of revolutionary states because that province did not have an enduring revolutionary government until the 1780s.) [32] This analysis, then, represents the history of 487 executive leaders holding 604 offices under both British and American sovereignty. Some of the men have familiar names, but many do not.[33]

Cross tabulations of measurable characteristics are the main thrust in establishing similarities and differences among the executive leaders. The combined group of 487 men may be broken down into three subgroups: the late colonial executives (231 men), the loyalist executives (134 men), and the revolutionary executives (308 men). The loyalist subgroup permits the evaluation of the characteristics of those who most adamantly opposed revolutionary activity, as compared to the late colonial and revolutionary subgroups. Cross-tabulated comparisons were run according to a whole range of standard variables, including occupations, levels of personal and family wealth, social origins, kinship ties, educational experiences, religious affiliations, ages, and places of birth.

Before turning to the problem of turnover and change and to the question why men rebel as it related to the American Revolution, however, one final point must be emphasized. The late colonial executives averaged 10.6 years in office before they fell from power, an average that would have been higher had not the coming Revolution cut their tenure short. The revolutionary executives averaged 5.9 years, representing a consecutive average for the two groups of 16.5 years (Table 1.1). Taking 1776 as the median year of turnover, the combined executive political elite was just coming to power when Parliament revoked the Stamp Act and approved the Declaratory Act and was just leaving office when General George Washington and his French allies defeated the redcoat forces of Lord Charles Cornwallis at Yorktown.

Table 1.1

*Average Years in Office of Late Colonial
and Revolutionary Executives*

Office	Late Colonial (Number)	Average	Revolutionary (Number)	Average
Governors	(12)	7.17	(9)	7.22
Lieutenant Governors	(4)	7.75	(4)	7.50
Secretaries	(13)	17.92	(12)	12.50
Treasurers	(16)	10.50	(19)	6.11
Attorneys General	(14)	8.50	(14)	6.14
Chief Justices	(12)	7.83	(14)	6.64
Associate Judges	(44)	7.14	(49)	9.71
Councilors / Senators	(152)	11.82	(216)	4.47
CUMULATIVE AVERAGE	(267)	10.64	(337)	5.88

Thus we are considering the lives and public careers of a large number of men who fought for and against the coming of the Revolution, as well as the lives of men who carried the revolution from its first phase to the conclusion of its military stage before the matter of creating a stronger national government overwhelmed the sages of Confederation America. Although much more in terms of leadership analysis remains to be done, the data that follow deal with the lives of men who were as instrumental as any group in molding the revolutionary experience, a point which becomes more obvious when the examination of public careers shows that at least 50 per cent of the revolutionary executives were in the lower houses of colonial Assemblies just before the old order vanished. Many such men were actively leading opposition to the acts of Parliament and the attempts of their late colonial counterparts in executive offices to implement Parliamentary legislation. The tensions between the two groups help us to understand why some were about to become men in rebellion.

Chapter One: Notes

[1] (Madison, 1909), p. 22. Actually Charles H. Lincoln published similar arguments before Becker in *The Revolutionary Movement in Pennsylvania, 1760–1776,* University of Pennsylvania Publications in History no. 1 (Philadelphia, 1901).

[2] Critical volumes written in the "Progressive" framework, besides Becker and Lincoln, include Carl Bridenbaugh, *Cities in Revolt: Urban Life in America, 1743–1776* (New York, 1955); Elisha P. Douglass, *Rebels and Democrats: The Struggle for Equal Rights and Majority Rule during the American Revolution* (Chapel Hill, 1955); J. Franklin Jameson, *The American Revolution Considered as a Social Movement* (Princeton, 1926); Merrill Jensen, *The Articles of Confederation: An Interpretation of the Social-Constitutional History of the American Revolution, 1774–1781* (Madison, 1940); Vernon L. Parrington, *Main Currents in American Thought* (2 vols., New York, 1927), esp. Vol. I entitled *The Colonial Mind, 1620–1800;* Arthur M. Schlesinger, Sr., *The Colonial Merchants and the American Revolution, 1763–1776* (New York, 1918). Two intelligent evaluations of fluctuating interpretations about the coming Revolution include Jack P. Greene, "Changing Interpretations of Early American Politics," *The Reinterpretation of Early American History: Essays in Honor of John Edwin Pomfret,* ed. Ray Allen Billington (San Marino, 1966), pp. 151–84, and George A. Billias, "The Revolutionary Era: Reinterpretations and Revisions," *American History: Retrospect and Prospect,* ed. George A. Billias and Gerald N. Grob (New York, 1971), pp. 34–84.

[3] Becker, *History of Political Parties,* pp. 8–12.

[4] A critique of Becker's assumptions about popular participation in New York politics may be found in Milton M. Klein, "Democracy and Politics in Colonial New York," *New York History* 40 (1959), pp. 221–46.

[5] *History of Political Parties,* p. 5.

[6] *Ibid.,* p. 11.

[7] One weakness in the Becker analysis was that he never explained how the masses came to power. He sidestepped that issue by pointing out that common citizens gained a broader range of political rights. But there is little evidence to demonstrate that common citizens took over leadership functions in New York's revolutionary government, which makes it questionable as to whether the people had emerged with the right to determine their own political destiny after 1776.

[8] (Ithaca, 1955). See also Robert E. and B. Katherine Brown, *Virginia, 1705–1786: Democracy or Aristocracy?* (East Lansing, 1964), in which the authors assert that the Old Dominion was a middle-class society.

[9] *Middle-Class Democracy,* p. 402. See also Chaps. 1–3.

[10] *Ibid.,* p. 401.

[11] *Ibid.,* p. 351. Other critical "consensus" studies constructed upon the

middle-class model include Bernard Bailyn, "Political Experience and En-lightenment Ideas in Eighteenth-Century America," *American Historical Review* 67 (1962), pp. 339–51; Daniel J. Boorstin, *The Genius of American Politics* (Chicago, 1953), pp. 66–98; Louis Hartz, *The Liberal Tradition in America: An Interpretation of American Political Thought since the Revolution* (New York, 1955), pp. 3–86; Edmund S. and Helen M. Morgan, *The Stamp Act Crisis: Prologue to Revolution* (Chapel Hill, 1953); Edmund S. Morgan, *The Birth of the Republic, 1763–1789* (Chicago, 1956); Richard B. Morris, "Class Struggle and the American Revolution," *William and Mary Quarterly*, 3rd Sers. 19 (1962), pp. 3–29; Frederick B. Tolles, "The American Revolution Considered as a Social Movement: A Re-evaluation," *American Historical Review* 60 (1954), pp. 1–12. Edmund S. Morgan probably stated the "consensus" thrust most succinctly when he wrote: "The most radical change produced in Americans by the Revolution was not a division at all but the union of three million cantankerous colonists into a new nation." See *Birth of the Republic*, p. 100.

[12] *American Suffrage from Property to Democracy, 1760–1860* (Princeton, 1960), pp. 20–39.

[13] The thrust of research by some political scientists in the recent years has produced rather negative conclusions about the ability of modern Americans to discern the subtleties of issues and to understand differences in candidates. Indeed, survey research findings indicate that most citizens are little more than functionally literate in their perception of issues and candidates. See Angus Campbell, *et al., The American Voter* (New York, 1960), pp. 188–265. This study by Campbell and his associates of the Survey Research Center at the University of Michigan concluded that less than 15 per cent of the voting electorate sampled during the 1950s comprehended issues in terms of the liberal-conservative continuum. One can only speculate about past times, but modern survey research findings force one to wonder whether historians consistently have overrated the political awareness and perception of citizens in other epochs. Have historians reflected themselves rather than the general populace? One cannot presume that the typical enfranchised voter in eighteenth-century America was conscious of issues, thought and reflected about political developments, or even bothered himself about politics, especially since political decision-making was considered to be in the jurisdiction of the upper classes. And when legislators wrote acts into law by imploring the name of the people, there is no reason to assume that they were acting for the people. The greater likelihood is that legislators were giving legitimacy to actions which most citizens cared little about or rarely thought about, unless legislative actions affected them *directly* and *personally*. Besides various studies produced by the Survey Research Center, see V. O. Key, Jr., *Public Opinion and American Democracy* (New York, 1961), pp. 182–202; Robert E. Lane, *Political Life: Why and How People Get Involved in Politics* (New York, 1959), pp. 3–42; Lester W.

Milbrath, *Political Participation: How and Why Do People Get Involved in Politics?* (Chicago, 1965), pp. 142–54.

14 Bernard Bailyn, *The Ideological Origins of the American Revolution* (Cambridge, 1967), pp. 67–76; Bailyn, *The Origins of American Politics* (New York, 1968), pp. 19–24; Richard Buel, Jr., "Democracy and the American Revolution: A Frame of Reference," *William and Mary Quarterly,* 3rd Sers. 21 (1964), pp. 165–90; Roy N. Lokken, "The Concept of Democracy in Colonial Political Thought," *William and Mary Quarterly,* 3rd Sers. 16 (1959), pp. 568–80; Gordon S. Wood, *The Creation of the American Republic, 1776–1787* (Chapel Hill, 1969), pp. 10–28.

15 The fear of popular anarchy became very real for many upper-class citizens during the years of developing revolution. Indeed, it was one element in the intellectual construction of some who remained loyal to the mother country. See, for example, the thoughts of Peter Oliver in Douglass Adair and John A. Schutz, eds., *Peter Oliver's Origin and Progress of the American Rebellion: A Tory View* (San Marino, 1961), pp. 93–112. See also Bailyn, *Ideological Origins,* pp. 301–19.

16 Bailyn, *Origins of American Politics,* pp. 52–58.

17 Leonard W. Labaree, ed., *Royal Instructions to British Colonial Governors, 1670–1776* (2 vols., New York, 1935), I, pp. 55–56. Spelling in all eighteenth-century quotations has been updated for purposes of consistency.

18 Some royal governors like Francis Bernard of Massachusetts were arguing for a titled American aristocracy to give even more balance to American governments and to hold the populace in greater check. Bernard had good reason to fear the common citizens of Boston. His desire to make the analogy between the home government and American governments more perfect was a logical response to the heightened mob activity of the 1760s in opposition to imperial programs. Consult Morgan and Morgan, *Stamp Act Crisis,* pp. 19–35.

19 "Historians and the Problem of Early American Democracy," *American Historical Review* 67 (1962), pp. 626–46.

20 Rind's *Virginia Gazette,* June 9, 1768.

21 "Historians and the Problem of Early American Democracy," *American Historical Review* (1962), p. 635. John B. Kirby, "Early American Politics—The Search for Ideology: An Historiographical Analysis and Critique of the Concept of 'Deference'," *Journal of Politics* 32 (1970), pp. 808–38, argues that deferential assumptions imply citizen satisfaction with upper-class leadership. Kirby contends that there is no hard evidence for such assumptions. Instead, he maintains that "one must also be able to say, without qualification, that that is what the lower classes did in fact believe, that had they been *perfectly* free to select any one they desired [for elective offices], their choice would have been no different. If men are unable to have legitimate alternatives in selecting individuals for public office, then they have been denied an important aspect of human freedom—the simple

but basic freedom of choice. Limiting the choices of men who can run for office is thus a direct means of controlling a people's liberties and does not simply reflect an attitude of deference." See p. 832. Whether because of deference or repression, it was a rare day when common citizens took important offices.

²² One important reason that citizens were less than central to the political process was that they could not vote for very many offices. Merrill Jensen has emphasized that "Aside from Massachusetts, Connecticut, and Rhode Island, the sole political right of the people in most colonies [before the Revolution] had been limited to voting for members of the lower houses of the legislatures." See "The American People and the American Revolution," *Journal of American History* 57 (1970), p. 24.

²³ What evidence there is suggests that men of standing, wealth, and reputation dominated in elections to lower houses. See Jack P. Greene, "Foundations of Political Power in the Virginia House of Burgesses, 1720–1776," *William and Mary Quarterly*, 3rd Sers. 16 (1959), pp. 485–506; Lucille Griffith, *The Virginia House of Burgesses, 1750–1774*, rev. ed. (University, Alabama, 1970), pp. 128–68; Jackson T. Main, "Government by the People: The American Revolution and the Democratization of the Legislatures," *William and Mary Quarterly*, 3rd Sers. 23 (1966), pp. 391–407; Robert M. Zemsky, "Power, Influence, and Status: Leadership Patterns in the Massachusetts Assembly, 1740–1755," *William and Mary Quarterly*, 3rd Sers. 26 (1969), pp. 502–20. For a dissenting opinion, worth comparing to Greene and Griffith, see Brown and Brown, *Virginia, 1705–1786*, pp. 215–42.

²⁴ Michael Zuckerman, *Peaceable Kingdoms: New England Towns in the Eighteenth Century* (New York, 1970), pp. 187–219, denies that oligarchies existed on the local level of Massachusetts politics. Zuckerman's definition of that term is to the point. Oligarchy in government represents "the occupancy of positions of power in the society. It entails a patterned concentration of power in an elite of considerable numerical constriction and significant stability of membership. It requires that these notables maintain a style of life set off at a distinctive distance from the rest of the community, and that their authority be acknowledged and unchallenged by those subject to it." See pp. 201–2. Although Zuckerman demonstrates that turnover was fairly high in the communities he investigated, he does not analyze the characteristics of those holding office which makes it impossible to judge whether officeholders were the socioeconomic elite. Furthermore, Edward M. Cook, Jr., "Local Leadership and the Typology of New England Towns, 1700–1785," *Political Science Quarterly* 86 (1971), pp. 586–608, questions the validity of Zuckerman's sample of representative towns.

²⁵ *Conservatism in Early American History* (New York, 1948), p. 28.

²⁶ For materials currently available, see the studies listed in the previous three footnotes along with Jackson T. Main, *The Upper House in Revolutionary America, 1763–1788* (Madison, 1967); James Kirby Martin, "A Model for the Coming American Revolution: The Birth and Death of the

Wentworth Oligarchy in New Hampshire, 1741–1776," *Journal of Social History* 4 (1970), pp. 41–60; Robert Zemsky, *Merchants, Farmers, and River Gods: An Essay on Eighteenth-Century American Politics* (Boston, 1971).

[27] Jesse Lemisch, "The American Revolution Seen from the Bottom Up," *Towards a New Past: Dissenting Essays in American History,* ed. Barton J. Bernstein (New York, 1967), pp. 3–45; Lemisch, "Jack Tar in the Streets: Merchant Seamen in the Politics of Revolutionary America," *William and Mary Quarterly* 3rd Sers. 25 (1968), pp. 371–407. See also the collected essays of Staughton Lynd, *Class Conflict, Slavery, and the United States Constitution: Ten Essays* (Indianapolis, 1967), pp. 3–132, and Bernard Friedman, "The Shaping of a Radical Consciousness in Provincial New York," *Journal of American History* 56 (1970), pp. 781–801.

[28] A general failure of the "consensus" group has been that of assuming that writings and thoughts expressed by the most verbal Americans represented the "mind" of all prerevolutionary citizens. What is important is that these thoughts, analyzed in studies by Bernard Bailyn, Edmund S. Morgan, and Gordon S. Wood, were ideas emanating from the elite. Then the thoughts make sense within the context of the crisis in the structural relationships of prerevolutionary politics. Consult Chapter Two.

[29] I drew upon those men who were resident in office during 1774 for twelve of the thirteen colonies. I used the year 1773 for Massachusetts because the royally supported government had begun to collapse in 1774 with the reaction of Parliament to the Boston Tea Party in passing and implementing the "Coercive" Acts. Thus by the middle of 1774 Massachusetts faced a military governor and a *mandamus* council, besides a series of legal restrictions on the normal operations of civil government. See *Appendix I* for a list of all executive officers involved in the outbreak of the Revolution.

[30] The term "executive" is less cluttering to the text than terms like "upper-hierarchy" officeholder or "higher official," although the latter expressions may be used in places. What I want to avoid is the constant repetition of all offices when discussing the data.

[31] Stability of tenure definitely characterized higher offices before the Revolution, if for no other reason than that the highest executive offices were appointive. For further comments about tenure rates and the role that they played in fomenting revolution, see Chapter Two.

[32] In the selection of revolutionary executives I took those men who assumed the offices which the late colonial executives vacated, either in 1776 or 1777 after the new governments began to operate in each state. In the case of Massachusetts where citizens did not ratify a new constitution until 1780, I chose those men who assumed the reins of leadership with the reinvocation of the 1691 charter in 1775. Rhode Island and Connecticut did not have new state constitutions; as a result, I selected the leaders who either were elected or appointed in 1776.

[33] Familiar names include those of John Wentworth, Thomas Hutchinson,

Andrew and Peter Oliver, Cadwallader Colden, Richard Stockton, Caesar Rodney, Robert Carter Nicholas, Martin Howard, Edgerton Leigh, Samuel Adams, John Adams, Benjamin Lincoln, Roger Sherman, Oliver Wolcott, George Clinton, John Morin Scott, John Jay, William Duer, Abraham Yates, William Livingston, William Paterson, David Rittenhouse, Joseph Reed, Luther Martin, Patrick Henry, Edmund Randolph, James Iredell, John Rutledge, Henry Laurens, and William Henry Drayton, to name but a few who would influence the course of revolution in America.

CHAPTER TWO

Political Immobility and the
Origins of the Revolution

I

PATTERNS of behavior among officeholders in the political arena tend to reflect their positions within the structure of political systems. Political structures normally are hierarchical; offices on higher levels by function usually have a broader range of authority, and they command greater prestige and respect than do offices on lower levels. By definition, then, offices on higher levels are fewer in number, making it impossible for all office seekers to attain them. Individuals making the decision to enter politics characteristically, though not always, begin political careers by fulfilling the responsibilities of lower-level offices. They perceive politics from that vantage point, but they hope to work their way up through the hierarchy so as to gain greater status and authority associated with higher-level offices. As mobility occurs, moreover, perceptions of responsibilities and political reality change. Ultimately few succeed in their drive to balance expectations with achievements, and levels of expectation do vary from person to person. Yet as long as fluidity in the form of mobility (opportunity for personal and group political advancement) denotes the system, both those who succeed and those who fail retain the sense that the system has some merit and should not be seriously modified except by chance, fortune, or political necessity through time.[1]

That some men should quest for political power is a normal part of the political process. The quest continues every day and gives momentum to political change and the rise and decline of political movements. Structurally, the process of officeholder interaction does not usually get out of hand and lead to coups, palace rebellions, and broader peoples' revolutions unless individuals seeking positions of greater power and prominence metamorphose into groups which feel that opportunity for advancement and upward political mobility is too narrowly confined, or worse yet, nonexistent. The "outs," collecting in lower-level offices and finding both security and unity in numbers, have two real alternatives open to them. They may aggrandize as much authority as possible at the highest level to which they may advance in the political structure, normally accomplished by cutting into the powers and prerogatives of higher officials. Or they may speak out against the right of the higher "in" group to rule. If those dominating at higher levels remain insensitive to "out" group pressures, do not find new avenues of mobility, or attempt to reassert lost authority, then they may very well precipitate rebellion. Clearly, the first pattern of "out" group response characterized colonial American politics after 1689, from the time of the Glorious Revolution in America to the end of the Seven Years' War in 1763. But after that date, the second pattern of response (potential rebellion) became the new mark of late colonial political reality.[2]

The hypothesis here is that political immobility caused stress in the colonial political systems and underlay much of the tensions giving motion to the developing American Revolution. Out factions had coalesced in one form or another in all of the colonies prior to 1763; they were devoted to circumscribing the prerogatives of higher royal officials in the provincial political structure. Such factions, coming together in lower houses of Assemblies, began to consider the possibility of rebellion after 1763 when reinvigorated imperial programs proscribed many of the prerogatives assemblymen had won.[3] Thus the "out" factions, sensing a relative loss of power and seeing no alternative avenues for political mobility, faced the bleak prospect of losing what had been gained or forcing the system open through rebellion. The latter course was the only viable alternative for lower-level officials collectively frustrated by political immobility.[4]

Before proceeding further, however, definitions are in order. If we define the prerevolutionary *political elite* as all those individuals who held political offices, whether on local, county, or colony-wide levels in the provincial political structures, then definite patterns emerge more clearly from the data. Tensions were building between "lesser" and "higher" officials causing increasing amounts of political instability and disequilibrium as the 1760s and 1770s unfolded. Lesser officials here are defined as those leaders carrying out the duties attached to local and county offices as well as legislators in the lower houses of the thirteen colonial Assemblies. In the years immediately prior to the disruption of colonial governments, many of them were at one and the same time political *incumbents* and political *insurgents*.[5] Such men were a major part of the late colonial political elite, but they were lesser officials theoretically subordinate to royal authority in that elite. Higher officials, on the other hand, were those favored few men who clustered around royal and proprietary governors. They were men in colony-wide offices above the Assembly level, men who normally gained their positions through appointive procedures and who represented the presumed monarchical and aristocratic social orders in government. The term "higher," derived from the eighteenth-century hierarchical conception of mixed government, is here specifically applied to those executive leaders under study. Prerevolutionary higher-level officeholders were a small but not insignificant number, given the reassertion of imperial authority after 1763, in the late colonial political elite.

Tensions among lesser and higher officials were manifest well before the decades of revolution. Political incumbents on the Assembly level and below often formed "country" or "whig" factions in their thrust toward expanding the powers and prerogatives of lower houses vis-à-vis royal and proprietary governors and councilors. Higher officials, on the other hand, usually congregated into "court" or "tory" factions in defensive reaction. Experiencing little or no support from uninterested and lackadaisical Crown officials in England until the 1760s, higher officials fought a losing battle to preserve and protect the prerogatives of royal and proprietary governments. Leaders in the lower houses persisted in their attempts to aggrandize authority, and the clash of factions resulted. Who would control financial matters and the distribution of tax monies? Would governors or Assembly leaders have the final authority to determine speakers of the house? Would governors or assemblymen have the power to decide what developing frontier regions would be represented in Assemblies? Would royal officials in the colonies be dependent upon Assemblies for salaries? Who would control Indian policies? The attempt to resolve such questions set the tone of factional disputes, at least until the early 1760s when home officials began to reassert royal authority through the implementation of more rigorous imperial programs. Then the nature, the quality, and the content of factional bickering changed.[6]

Though setting the tone of eighteenth-century politics, factionalism in itself does not have the power to explain the dynamics of the coming Revolution. We must ask what factors served to shape factional lines and ultimately to make political reconciliation impossible. Remembering that offices and individual political careers were as much at stake as were royal and proprietary prerogatives, we may say that political immobility was both a *precondition* of party factionalism as well as a *precipitant* of revolution once British policy changed course after the Seven Years' War.[7] We must now investigate why lesser officials found themselves frustrated by advancement procedures prior to the outbreak of fighting revolution.

II

William Gordon, the patriot historian of New England, wrote during the 1780s that the beginning of the revolutionary movement in Massachusetts could be traced to 1760 and a festering controversy between the Otis family and Thomas Hutchinson about the successor to the deceased Stephen Sewall as chief justice of the superior court of judicature. According to Gordon's account, Governor William Shirley had promised the office to James Otis, Sr.; but when a vacancy occurred, Shirley made his apologies and appointed another to whom he also had promised the chief judgeship. Shirley assured Otis that he would receive the office next time around, but that day came long after Shirley had passed from the scene and just after Francis Bernard had taken over the Massachusetts governorship. Governor Bernard weighed the evidence and considered available candidates. In the meantime, James Otis, Jr., let it be known that if his father was not appointed he would personally "kindle such a fire in the province as shall singe the governor, though I myself perish in the flames." [8] Governor Bernard selected Thomas Hutchinson.

James Otis, Jr., sought to live up to his apparent threat. William Gordon noted that young Otis "joined himself to the party which was jealous that the views of administration were unfavorable to the rights of the colony . . . and soon became its chief leader." [9] For young James Otis his commitment to public principles and his frustration with procedures of political advancement meshed into one, producing his insurgent behavior and his sporadic diatribes against British rule in Massachusetts. Shortly after the chief judgeship controversy, he was pleading against the granting of writs of assistance to customs house officials as a known violation of the liberties of Englishmen, an amorphous body of rights guaranteed to all subjects through the equally amorphous and unwritten British constitution. Only a few months before the elder James Otis had been pleading his case before Governor Bernard. Now his son was striking back by charging that Bernard and Hutchinson were corrupting and suppressing the inalienable rights of Englishmen.

The Hutchinson-Otis controversy is but one example of how personal political frustrations formed the texture of factional alignments. The elder James Otis was the product of a fairly prominent Barnstable family. He was a militia colonel and had served in the Massachusetts General Court. In 1760 he became speaker of that body. Yet Bernard had denied him the prominence and the prestige of being chief justice. The Otises no longer remained friends to British rulers in Massachusetts.[10]

It must have been particularly galling to have lost a major judicial appointment to a man like Thomas Hutchinson, "plural officeholder" par excellence in prerevolutionary Massachusetts. In 1760 Hutchinson controlled a variety of local, county, and upper-hierarchy offices. A former speaker of the lower house in the General Court himself, Hutchinson became a councilor in 1749 and continued to serve in that capacity until his unwanted association with the formulation of the Stamp Act cut off his tenure in 1766. Also holding a commission to command the fort on Castle Island in Boston Harbor, he had served since 1752 as a probate judge as well as a justice of the Suffolk County court of common pleas. Hutchinson, then, in 1760 was not only a local official but also was the president of the council, lieutenant governor, and chief justice.[11] During the 1760s the new chief justice became one symbol of oppression in British-endorsed leadership. Early in the next decade Hutchinson secured the governor's commission for himself, thus leading whig leaders like sullen John Adams to write that he was becoming "one determined Enemy to those Principles and that Political System to which alone he [Hutchinson] owes his own and his Family's late Advancement—one who thinks that his Character and Conduct have been the Cause of laying a Foundation for perpetual Discontent and Uneasiness between Britain and the Colonies, of perpetual Struggles of one Party for Wealth and Power at the Expense of the Liberties of this Country." [12]

Indeed, plural officeholding in higher-level offices was a reason in itself for political immobility. With few upper-hierarchy offices available and fewer men holding them, it was exceedingly difficult for American community leaders who had reached the Assembly level of politics to move to the top of the prerevolutionary hierarchy of offices. Men such as Hutchinson were in their way and apparently not about to step aside.

A second practice constricting opportunities for political advancement had to do with British "placemen" in high office. The term "placeman" was used rather indiscriminantly during the heated debates leading to revolution and was meant to deride all kinds of royal officeholders. But for our purposes we need a more exacting definition. The term here is applied to all those men, usually born outside the colonies and therefore intruders from without into colonial offices, who used contacts in England to acquire lucrative colonial positions in the customs service, the Vice-Admiralty court system, and/or the administrative, judicial, and legislative branches of the provincial governments. Placemen were men who wanted offices as much for personal profit as for political power and prestige. They were a class of professionals when most politicians were amateurs. Men like Thomas Hutchinson often were slurred as placemen, but they were hardly outsiders invading the colonial political arena. [13]

The presence of placemen holding high office caused particular bitterness in South Carolina prior to the Revolution. The native socioeconomic elite families had long been disenchanted with patronage decisions made by ministers in England which placed nonnative favorites on the governor's council and in other appointive positions. The wealthy merchant and future revolutionary leader, Henry Laurens, for example, refused an appointment to the council in 1764 because of the presence of placemen. He remained with others of the native socioeconomic elite in the commons house of Assembly. There he lent support in opposition to both British policies and British placemen in South Carolina government.[14]

William Henry Drayton, on the other hand, represented one exception to native elite attitudes in South Carolina. Drayton was born into an old and wealthy family, studied at Oxford, and returned home as a young man ready to assume positions in the governmental hierarchy. He entered the commons house in 1765 where he soon made it clear that he was no patron of rebellious sentiments. The ministry eventually sanctioned his loyal behavior by appointing him to the council, essentially through the urging of his uncle, Lieutenant Governor William Bull II. In 1774 Drayton's uncle gave him a temporary commission to South Carolina's circuit court (the highest court in the province). Drayton learned shortly thereafter, however, that the ministry had offered a permanent appointment to William Gregory, former chief justice of Quebec and not a South Carolina native. Drayton's conversion to the revolutionary cause had begun.[15]

When Drayton realized that he too, despite his loyal behavior, was to be barred from offices that he desired and would be penalized in favor of outsiders for whom the ministry had higher regard, he struck back. Drayton gave vent to some of his anger in a pamphlet addressed to the first Continental Congress assembling in Philadelphia. He listed several grievances against the Crown. The first naturally dealt with "taxing those American Freeholders, *although* they have not any representation, *of their own election,* in Parliament." The other grievances got more directly to what was upsetting Drayton. He complained that "Placemen dependent upon the Crown, being Strangers *ignorant* of the interests and laws of the Colonies, are sent from England to fill seats in Council, where they often form a majority;—as Legislators, determining the most weighty affairs of the Colony—and as Chancellors, decreeing in Suits relating to the most valuable property of the Subject." Drayton also spoke out against ministry-appointed judges who held their positions during the Crown's pleasure which was "a tenure dangerous to the liberty and property of the Subject; and *therefore* justly abolished in England." Young Drayton related with some accuracy that at one time South Carolinians had enjoyed a council as well as courts which had consisted "of Men *of property established* in the Colony." Native local elite leaders "stood in no awe of a Minister, yet they rendered the most essential services to the Crown, as well as to the People." But with more imperial favoritism in appointments, the council and the courts consisted of "more strangers from England, than Men of rank in the Colony!" No longer did common citizens look for justice to the *"independent and well-informed Bench* of Judges" made up of local elite leaders. Those wanting adjudication of disputes had to face judges dependent upon "the Crown for their daily bread." The only way to regain judicial independence was to turn the court system back over to the native socioeconomic elite.[16]

When the local South Carolina elite instituted a new revolutionary government in 1776, Drayton received the appointment as chief justice of the circuit court. Thus the coming Revolution ended Drayton's frustrations about losing an important and scarce upper-hierarchy political office to an outsider; it also ended sycophantic careers of placemen in South Carolina and elsewhere.

There were other factors causing political immobility for aspiring lesser officials beyond those of placeman appointments and plural officeholding. One crucial factor had to do with unchecked tenure limitations on appointments. Once in an upper-hierarchy office, the favored elite leader could presume that the position was his to use or to exploit until he wished to retire or until he died. Sickness, old age, lack of interest, or occasionally even disputes with governors, but not constituency recall, opened high offices, yet at a frustratingly slow rate. The normal practice in royal and proprietary provinces was to have twelve councilors. Leonard W. Labaree has estimated that on the average less than one new councilor was appointed each year in any given province, which meant that there was a relatively low turnover rate of between 5 and 10 per cent a year. Councilors of Virginia, where appointed by the Crown, averaged 12.6 years in office, yet in the charter colony of Connecticut councilors averaged 14 years, even though elected by the local voting citizenry.[17] Thus opportunity for advancement was further narrowed under conditions of open-ended, unchecked tenure.

As colonial society matured, moreover, and as population increased (jumping from just over 250,000 individuals to over 1,500,000 people between 1700 and 1760), there was an absolute increase in the numbers of citizens with wealth and social standing, the standard requirements for leadership selection. Yet the number of colonial executive offices remained fixed through time. In the mid-eighteenth century most colonies still had only one secretary, three or four associate judges of superior courts, and twelve councilors. Population expansion, then, produced a glut of available candidates on the officeholding market. Men who wanted high office and had the socioeconomic qualifications found it more difficult to come to the attention of governors or those with the power of appointment in England. They had to satisfy their penchant for leadership with local and county offices, serving variously as justices of the peace, town selectmen, militia officers, and probate judges. Established community leaders could realistically aspire to election to the provincial Assembly, but beyond that point there was little hope. Unless the individual had special influence or contacts with the governor or ministers in England, his chances for appointment to high office were nil. Thus opportunity for political advancement decreased as the population increased and the ranks of the upper class swelled with ever greater numbers of less visible community leaders, only giving greater intensity to the problem of political immobility above the Assembly level of politics.[18]

Given such factors plus the appointive nature of most higher offices, the real key to advancement depended upon influence and contacts. Before the Revolution, for example, royal governors recieved specific instructions from the Board of Trade outlining rules to follow in nominating and selecting other executive officers. The Board of Trade wanted an up-to-date list of prospects for each royal council containing "the names and characters of three persons inhabitants . . . whom you shall esteem the best qualified for that trust." [19] The royal governors nominated from among those upper-class citizens in their favor. Influential members of the British ministry confirmed candidates either from the governor's nomination list or from names presented by other powerful cabinet members. The royal governor, moreover, had to consult with at least three members of his council for advice in appointing men "to be judges, justices of the peace, or other necessary officers." Thus in royal colonies the prerogative of upper-hierarchy leadership selection lay with the governor in consultation with his council or in conjunction with higher officials in England.[20] The same general pattern held true for proprietary colonies, except that the chief proprietor had the final voice in filling executive positions.[21]

Thus a very few privileged provincials coming from the most visible and trustworthy families potentially controlled more than their share of higher offices. Men with somewhat lesser status or influence had more difficult problems because of lower visibility levels and direct competition with men from families who had already established contacts. As a result, the channels to high office were clogged with colonial favorites and nonnative placeman interlopers who took more than their share of offices (plural officeholding) over extended periods of time (unchecked tenure). If a prominent citizen wanted to acquire a higher office, he had to know the right people. If he did not, then his fate, at best, was likely to be permanent consignment (depending upon voter attitudes) to the provincial Assembly. And it was on that level of the political structure that dissatisfaction was building.

Keeping appointive procedures in mind, we may interpolate the distinction between lesser and higher officials and expand the original definition of these two types within the prerevolutionary political elite. Higher officials normally were men within the elite who had imperial influence and contacts; therefore, many of them were able to move up the hierarchy. Lesser officials usually lacked such contacts. Such men found themselves stymied at the Assembly level because of the narrower range of their life experiences, interests, and contacts.[22] They were not in the position to gain the attention of high officials with appointive powers. Yet as assemblymen they were able to come into contact with others like themselves, coalesce into opposition factions, cut into the prerogatives of the favored few on the top, and challenge the whole scheme of imperial politics when the time came. For such men lack of mobility undergirded their sense of consciousness that new imperial restraints were undesirable. Lack of mobility thus served as a precondition to the creation of factional lines as well as a precipitant to greater instability in prerevolutionary politics, that is once the favored few in upper-hierarchy offices had to execute the provisions of new imperial programs. Higher officials became the particular targets of insurgent lesser official wrath.[23]

III

Immobility among lesser officials became one working factor in precipitating rebellious behavior when various British cabinets after 1763 urged Parliament to tighten up imperial controls by passing such infamous pieces of legislation as the Sugar and Currency acts of 1764, the Stamp Act of 1765, the Townshend duties of 1767, and the Tea Act of 1773. Insurgent whig leaders, many of whom were holding local, county, and Assembly-level positions, sensed that an assault upon new ministerial schemes also would serve to embarrass the very men who stood as roadblocks to their political advancement. What insurgent leaders needed, then, was a vocabulary with the potential to enunciate their worldview in challenging Parliamentary legislation and attacking their opponents in higher offices. They modeled that vocabulary, most notably after 1763, on the English radical Whig opposition tradition.[24]

English opposition Whigs had argued earlier in the eighteenth century that balance among the traditional social orders in government was being overturned because of the corrupted dealings of powerful cabinet ministers. Power was unchecked, and tyranny was on the horizon, or so the radical Whigs maintained in their publications, most especially during the years when Sir Robert Walpole was the master of the realm (1721–1742). Walpole and his followers used electoral bribery and collusion in Parliamentary elections and favoritism in filling sinecures to insure that there would be a coalition of leaders willing to support Walpolean policies. According to the radical Whigs, liberties were vanishing because ministers were seizing power from the traditional orders in government. Walpolean politics represented a conspiratorial hand which was corrupting the normal operation of English politics. Bernard Bailyn has written that radical Whigs and American insurgents (well versed in radical Whig writings and seeing themselves in the position of opposition) believed that such

> Threats to free government . . . lurked everywhere, but nowhere more dangerously than in the designs of ministers in office to aggrandize power by the corrupt use of influence, and by this means ultimately to destroy the balance of the constitution. Corruption, especially in the form of the manipulation and bribery of the Commons by the gift of places, pensions, and sinecures, was as universal a cry in the colonies as it was in England.[25]

Vocal American lesser officials charged in their own pamphlets and newspaper editorials with ever greater frequency after 1763 that a ministerial "conspiracy" had been launched to "corrupt" and subvert American "liberties." Those in upper-hierarchy offices, the insurgents claimed, were a part of the plot. Governors and other court party leaders, dependent upon Crown patronage to remain in their offices, would most willingly carry out new imperial laws, thereby eliminating liberties in their unquenchable thirst for political preference. Insurgents believed that power corrupted; they were concluding by the early 1770s that if higher officials remained much longer in office, the colonial governments would become little more than functioning "tyrannies." [26]

The insurgent whig ideology had a frenzied, even paranoid cast to it, demonstrating that serious tensions lay below the surface of politics, tensions generated by the minds of lesser officials who were giving vent to their own political frustrations.[27] The choice of vocabulary is revealing in that it so neatly fit the insurgents' dual drive against toughened Crown policies, on the one hand, and against favored royal and proprietary higher officials standing in the path of political ascendancy, on the other hand. If the colonial insurgents within the elite had been able to move up and into higher offices, then the vocabulary would have been more in contradiction to their perception of political reality at the time of dawning revolution. But the lack of mobility intensified such conceptions, making heightened confrontation almost inevitable without some reversal in the nature of home government legislative policies and appointment procedures. In this specific sense, then, the English Whig opposition worldview expressed the frustrations of insurgent lesser officials. The ideology supported the final formulation of notions that the only way to save American liberties was to overthrow those men who were agents in the conspiracy that was corrupting American governments. That assault came with force following Parliament's promulgation of the Coercive Acts in 1774.[28]

IV

The observation has been made that many of those who led the surge against British sovereignty after 1774 were simultaneously incumbents and insurgents within the late colonial political elite. It has been suggested, moreover, that lesser officials were anxious to acquire higher offices. Career-line analysis in conjunction with an investigation of the executive turnover rate following the collapse of British authority substantiates the pattern. Of the 487 late colonial and revolutionary executives, each held an average of three offices before the outbreak of the Revolution. We find that there was a fairly even distribution among some offices and great imbalance among others (Table 2.1).[29] Future revolutionary executives were somewhat more successful in obtaining officers' commissions in local militia units prior to 1776 whereas late colonial and loyalist executives surpassed the former group in acceding to such appointive colony-wide and intercolonial positions as Vice-Admiralty court judges, collectors of quit rents, surveyors general, and customs commissioners. Late colonial and loyalist leaders simply had more appointive favor than did future revolutionary executives— many lesser official insurgents were elected leaders in militia units.

Surprisingly, 48 per cent of the late colonial executives had served in colonial Assemblies before moving up in the hierarchy, demonstrating mobility for some. The question, though, had to do with what kinds of men, and we will see that they were those who fell on the intercolonial side of the community-imperial continuum of interests and contacts. Thomas Hutchinson and William Henry Drayton were cases in point. Men who may be placed on the community end of the continuum rarely experienced mobility beyond the Assembly level before the Revolution. Only 36 per cent of

Table 2.1

*Sampling of Other Offices Held
by Political Elite Leaders before the Revolution*

Office	Late Colonial (Number)	%	Loyalist (Number)	%	Revolutionary (Number)	%
Militia Officer [1]	(73)	31.6	(40)	29.9	(146)	47.4
Justice of the Peace [2]	(78)	33.8	(36)	26.9	(97)	31.5
County Offices [3]	(69)	30.0	(27)	20.2	(81)	26.2
Assemblymen	(111)	48.1	(48)	35.8	(155)	50.3
Miscellaneous Colony-wide Offices [4]	(45)	19.5	(37)	27.6	(15)	4.9
Revolutionary Conventions and Congresses [5]	(21)	9.2	(4)	3.0	(192)	62.3
Continental Congress [6]	(26)	11.2	(4)	3.0	(82)	26.2

[1] Includes all those with rank of captain or above.

[2] Oftentimes upper-hierarchy offices included an appointment as justice of the peace. These figures relate to known cases before an individual was elevated to an upper-hierarchy office.

[3] Including such positions as sheriff, probate judge, commons pleas court judge, country treasurer, and the like.

[4] This category includes such appointive positions as colony agent, surveyor general, receiver general, customs official, and the like.

[5] The percentages count the attendance of each individual at one or more conventions or congresses.

[6] The figures include both Continental Congresses throughout the revolutionary period.

those who showed signs of loyalism, moreover, had served in Assemblies. They were much more dependent in officeholding patterns upon appointive favor from above. Slightly over 50 per cent of the future revolutionary executives were incumbent in lower houses prior to the end of British authority. Such men were in the thick of the fight with higher authorities after 1763 and did not hesitate, it might be added, to move into executive positions in 1776 and 1777 after the formation of new state governments.

Lesser officials on the whole, given their broad range of political experiences in lesser offices before 1776, were not reluctant to assume the highest offices for themselves after that time. They had broken the pattern of political immobility.

Between 1774 and 1777 ten of the thirteen rebellious American colonies—Massachusetts, Rhode Island, and Connecticut were exceptions—not only shed themselves of British sovereignty, but also formulated new state constitutions, vesting sovereignty in the American citizenry. The Massachusetts Revolutionaries, confronted with a military governor, a *mandamus* council, and British troops in reprisal for the Boston Tea Party, reaffirmed their 1691 charter in 1775 and used it as a basis for government until a new constitution won a semblance of popular ratification in 1780. Connecticut and Rhode Island, the two charter colonies, simply retained their charters as the basis of their state political systems while dropping all references to British sovereignty.[30] Elsewhere British sovereignty vanished as the legitimate royal and proprietary governments gave way to revolutionary conventions and congresses. Insurgent assemblymen in the last of the colonial Assemblies and the first of the extra-legal provincial conventions elected representatives to the first Continental Congress. The extra-legal conventions, originally called into session because loyalist governors refused to allow regular legislative meetings to select Congressional delegates, became self-perpetuating bodies in the face of higher official intransigence. Conventions met for specific purposes, then disbanded, but not before issuing orders for the election of community representatives to the next congress, if conditions warranted it. As a result there were five such congresses in New Hampshire before the last one resolved itself into a constitutional convention and then into an interim revolutionary government. New Jersey made the transition through four congresses; North Carolina's first two conventions met to elect delegates to the Continental Congress, and the last three, like congresses elsewhere, made decisions about organizing resistance through local militia forces, about financing opposition, about controlling and suppressing outspoken loyalists, and ultimately about working out the details of a new state government. Everywhere the constitutions divested the Crown of sovereignty and placed it in the hands of the commonalty of Americans.[31]

Contemporaries recognized that the formation of new governments would result in changes in the types of men holding high offices. One prominent Maryland planter-lawyer, attending the Continental Congress in the spring of 1776 when some still hoped for
resolution of differences, stated that

> If the Commissioners do not arrive shortly [from Great
> Britain] and Conduct themselves with great Candor and
> Uprightness to effect a Reconciliation, a Separation will most
> undoubtedly take place and then all Governors and Officers
> must quit their Posts and New Men must be placed in the Sad-
> dle of Power." [32]

He wrote about "New Men" in high offices; but most would be
old and wise men in terms of political experience.

John Adams too hinted at changes in leadership types when he
wrote shortly after the Declaration of Independence:

> The Colonies to the South, are pursuing the same Maxims,
> which have heretofore governed those to the North. In consti-
> tuting their new Governments, their Plans are remarkably
> popular. . . . And in the choice of their Rulers, Capacity,
> Spirit, and Zeal in the Cause, supply the Place of Fortune,
> Family, and every other consideration, which used to have
> Weight with Mankind. [33]

Adams argued that "Zeal in the Cause" now meant more than
visible characteristics like "Fortune" and "Family" in gaining offices. Apparently nontraditional American aristocrats of wealth
were not faring well in competition with zealous community leaders. Adams' observations essentially were correct.

What John Adams suggested was a high turnover rate among executive leaders resulting from the changeover in governments. He
felt that the movement away from "idolatry to Monarchs, and ser-
vility to Aristocratical Pride" would produce new methods of leadership selection and promotion. He declared in a letter to Patrick
Henry:

> The dons, the bashaws, the grandees, the patricians, the sach-
> ems, the nabobs, call them by what name you please, sigh,
> and groan, and fret, and sometimes stamp, and foam, and

curse, but all in vain. The decree is gone forth, and it cannot be recalled, that a more equal liberty than has prevailed in other parts of the earth, must be established in America. That exuberance of pride which has produced an insolent domination in a few, a very few, opulent, monopolizing families, will be brought down nearer to the confines of reason and moderation.[34]

Adams seemed to relish the humiliation of some within the political elite. Yet he would not hesitate to take higher offices than he had held before in the new governments.

John Adams was not singular among the articulate insurgent leaders in praising the shift away from "Aristocratical Pride" in the organization of governments. Thomas Jefferson, communicating with Benjamin Franklin in 1777, commented on the impact of leadership turnover and constitutional change in the minds of revolutionary Virginians. Jefferson related that

the people seem to have deposited the monarchical and taken up the republican government with as much ease as would have attended their throwing off an old and putting on a new suit of clothes. . . . A half dozen aristocratical gentlemen agonizing under the loss of preeminence have sometime ventured their sarcasms on our political metamorphosis. They have been thought fitter objects for pity than punishment.[35]

Apparently there were some who did not care for the leveling aspects of insurgent programs.

David Ramsay, the well-known South Carolinian and historian of the American Revolution, put the dynamics of political transformation as it pertained to leadership change in clearest perspective when he joined many other Charlestonians in celebrating the second anniversary of the Declaration of Independence. Ramsay spoke to the throngs of celebrants; he told them that

it is the happiness of our present [state] constitution, that all offices lie open to *men of merit,* of whatever rank or condition; and that even the reins of state may be held by the *son of the poorest man,* if possessed of abilities equal to the important station. We are no more to look up for the blessings of government to hungry courtiers [Ramsay exclaimed], or the *needy dependents of British nobility;* but we must educate our children for these exalted purposes.[36]

Ramsay sensed that the coming Revolution, the transition from Crown colonies to American states, and the formation of new standards of leadership selection had opened up offices in government to "men of merit" at the expense of "hungry courtiers." The possibility of political mobility for men who thought of themselves as talented, virtuous, and wise, regardless of family backgrounds, personal wealth, or imperial connections, was to become a notable feature in the operation of advancement procedures in new state governments. "Men of merit" would no longer have to defer their expectations of achieving high positions.

One key, but by no means the only one, to the rapid advancement of so many men who perceived themselves as talented, was the high turnover in executives coming in the wake of revolution. Of those 231 higher officials holding the 267 executive offices in the thirteen colonies just before the collapse of British authority, 77.5 per cent fell from power. Only fifty-two (22.5 per cent) found themselves in the position to move into the revolutionary ranks. Decisions had to be made by each of the late colonial executives about whether to remain loyal to the mother country, to assume the guise of neutrality, or to join the revolutionary cause. Strong tendencies toward loyalism or out-and-out toryism accounted for fully 70.9 per cent of the actual turnover rate. Men in high office who were particular targets of insurgent wrath often had little alternative but to remain loyal, to flee for their personal safety behind British military lines, or to leave the colonies.[37] Court party leaders, for years the most visible opponents of popular party rhetoric and wrath, could not shed their associations with the old regime and with charges of having corrupted the rights and liberties of American citizens. Men with names like Wentworth, Hutchinson, Oliver, De Lancey, Penn, Dulany, Randolph, and Bull could not break with the past; they could only hope that it and they would be restored to power through British military intervention.

Those choosing to remain loyal or finding themselves condemned to the tory camp were of several types and kinds. There were variations in the latitude that each individual had in making decisions, and there were individual depths of equivocation according to particular circumstances. Thomas Hutchinson, the last royal governor of Massachusetts (1771–1774), renowned plural office-holder, and target of insurgent anger, never had the opportunity to consider alternatives. He easily stood as the archetype loyalist who left home and native country never to return.

But some other late colonial executives equivocated, demonstrating tendencies, though no commitment, to the loyalist position. One such person was Judge William Potter of South Kingston, Rhode Island.[38] The Judge was a local leader who had inherited a large commercial farm from his father, thus setting himself up as a person of economic standing in South Kingston. Above average in family resources and personal wealth, Potter was elected to the Rhode Island Board of Assistants (upper house of the Assembly) in 1774—he had served terms in the lower house.[39] As an assistant Potter mouthed normal attitudes of disgust with imperial policies. Yet within a few days after the battles of Lexington and Concord when the Rhode Island Assembly hastily gathered to authorize an army of observation to protect Rhode Island borders against possible British military forays, Potter joined Governor Joseph Wanton (1769–1775), Lieutenant Governor Darius Sessions (1769–1775), and Assistant Thomas Wickes (1767–1768, 1769–1771, 1772–1775) in protesting the Assembly's action. The four leaders sent a remonstrance to the popular branch maintaining that warlike measures such as organized military opposition would "be attended with the most fatal consequences to our charter privileges; involve the country in all the horrors of civil war; and, as we conceive, is an open violation of the oath of allegiance which we have severally taken, upon our admission into the respective offices we now hold in the colony." [40]

In the aftermath of tensions caused by Lexington and Concord, the four executives had gone too far; they had indicated loyalist sentiments. Potter was not reelected to the Board of Assistants, but Governor Wanton again took the governorship and continued to hold out and to deny the Assembly's right to organize an army of observation. In November 1775 the Assembly deposed Wanton and named a new governor. In the meantime, Judge Potter recanted by sending a personal petition to the Assembly apologizing for his untoward behavior. He now claimed that his real motivation in signing the remonstrance had nothing to do with personal loyalty to the Crown; far from it. He really had opposed a show of militarism because "trade, and particularly the town of Newport, would be greatly distressed, which a little longer time might prevent. . . . Sorry, I am," Potter went on, "if any of the good people of this colony should have conceived otherwise of me; and I greatly lament, that the unguarded expressions in that protest, should give cause therefore." Judge Potter promised to be loyal to all "friends of liberty" henceforth, but never to British oppressors.[41]

In response the Assembly voted to welcome Potter back into its good standing, and in 1776 the Judge again returned to the Board of Assistants, serving through 1778. In later years, it might be noted, the Judge became a devoted follower of Jemima Wilkinson, a religious enthusiast who believed that she had the power to bring a recently deceased daughter of the Judge back to life. Few were surprised when Jemima failed, but Judge Potter had not faltered in renewing his own political life in Rhode Island some years before, but only because he had not passed beyond the point of resuscitation. He had only shown tendencies toward loyalism, certainly a curable disease, not the malignant toryism of a Thomas Hutchinson, which in final form ended Hutchinson's political life in America.[42]

Yet we must also consider those late colonial executives who left office but did not evidence at least visible signs of loyalism. We are talking about 29.1 per cent of the late colonial group. The behavior of most of these men, best described as outward "neutrality," may be epitomized in the career of the wealthy Virginia planter Robert Carter of Nomini Hall. Carter met with other favored individuals from Virginia's tobacco planting elite as a councilor for the first time in 1758, assuming duties as gubernatorial adviser, legislator, and final arbiter in Virginia's judicial system. From one of Virginia's most distinguished families and properly educated in England, Carter quite naturally fitted into his new role as councilor. The underlying assumption in his training since boyhood was that he would one day fill high offices and rule with a wise and benevolent hand.[43] Yet after 1772 Carter's trips to Williamsburg became less frequent; he seemingly had lost his taste for official duties. Carter found himself in the awkward position of having to resolve a personal loyalty crisis. Did his mind belong to Great Britain or to his native Virginia? In the end, unable to decide, he retreated from government, minimized his political activities and associations, and spent more time than ever working on his vast tobacco estates. During the Revolution Carter kept his financial interests solvent by selling supplies to the American army, but after 1774 he no longer bothered himself with an active part in political decision-making. Neutrality in politics solved the dilemma of his allegiance crisis.[44]

Another neutral with awkward circumstances was Mark Hunking Wentworth of New Hampshire. His reasons for choosing neutrality, however, were somewhat different from those of Robert Carter. Before the Revolution one almost literally had to be related to the Wentworth clan if one wanted to hold upper-hierarchy executive offices in New Hampshire. Mark Hunking, a wealthy merchant who made his personal fortune by supplying the British navy with masts and spars from New Hampshire's virgin timber regions, lived in Portsmouth, the center of the province's social and political life. His brother Benning was royal governor from 1741 to 1767, and Mark Hunking's son John took over from his uncle in the latter year and filled the governor's post until driven from the province by New Hampshire insurgents in 1775. Mark Hunking obtained a councilor's commission in 1759, obviously through the recommendation of brother Benning, yet after 1767 Mark Hunking attended few council meetings, apparently out of a sense of delicacy—his son was governor—and because of increasing age. Even though local revolutionaries forced his son to flee the province, they never took aggressive actions against Mark Hunking. The latter was old, suffered from bad health, and represented no real threat to the aggrandizing tendencies of New Hampshire insurgents. They allowed Mark Hunking to live on quietly in Portsmouth until he died in 1785, never having taken an active part in working for or against the Revolution.[45]

To assume loyalist tendencies or overt toryism in the Carter and Wentworth examples would be misleading. They and other late colonial executives like them left offices for a variety of reasons, whether because of old age and the lack of energy to resist change, personal crises in allegiance, or the effects of pressure coming from insurgent lesser officials. We must keep in mind that of the revolutionary executives who replaced Carter and Wentworth types, 50.3 per cent were assemblymen and 62.3 per cent attended one or more provincial congresses before rising to executive offices. They exerted pressure; loyalists and neutrals fell by the wayside in the upheaval of leadership.

V

Not only did personal decisions affect the overall pattern of turnover in executives, but the rate also fluctuated according to political conditions in each colony (Table 2.2 and Chart 2.1). The internal political climate often dictated the extent of upheaval in upper-hierarchy leadership. In three colonies—New York, Pennsylvania, and Georgia—the turnover was complete. In five provinces —North Carolina, South Carolina, Virginia, Maryland, and New

Table 2.2

Turnover of Late Colonial Executive Leaders

Colony	Number	Loyalist Turnover (Number)	%	Other Turnover (Number)	%	Total Turnover %
New York	19	(18)	94.7	(1)	5.3	100.0
Pennsylvania	17	(13)	76.5	(4)	23.5	100.0
Georgia	15	(11)	73.3	(4)	26.7	100.0
North Carolina	16	(12)	75.0	(3)	18.7	93.7
South Carolina	20	(13)	65.0	(5)	25.0	90.0
Virginia	14	(8)	57.1	(4)	28.6	85.7
Maryland	19	(8)	42.1	(8)	42.1	84.2
New Hampshire	17	(13)	76.5	(1)	5.9	82.4
New Jersey	17	(11)	64.8	(2)	11.7	76.5
Massachusetts	34	(14)	41.2	(10)	29.4	70.6
Rhode Island	20	(4)	20.0	(7)	35.0	55.0
Delaware	6	(1)	16.7	(1)	16.7	33.4
Connecticut	17	(1)	5.9	(2)	11.7	17.6
TOTAL AND AVERAGE	231	(127)	55.0	(52)	22.5	77.5

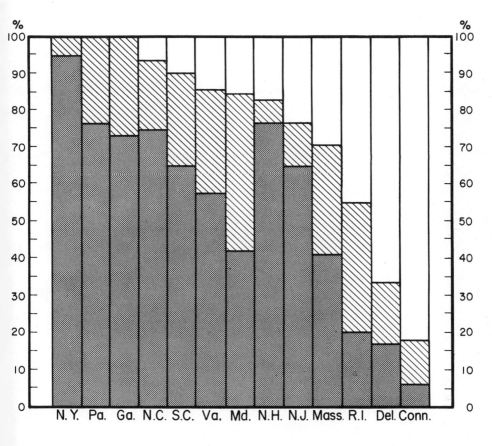

CHART 2.1

A VISUALIZATION OF LATE COLONIAL TURNOVER

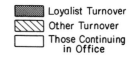

Loyalist Turnover
Other Turnover
Those Continuing
in Office

Hampshire—the turnover percentage was above 80 per cent. Yet in the charter colonies of Connecticut and Rhode Island the rate was low, as it was in the proprietary province of Delaware. There must have been reasons for so much internal variance.

The turnover rate in Connecticut was lower (17.6 per cent) than in any other colony. Connecticut, however, had experienced its real upheaval in executive leadership several years before at the time of the Stamp Act crisis. Political factionalism in Connecticut during the 1760s involved the usual squabbling about prerogatives and powers and was underscored by different orientations toward British policies. Governor Thomas Fitch headed the more imperial-oriented court faction while the future revolutionary governor, Jonathan Trumbull (1769–1784), emerged as the leader of the American rights country faction. Fitch and a coterie of his followers were in higher offices when Parliament passed the Stamp Act; they found themselves in the rather unpleasant position of having to implement the new legislation. Even though the Fitch group reluctantly, and only reluctantly, tried to administer the Stamp Act in Connecticut, Trumbull and his followers, many of whom were active organizers of the Connecticut Sons of Liberty, used the controversy to vote the Fitch faction out of office during the spring 1766 elections. That was the last time when any real amount of executive turnover occurred in that charter government, before or during the Revolution.[46]

Thus there was no reason to oust the Connecticut officialdom in the mid-seventies because it already favored and actively supported American interests. The conflict of officeholding interests did not have the potential, or the issue base, to turn into an all-out attack upon those favored few in high political offices. In Connecticut, then, the leading lesser officials of the 1760s had already become higher officials, long before the same process caused executive turnover and change in other provinces.

There was an additional factor which held down Connecticut as well as Rhode Island executive turnover. The legal bases of these governments, their seventeenth-century charters, provided a degree of openness and fluidity in upward political mobility for those desiring the highest provincial offices. To be specific, political advancement was not controlled by ministry-appointed governors or by influential politicians in England. Local Connecticut freemen possessed the right to determine what officials held most upper-hierarchy offices. Thus aspiring citizens knew that the possibility existed for political mobility, even if they lacked great wealth or important political connections. Movement to the top of the hierarchy was slow and arduous, and Connecticut richly deserved its title as "the land of steady habits." Yet opportunities to advance for those unfavored with imperial connections did exist. In the autumn freemen voted for twenty nominees who became candidates for the governorship, the lieutenant governorship, and the twelve assistant positions. In the following spring freemen formally elected fourteen of the twenty candidates. Once on the list and once in office, tenure became synonymous with renomination and reelection, since nominations invariably went to those already in office.[47] Young aspirants realized that some possibility existed to work up through the political system and eventually to gain nomination and election to the highest offices, even though they personally lacked imperial connections so necessary for political ascendancy in royal and proprietary colonies. Connecticut leaders had to earn community status but not the favor of English patrons. Thus opportunity for political mobility was present, however slight, in the Connecticut hierarchy of offices; it was the product of the charter basis of government which sanctioned community-wide and colony-wide decisions by which individuals rose in politics.

Rhode Island also experienced a low turnover rate (55 per cent), relative to royal and proprietary colonies, but it was much higher than the other charter colony of Connecticut. Two factors help to explain the difference between Connecticut and Rhode Island. First, Rhode Island's late colonial executives with loyalist leanings, such as Governor Joseph Wanton and Lieutenant Governor Darius Sessions, had not been purged from power at a previous point in time. Party factionalism, second, had a slightly different cast in Rhode Island. Lines did not follow the usual imperial-local division as they did in Connecticut at the time of the Stamp Act crisis. Factionalism in Rhode Island tended more to represent geographical interests. Factions centered upon men from Providence and men from Newport and environs. The question was what geographic region would utilize the economic perquisites of government. Each region wanted to control Assembly rewards that would affect economic development in that region.[48] Factional tensions eased during the early 1770s, yet some higher officials found themselves turned out of office after 1774 because they were on the losing side of the ballot, not because of growing revolutionary ferment.

Rhode Island, in fact, had an open and thriving political arena, when compared to others. Party factionalism caused high rates of annual turnover in some elective upper-hierarchy offices, given the general balance between the factions. Unlike Connecticut, individual candidates did not have to slowly move up according to a rigid nomination system. Since factions were of relatively equal strength, and since elections came every year, no one could presume that an office was his for longer than a year.[49] Thus there was a continuing turnover in leadership, reflecting heated party factionalism. Leaders could not complain about the quantity of fluidity in the system, and they did not write a new state constitution after 1774. The seventeenth-century charter, providing for a relatively open system, remained the basis of the revolutionary and postrevolutionary government.

Massachusetts, like Connecticut, had a higher than usual turnover in some executive offices resulting from local opposition to the Stamp Act. Ministerial supporters like Thomas Hutchinson and Andrew and Peter Oliver lost their seats in the upper house of the General Court in 1766 because they had gone along with the Stamp Act, that is until forced to submit to Boston mob rule. Barring them from the council was possible because Massachusetts had a unique charter provision whereby the lower house of the General Court elected the upper house of councilors annually. (In every other royal province the governor nominated and the ministry in England sanctioned council appointments.) Intransigent delegates in the lower house, therefore, used the Stamp Act issue to oust the imperial-oriented Hutchinson faction from the council, thereby weakening the influence of Governor Francis Bernard in the General Court. Bernard still had the power to veto the lower house's choices, and he did so in 1766, but his veto prerogative did not win back the seats for his supporters. Because of the 1766 purge and because the lower house had the legal right to name councilors, future revolutionary activists like John Hancock and James Bowdoin were already on the council in the early 1770s before the end of royal government after the Boston Tea Party. It is more than probable that the Massachusetts executive turnover rate (70.6 per cent) would have been higher had Massachusetts royal governors possessed the right to nominate men for council appointments, men who more willingly would have supported imperial policies. Hence a unique charter provision held down turnover in Massachusetts resulting from revolution.[50]

The only other province with a relatively low turnover rate was Delaware, but the figure (33.4 per cent) was more a reflection of the means of calculation than of the actual turnover in Delaware's executive leaders. Delaware was an exception in that it had a partially developed stratum of upper-hierarchy offices before the Revolution. Delaware had an attorney general and a supreme court, but Penn family proprietary appointees—the governor, secretary, treasurer, and councilors of Pennsylvania—did double duty in Delaware, since the three lower counties were under the jurisdictional control of the Penn interests. Thus these late colonial Pennsylvania officials made occasional sojourns to Delaware to meet with the popularly elected delegates in the lower house of the General Assembly. Together the Penn executives and the lower house handled local problems. So as not to overweight the rate of turnover among upper-hierarchy Pennsylvania officials (remembering that Pennsylvania turnover was 100 per cent), the Delaware figure is based solely upon the attorney generalship and the supreme court. If the other Penn officeholders are counted, then the actual turnover rate in Delaware jumps to 81 per cent. Including Pennsylvania leaders twice in the overall calculations, however, would tend to distort the cumulative figure, since all other leaders are tabulated only once. Thus the incomplete nature of the executive office structure in late colonial Delaware was primary to making it a deviant case and holding down the turnover percentage.

Four provinces—Connecticut, Rhode Island, Masschusetts, and Delaware—evidenced prerevolutionary internal political circumstances which muted the overall executive turnover rate of 77.5 per cent. If, for the sake of analysis, we eliminate these four provinces from the calculations, the rate jumps from 77.5 to 90.2 per cent in the remaining nine royal and proprietary colonies; also, 69.5 per

cent of the late colonial turnover in these nine colonies was attrib-
utable to loyalist identifications, as opposed to 55 per cent in all
thirteen. Such calculations support the observation that those late
colonial provinces with royal and proprietary structures (those al-
lowing for little mobility above the Assembly level of politics) had
much higher rates of executive turnover than did those provinces
with hierarchies permitting some degree of internally based and internally controlled political advancement. The turnover rate was
highest where community socioeconomic leaders who were present
in lesser offices had little or no voice in the selection of upper-hierarchy officeholders.

This general observation becomes even clearer when the rate of
turnover in the southern colonies is compared to that of the northern colonies (Chart 2.2). The southern provinces, contending with
greater numbers of placemen, had consistently higher percentages
of turnover than did the northern provinces where charter provisions and electorate and Assembly control produced greater fluc-
tuations in rates. The overall executive turnover rate in the six
southern provinces was 86.7 per cent, whereas in the seven northern provinces it was 71.6 per cent. In the South fully 47 per cent of
the executives in office before the Revolution were born outside the
colonies as compared to 15 per cent for the North. Even though
foreign birth does not necessarily mean that the individual was a
placeman, the percentage difference indicates that more outsiders,
many of whom were placemen, were holding offices particularly in
North Carolina, South Carolina, and Georgia.[51] Such men, lacking
extensive ties in the colonies and more dependent upon the British
ministry for their offices, tended more naturally toward loyalism.
Their presence did irritate native socioeconomic leaders, many
of whom had imperial connections. Southern community leaders
felt that they must gain full control of all offices in their governments, especially if political mobility beyond the Assembly level
was to be their lot. The coming Revolution gave them their chance;
experiencing less mobility than their northern counterparts, southern community leaders pushed late colonial executives aside in
greater numbers.

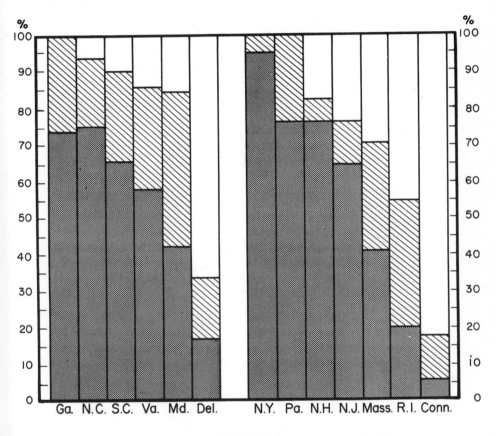

CHART 2.2

A VISUALIZATION OF LATE COLONIAL TURNOVER
BY SECTION – SOUTH AND NORTH

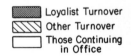

Loyalist Turnover
Other Turnover
Those Continuing
in Office

VI

Our discussion of political immobility and turnover in high executive offices would be incomplete without mentioning Assembly turnover. Though there was much turnover among assemblymen between 1774 and 1777, it was rarely a product of loyalist leanings and sentiments. Assembly turnover more often reflected movement up, not out, of the political hierarchy. Fifty per cent of the revolutionary executives had seats in lower houses prior to the disruption of colonial governments. Not all of the 155 men were incumbent in Assemblies during 1773 or 1774, but all of them were in some way involved in prerevolutionary factional disputes. They and others contended with court faction leaders, and they most specifically took advantage of new-found avenues to higher offices once insurgent opposition turned to full-scale rebellion.

The new revolutionary executives, for years having put up with frustrations in terms of political advancement, contributed in varying individual degrees to the first revolutionary settlement as embodied in the constitutions of 1776 and 1777. Their political experiences, expectations, and frustrations served as common reference points in establishing new constitutional procedures for political advancement. Insurgent leaders thought in terms of popular sovereignty; they had no other way to turn. Moreover, they carefully implemented popular sovereignty by giving the democracy of citizens a larger voice in determining who would hold high offices. They expanded the political rights of the common citizenry to make sure that men like themselves, established community socioeconomic leaders, would have open access to all offices in government. They worked within the framework of mixed government, but insurgents tipped the balance to favor the democracy of citizens.

With this overall pattern of leadership turnover and change in mind, we now must focus our attention on the collective analysis of all those executives under study here. The specific characteristics of each group (late colonial, loyalist, and revolutionary) will permit us to understand why lesser officials felt frustrations about political immobility prior to the Revolution. The constitutions of 1776 and 1777 became the channels through which insurgent lesser officials alleviated their political frustrations. The following pages, furthermore, propose to explain why the crisis within the late colonial political elite became a democratizing movement in American political development while not necessarily being a movement arising from the democracy of citizens.

Chapter Two: Notes

[1] The relationship between political perceptions and levels of officeholding as critical factors in political behavior has been discussed by Samuel P. Hays, "Political Parties and the Community-Society Continuum," *The American Party Systems: Stages of Political Development,* ed. William N. Chambers and Walter D. Burnham (New York, 1967), pp. 152–81. For the period of the American Revolution, see William A. Benton, "Pennsylvania Revolutionary Officers and the Federal Constitution," *Pennsylvania History* 31 (1964), pp. 419–35, and Stanley M. Elkins and Eric McKitrick, "The Founding Fathers: Young Men of the Revolution," *Political Science Quarterly* 76 (1961), pp. 181–216.

[2] The out-group and in-group thesis (that is within the elite) generally has been ignored by those who study the history of American politics. An important exception, however, is Bernard Bailyn, "Politics and Social Structure in Virginia," *Seventeenth-Century America: Essays in Colonial History,* ed. James Morton Smith (Chapel Hill, 1959), pp. 90–115. Consult also James Kirby Martin, "A Model for the Coming American Revolution," *Journal of Social History* (1970), pp. 41–60. Historians of Europe, however, have related such theses to the great revolutions sweeping through Europe in the eighteenth and nineteenth centuries. See in particular Alfred Cobban, *The Social Interpretation of the French Revolution* (Cambridge, 1964), pp. 8–24, 54–67; John R. Gillis, "Political Decay and the European Revolutions, 1789–1848," *World Politics* 22 (1970), pp. 344–70; Jeffrey Kaplow, "Introduction," *New Perspectives on the French Revolution: Readings in Historical Sociology,* ed. Jeffrey Kaplow (New York, 1965), pp. 12–22. Kaplow maintains that those who gave impetus to the French Revolution included citizens "engaged in economic activities that the nobility disdained" and men in the professions who "were assigned certain roles which nobles did not care to play." Revolutionary leaders were neither of the nobility nor of the people, but they were above the general citizenry because of "their wealth, their contacts, their access to local political power." Although not a conscious class, what such individuals "had in common [was] their exclusion from the consecrated power structure, their favorable disposition toward change, their potential revolutionism." See p. 14. They were quite similar to lesser officials who rose up two decades before in revolutionary America.

[3] Jack P. Greene, *The Quest for Power: The Lower Houses of Assembly in the Southern Royal Colonies, 1689–1776* (Chapel Hill, 1963), is the most thorough treatment of aggrandizing Assemblies. See also Leonard W. Labaree, *Royal Government in America: A Study of the British Colonial System before 1783,* Yale Historical Publications Studies Vol. VI (New Haven, 1930).

[4] Greene, *Quest for Power,* p. 11, points out that there was "a marked

correlation between the appearance of economic and social elites produced by growth in colonial wealth and population on the one hand and the lower houses' demand for increased authority, dignity, and prestige on the other." One reason that the native socioeconomic elite solidified prerogatives at that level was that it was difficult for them to proceed to higher-level offices. The pattern might have been different had the Crown been more sensitive to the officeholding needs of rising native elites during the eighteenth century.

[5] This terminology has been taken from a brilliant theoretical essay by Harry Eckstein, "On the Etiology of Internal Wars," *History and Theory* 4 (1964), pp. 133–63. Eckstein argues that tensions within European political elites boiled over into revolutions during the eighteenth and nineteenth centuries.

[6] For the shift in Crown policies as it affected the lower houses and factionalism, see Greene, *Quest for Power,* pp. 355–453.

[7] Eckstein, "On the Etiology of Internal Wars," *History and Theory* (1964), pp. 140–43.

[8] William Gordon, *The History of the Rise, Progress and Establishment of the Independence of the United States of America* (4 vols., London, 1788), III, pp. 140–41. Gordon claimed that Hutchinson actively sought the chief judgeship, but Governor Bernard stated that James Otis, Sr., was the only solicitor. See the quote in Ellen C. Brennan, *Plural Office-Holding in Massachusetts, 1760–1780* (Chapel Hill, 1945), p. 30.

[9] Gordon, *History,* III, p. 141.

[10] There is much commentary on the controversy. Consult in particular John J. Waters and John A. Schutz, "Patterns of Massachusetts Colonial Politics: The Writs of Assistance and the Rivalry between the Otis and Hutchinson Families," *William and Mary Quarterly,* 3rd Sers. 24 (1967), pp. 543–67; John C. Miller, *Sam Adams: Pioneer in Propaganda* (Boston, 1936), pp. 22–47; John M. Murrin, "The Legal Transformation: The Bench and Bar of Eighteenth-Century Massachusetts," *Essays in Politics and Social Development: Colonial America,* ed. Stanley N. Katz (Boston, 1971), pp. 415–49. Murrin treats the dispute in the context of the Anglicization (professionalization) of the Massachusetts legal profession. Yet Hutchinson was not a trained attorney. Here is another reason for "outs" sensing political immobility. The highest offices were not going to men who were in the profession. For the life and public career of James Otis, Sr., see John J. Waters, *The Otis Family in Provincial and Revolutionary Massachusetts* (Chapel Hill, 1968), pp. 76–131.

[11] Allen Johnson and Dumas Malone, eds., *Dictionary of American Biography* (22 vols., New York, 1928–1944), IX, pp. 439–43. (Hereafter cited *D. A. B.*). Clifford K. Shipton, *Sibley's Harvard Graduates: Biographical Sketches of Those Who Attended Harvard College, 1690–1763* (12 vols. to date, Cambridge, 1933–   ), VIII, pp. 149–216. See also Brennan, *Plural Office-Holding,* pp. 31–33.

[12] Diary entry, June 13, 1771, L. H. Butterfield, *et al.*, eds., *The Adams Papers: Diary and Autobiography of John Adams* (4 vols., Cambridge, 1961), II, pp. 34–35.

[13] For more information about placemen, consult Jackson T. Main, *The Upper House in Revolutionary America*, pp. 3–42.

[14] George C. Rogers, Jr., *Evolution of a Federalist: William Loughton Smith, 1758–1812* (Columbia, 1962), pp. 36–43.

[15] William M. Dabney and Marion Dargan, *William Henry Drayton and the American Revolution* (Albuquerque, 1962); *D. A. B.*, V, pp. 448–49; John Drayton, *Memoirs of the American Revolution* (2 vols., Charleston, 1821), I, pp. xxiii–xxvii; W. Roy Smith, *South Carolina as a Royal Province, 1719–1776* (New York, 1903), pp. 133–41, 333–34. For William Gregory's life, see E. Alfred Jones, *American Members of the Inns of Court* (London, 1924), p. 89.

[16] *A Letter from Freeman of South Carolina to the Deputies of North-America, Assembled in the High Court of Congress at Philadelphia* (Charleston, 1774), pp. 9–10, 18–20.

[17] *Conservatism in Early American History*, pp. 21–22. Legislators in Assemblies usually had lower tenure averages, but there is also evidence which demonstrates that powerful Assembly leaders enjoyed virtually unchecked tenure. See Jack P. Greene, "Foundations of Political Power in the Virginia House of Burgesses," *William and Mary Quarterly* (1959), pp. 485–506; Lucille Griffith, *The Virginia House of Burgesses*, pp. 141–51; Waters, *Otis Family*, p. 85; Robert M. Zemsky, *Merchants, Farmers, and River Gods*, pp. 285–328. Sir Lewis Namier, by comparison, analyzed the turnover rate in the general Parlimentary elections of 1747, 1754, and 1761. He found that approximately 25 per cent of the Commons membership was new after each election. Namier also calculated the average number of years of Parliamentary service for those elected to the 1761 House of Commons. He found that tenure in Parliament averaged twenty-two years per man. Average years of service, of course, was higher with erratic elections. See *England in the Age of the American Revolution*, 2nd ed. (New York, 1966), pp. 216–19, and *The Structure of Politics at the Accession of George III*, 2nd ed. (New York, 1965), pp. 158–59. I have done some investigation of legislative turnover in New Hampshire prior to the Revolution. Of those elected to the 1765 Assembly, 77.4 per cent returned in 1768. Of those elected in 1768, 70.6 per cent retained seats in the 1771 elections. After that the coming Revolution speeded up Assembly turnover. What voters appeared to be doing was ratifying the right of local socioeconomic leaders to represent them in the Assembly.

[18] The shortage of offices on any level of government, relative to population expansion, is a critical concept to understanding greater amounts of political rancor, as pointed out by Kenneth A. Lockridge and Alan Kreider, "The Evolution of Massachusetts Town Government, 1640 to 1740," *William and Mary Quarterly*, 3rd Sers. 23 (1966), pp. 549–74.

[19] Leonard W. Labaree, ed., *Royal Instructions to British Colonial Governors*, I, pp. 50–51.

[20] *Ibid.*, I, p. 367. See also Labaree, *Royal Government in America*, pp. 100–103, 123–28.

[21] Donnell M. Owings, *His Lordship's Patronage: Offices of Profit in Colonial Maryland*, Studies in Maryland History no. 1 (Baltimore, 1953).

[22] Samuel P. Hays, "Political Parties and the Community-Society Continuum," *The American Party Systems*, pp. 152–57, analyzes the pattern between positioning in the social system and perception in politics. Hays points out that "social institutions" are one variable in locating individuals on the community-society continuum, including those in office.

[23] In terms of targets one need only consider the selective violence directed toward the Olivers and Thomas Hutchinson in Boston during the 1760s and 1770s. Mobs operated in extra-institutional rather than anti-institutional fashion, according to Pauline Maier, "Popular Uprisings and Civil Authority in Eighteenth-Century America," *William and Mary Quarterly*, 3rd Sers. 27 (1970), pp. 3–35. Such mobs, though, had leaders, and many leaders came from the lesser official ranks of the political elite.

[24] The parameters of the Whig opposition ideology are captured in Caroline Robbins, *The Eighteenth-Century Commonwealthman* (Cambridge, 1959); J. G. A. Pocock, "Machiavelli, Harrington, and English Political Ideologies in the Eighteenth Century," *William and Mary Quarterly*, 3rd Sers. 22 (1965), pp. 549–83; Bernard Bailyn, *The Ideological Origins of the American Revolution*, pp. 22–54; Bailyn, *The Origins of American Politics*, pp. 3–58; Gordon S. Wood, *The Creation of the American Republic*, pp. 3–45.

[25] *Origins of American Politics*, p. 56.

[26] A debate has developed between Professors Bailyn and Jack P. Greene about what English ideological source American political leaders drew from in responding to imperial policies. Greene has argued in favor of the prerogative tradition, culminating in the Glorious Revolution against James II in England during 1688–1689. Bailyn has responded by reasserting the influence of radical Whig opposition writers in the formation of ideology making for the American Revolution. Any search for origins is valuable, but it is equally important to know what structural characteristics of the colonial political systems undergirded the enunciation of ideology. See Jack P. Greene, "Political Mimesis: A Consideration of the Historical and Cultural Roots of Legislative Behavior in the British Colonies in the Eighteenth Century," *American Historical Review* 75 (1969), pp. 337–67, including a "Comment" by Bailyn and a "Reply" by Greene.

[27] Gordon S. Wood, "Rhetoric and Reality in the American Revolution," *William and Mary Quarterly*, 3rd Sers. 23 (1966), pp. 3–32, suggests that the frenzied character of insurgent commentary betrayed serious social tensions below the surface of politics. In *Creation of the American Republic*, pp. 46–124, Wood implies that the source of tension was a feeling that the

values and the norms of American communities were collapsing. Only "virtue" and a dedication to "republicanism" would once again unite the people. Given that so much of the ideology came from the ranks of the elite, it seems equally probable that the frenzied tone of insurgent words was an expression of the political frustrations of men in the elite, especially those who saw themselves as politically immobile.

28 My feeling is that both the prerogative tradition and the radical Whig opposition tradition served colonial lesser officials well in their contest with higher officials. The prerogative vein was the primary line of thought in stripping more favored upper-hierarchy officials of powers after 1689. The translation of the Whig tradition into the colonial situation represented a means of attacking the "corrupting" hand of British officials, especially after 1763 when higher officials were attempting to regain lost authority. If we take pamphlet literature as the measure, the latter tradition was more important in mounting a direct assault upon the whole system, which implied removing the power-hungry corruptors from high office. Unless pamphleteers wanted tyranny, they had to consider the alternative of revolution.

29 I have made a systematic effort to collect data about the full range of offices held by political elite leaders. Unfortunately, the known percentage of men holding any particular office more than likely will be an understatement because of the incompleteness of extant records. Militia officer percentages will be less accurate than percentages for assemblymen, since Assembly records are far more complete. The accuracy of percentages will vary directly with the prominence and visibility of the particular office. For more data see *Appendix II.*

30 For the change in Rhode Island government, consult David S. Lovejoy, *Rhode Island Politics and the American Revolution, 1760–1776,* Brown University Studies Vol. XXIII (Providence, 1958), pp. 174–94; for Connecticut, see Oscar Zeichner, *Connecticut's Years of Controversy, 1750–1776* (Chapel Hill, 1949), pp. 219–35.

31 Richard F. Upton, *Revolutionary New Hampshire* (Hanover, 1936), pp. 32–45; Donald L. Kemmerer, *Path to Freedom: The Struggle for Self-Government in Colonial New Jersey, 1703–1776* (Princeton, 1940), pp. 316–51; Robert O. DeMond, *The Loyalists in North Carolina during the Revolution* (Durham, 1940), pp. 62–82.

32 Thomas Stone to Daniel of St. Thomas Jenifer, Philadelphia, April 24, 1776, Edmund C. Burnett, ed., *Letters of Members of the Continental Congress* (8 vols., Washington, 1921–1936), I, pp. 431–32; For similar comments, see Dr. William Shippen to Judge Edward Shippen, July 27, 1776, *Pennsylvania Magazine of History and Biography* 44 (1920), p. 286.

33 To Abigail Adams, June 10, 1776, L. H. Butterfield, *et al.,* eds., *The Adams Papers: Adams Family Correspondence* (2 vols., Cambridge, 1963), II, p. 42.

34 John Adams to Richard Cranch, August 2, 1776, *ibid.,* II, p. 74;

Adams to Henry, June 3, 1776, Charles Francis Adams, ed., *The Works of John Adams* (10 vols., Boston, 1856), IX, pp. 387–88.

[35] August 13, 1777, Julian P. Boyd, *et al.,* eds., *The Papers of Thomas Jefferson* (18 vols. to date, Princeton, 1950–   ), II, p. 26.

[36] "An Oration on the Advantages of American Independence, spoken before a Public Assembly of the Inhabitants of Charleston, in South Carolina, on July 4th, 1778," Hezekiah Niles, *Principles and Acts of the Revolution in America,* 2nd ed. (New York, 1876), p. 375. *Italics mine.*

[37] For further information about the political careers of executive loyalists after the outbreak of revolution, see *Appendix III.*

[38] In terms of categorization of leadership behavior, I allowed for two possibilities in classifying loyalists. If an individual evidenced prominiserial feelings, then I considered whether his leanings were strong enough to disrupt his life in the colonies, or permanently change the pattern of his economic, social, and political career. If so, the individual, like Thomas Hutchinson or John Wentworth, fell into the definite loyalist category. In some cases such as that of Judge William Potter, however, only tendencies were present because of personal actions or public accusations. Such men were classified as leaning toward loyalism. Whenever the loyalists are set apart as a distinct quantitative group, no such qualitative distinction has been drawn, since we are really dealing with definitions as well as degrees of loyalist expressions. For a different categorization scheme, describing leaders as "Whigs," "Whig-Loyalists," and "Tories," see William A. Benton, *Whig-Loyalism: An Aspect of Political Ideology in the American Revolutionary Era* (Rutherford, 1969).

[39] Wilkins Updike, *A History of the Episcopal Church in Narragansett Rhode Island,* 2nd ed. (3 vols., Boston, 1907), I, pp. 263–73; Caroline E. Robinson, *The Hazard Family of Rhode Island, 1635–1894* (Boston, 1896), pp. 57–60.

[40] John R. Bartlett, ed., *Records of the Colony [and State] of Rhode Island and Providence Plantations, in New England, 1636–1792* (10 vols., Providence, 1856–1865), VII, pp. 307–12. The remonstrance, dated April 25, 1775, appears in *ibid.,* VII, p. 311.

[41] Potter's memorial, South Kingston, June 1775, *ibid.,* VII, pp. 347–48.

[42] Updike, *History of the Episcopal Church in Narragansett,* II, pp. 266, 574–77.

[43] For such attitudes, consult Louis B. Wright, *The First Gentlemen of Virginia: Intellectual Qualities of the Early Colonial Ruling Class* (San Marino, 1940), pp. 38–94.

[44] Louis Morton, *Robert Carter of Nomini Hall: A Virginia Tobacco Planter in the 18th Century* (Williamsburg, 1941); Thomas A. Glenn, *Some Colonial Mansions and Those Who Lived in Them* (Philadelphia, 1899), pp. 217–94.

[45] John Wentworth, *The Wentworth Genealogy* (2 vols., Boston, 1870), I,

pp. 183–84, II, pp. 339–41; Lorenzo Sabine, *Biographical Sketches of Loyalists of the American Revolution* (2 vols., Boston, 1864), II, pp. 409–10, erroneously lists Mark Hunking as a loyalist, for no other ostensible reason than that his son John was a tory.

[46] Zeichner, *Connecticut's Years of Controversy*, pp. 52, 70–75; Lawrence Henry Gipson, *Jared Ingersoll: A Study of American Loyalism in Relation to British Colonial Government* (New Haven, 1920), pp. 149–228.

[47] Labaree, *Conservatism in Early American History*, pp. 20–24.

[48] This is the assessment of Mack E. Thompson, "The Ward-Hopkins Controversy and the American Revolution in Rhode Island: An Interpretation," *William and Mary Quarterly*, 3rd Sers. 16 (1959), pp. 363–75. For a different emphasis, see Lovejoy, *Rhode Island Politics*.

[49] Factional disputes and annual elections did not produce high turnover in some executive offices. The secretary, Henry Ward, served from 1760 until 1797, and the treasurer, Joseph Clarke, was in office from 1761 until 1792. But these offices were not directly elective.

[50] Francis G. Walett, "The Massachusetts Council, 1766–1774: The Transformation of a Conservative Institution," *William and Mary Quarterly*, 3rd Sers. 6 (1949), pp. 605–27; Peter O. Hutchinson, ed., *The Diary and Letters of His Excellency Thomas Hutchinson, Esq.* (2 vols., Boston, 1884–1886), I, pp. 73–75.

[51] For further data about the place of birth variable, consult Chapter Six.

CHAPTER THREE

Divergence in the Elite: The Community-Imperial Continuum of Economic Interests

I

Eighteenth-century leaders usually engaged in politics and sought colony-wide offices of power and prominence only after they had accumulated great personal wealth from high-income-producing occupations or from family inheritances. Such individuals, moreover, normally rose into the colony-wide hierarchy of offices after filling local and county positions. The provincial citizen seeking involvement in politics had to follow the kind of occupation that set him off from the rest of the community, an occupation that gave him substantial economic rewards and commensurate community social status. Such tendencies are normal in developing societies where the vast majority of citizens struggle with the vicissitudes of nature each day to remain economically solvent, leaving them little time for political action, and in societies which lack titled aristocrats but which honor wealth as the essential basis of distinction between the higher and lower classes of citizens. In the American provinces the commonalty tilled the soil or earned daily wages in towns; they were expected to defer to their socioeconomic betters in matters pertaining to the prerogatives of political decision-making. And they normally deferred, whether willingly or unwillingly.[1]

Those individuals with the greatest wealth in community settings had the greatest opportunity to build political careers. Yet if the community socioeconomic and political leader aspired to the higher offices in colony-wide governments, he needed much more than community preference. He had to have some quality that linked him with imperial interests, given the appointive nature of upper-hierarchy offices. He usually had to engage himself in an occupation which had the residual effect of bringing him into contact with imperial leaders, men who had the connections to promote him for a councilor's commission, a secretary's appointment, or perhaps even a governorship. Community socioeconomic standing served local leaders well in Assembly elections, but imperial socio-economic status, involving a much larger range of contacts and in-terests on the community-imperial continuum, was the only sure way to receive consideration for offices above the Assembly level, that is before the American Revolution. Once in high office as a re-sult of imperial contacts, the executive in turn would view the polit-ical arena from the imperial perspective, and the imperial perspec-tive would govern his political actions.[2]

Occupations were one key to an elite leader's location on the community-imperial continuum. To take an example, those mer-chants in "primary trading orbits" like Boston, New York City, or Philadelphia, were more likely to have developed imperial contacts, standing, and connections than those merchants who were commu-nity political leaders in "secondary orbits of trade." [3] The latter type did not barter within the trans-Atlantic imperial community but more than likely dealt with merchants in primary trading or-bits. Therefore, they had few chances to make or sustain important contacts beyond local communities. In terms of political advance-ment in prerevolutionary decades, then, where one worked was more often important than at what one worked. The collapse of British authority in America changed that pattern.

II

American Husbandry, a lengthy volume about the unscientific state of provincial American agricultural practices, described the prevailing occupational structure with an understandable agricul-tural bias. The anonymous author claimed that New England had three social classes predicated upon agricultural occupations and resulting levels of wealth. Those citizens in the upper class lived in "the most ancient settled parts of the province," and they owned "considerable land estates, upon which the owners live much in the style of country gentlemen in England." Such individuals, typified by Judge William Potter of Rhode Island, had overseers who carried out farming operations; moreover, those with estates often rented

their lands to tenants, "the rents paid for such farms being the principal part of the landlord's income." Advantages in landholding
permitted a "genteel, hospitable, and agreeable" life style, and it
might be added, afforded extra time to participate in politics. Middle-class citizens did not live so well. They were those "who rent
lands of others, but also the little freeholders who live upon their
own property." In actual numbers the middle group made up "the
considerable part of the whole province." Unlike lower-class inhabitants, the middle-class citizen enjoyed at least "the necessaries of
life." The lower class consisted of individuals temporarily out of
work or people who had just migrated to the colonies and were
looking for employment. But theirs was a temporary plight; land
was plentiful on the frontier, and labor was always scarce. Thus
employment could be found, and high wages, the result of labor
shortages, made it possible for individuals to earn the small amount
of capital necessary to purchase land. Few in New England, then,
remained long without property in that "destitute state of poverty,
which we see so common in England." [4]

Besides arguing that the colonies held out abundant prospects
for economic and social improvement, the author of *American
Husbandry* visualized a three-tiered socioeconomic structure based
on the acreage size of individual economic units. The author of
American Husbandry, however, did bias his conceptualization of
the occupational structure by ignoring other kinds of economic
pursuits.[5] Cadwallader Colden, the last royal lieutenant governor
of New York (1761–1776), made up for such deficiencies in comments about the American class structure that he forwarded to the
Board of Trade during the 1760s. Colden distinguished four sepa-
rate occupational classes in New York. Those in the upper class
were "the Proprietors of the large Tracts of Land, who include
within their claims from 100,000 acres to above one Million of
acres under one Grant." Typically, one intertwined family nexus
—De Lanceys, Livingstons, Schuylers, Morrises—controlled these
grants. Just below the great landholding families were "the Gentlemen of the Law [who] make up the second class in which properly
are included both the Bench and the Bar." Next, according to Colden, came the merchants. They were not as respectable because
they represented new wealth, citizens who had risen "suddenly from

the lowest Rank of the People to considerable Fortunes, and chiefly by illicit Trade in the last War [French and Indian]." Finally, on the bottom "in the last Rank may be placed the Farmers and Mechanics." The freeholders, tenants, town artisans, and wage earners comprised "the bulk of the People, and in them consists the strength of the Province." Though one indiscriminate class, Colden felt that they were "the most useful and the most Moral, but always made the Dupes of the former [merchants and lawyers]; and often are ignorantly made their Tools for the worst purposes." [6]

In commenting on the occupational structure Colden was complaining to the Board of Trade about the political aspirations of the lawyer group. In his mind whig lawyers were becoming uncontrollable in their drive for power. Colden's real and legitimate fear was that such men would take for themselves the political privileges which he had so long enjoyed as councilor (1721–1776) and lieutenant governor. Colden considered himself a member of the high and prestigious landholding class, and therefore he was more deserving of deference, power, and political authority than were rising lawyers. After all he held title to many thousands of acres, had a daughter who married into the De Lancey family, and maintained a beautiful estate, Coldenham, in Orange County. Colden simply did not want to lose his share of the available political resources in New York to lawyer insurgents.[7]

The Lieutenant Governor also demonstrated through his report the normal predilection to overstate the familiar and to underconceptualize the distant and unfamiliar. Hence landholders, lawyers, and merchants made up three of the four classes while the remaining 90 per cent or more of the population was one very large and amorphous group. Compared to the author of *American Husbandry*, though, Colden pointed out that some eighteenth-century Americans worked at other occupational pursuits besides tilling the soil. Many were merchants, professional men, manufacturers, and skilled and unskilled wage laborers. Numbers within each occupational category fluctuated from time to time and from place to place, but on the whole such individuals made up approximately 10 per cent of the provincial working force.[8]

Neither Colden's generalized description like "merchant" nor *American Husbandry*'s use of a term like "husbandman" should be misconstrued to mean that all colonial merchants or agriculturalists were of the same general kind or performed the same functions. Some merchants in "primary trading orbits" engaged in imperial and foreign commerce while others maintained outlets for imported goods in "secondary orbits of trade" far from the seacoast. Some manufacturers distilled rum in New England, and others forged iron in New Jersey and Pennsylvania. No two businesses were of the same capitalization, size, or extent in operations. Such variation within occupational groupings almost defies systematic classification; necessarily then, it must be understood that the following occupational categories are not intended to be undiscriminating. They are included as a general means to classify otherwise raw and disorganized data.

Some occupational categories may be broken down into subgroups, including the agricultural and professional groupings. In relation to agriculture, estimates suggest that between 10 and 15 per cent of prerevolutionary agricultural laborers were black slaves working on southern (and more rarely northern) plantations and commercial farms. About 2 to 5 per cent of the agriculturalists engaged in large-scale planting (tobacco, rice, indigo) employing dozens or even hundreds of slaves. From 5 to 10 per cent farmed commercially, producing a variety of foodstuffs (wheat, corn, livestock) primarily for market. Occasionally using slave labor, commercial farmers were larger operators than the numerically dominant freehold or yeoman farmers. The latter grew crops first for subsistence, and only secondarily for markets, that is if a surplus existed. Yeoman farmers made up perhaps 40 to 55 per cent of the agricultural population. Commercial farmers, corresponding roughly with the highest class in New England as discussed in *American Husbandry,* were economically a step above freehold farmers because their primary orientation was toward the marketplace. On the bottom of the free agricultural group was the tenant farmer, consisting of approximately 10 to 15 per cent of the agricultural force. As renters they were concentrated on the great manors of New York and commercial farms in New England and the middle colonies. In terms of overall acreage, plantations generally were the largest economic units, tending to range over one thousand acres in size even if only a few hundred acres were under cultivation at one time; commercial farms filled a middle position, normally larger than one or two hundred acres; freehold farmers gained livings from rather small plots, in many places averaging less than fifty acres.[9]

If the yeoman farmer tended to be dominant by absolute measures in the agricultural occupational group, then lawyers completely outdistanced all others in the professional category. Lawyers at most constituted less than 1 per cent of those gainfully employed in the provinces, yet they made up 70 per cent or more of the professional group. Physicians accounted for another 15 to 25 per cent of the professional class while ministers were even fewer in raw numbers, ranging from 2 to 5 per cent in that group. College professors or common school teachers were hardly present in any measurable sense. Professional colonists, on the whole, had very little numerical impact on the occupational structure; their weight must be measured in other ways.[10]

It cannot be emphasized enough that the prerevolutionary American occupational structure bears little or no relationship to the primary occupational activities of the late colonial and revolutionary executive elite (Table 3.1). Elite leaders were much more heavily oriented toward the professions and commercial activity than was the population. Whereas 1 to 2 per cent of all citizens were professional men or merchants, fully 33 per cent of the combined executive elite was professional and 21 per cent mercantile. The dominant agricultural group strikingly was underrepresented, making up only 36 per cent of the combined elite. Plantation owners were overweighted in the agricultural subgroup (67 per cent), and lawyers represented the vast majority (88 per cent) in the professional subgroup. The logical conclusion is that lawyers and merchants had real advantages in the process of executive appointment and election; they were following occupations most likely to yield substantial personal wealth. In the North lawyers and merchants far outnumbered all other occupational types, and in the South lawyers and plantation owners dominated in upper-hierarchy offices.[11]

The agricultural interests of the late colonial and revolutionary American commonalty were not represented in any proportional sense; the rise of new revolutionary executives to high offices, moreover, did not alter that pattern significantly. Comparisons among the late colonial, loyalist, and revolutionary executives reveal minimal occupational change, despite the high numerical transition in leadership. The loyalists tended more generally to be plantation owners (nearly 94 per cent of the loyalist agriculturalists were planters) and lawyers (nearly 96 per cent of the loyalist professional men were lawyers) than either of the other two groups. The revolutionary executives witnessed an influx of freehold farmers (just over 23 per cent fell into that category) which does suggest a certain leveling of barriers in terms of leadership selection. Fourteen per cent of the late colonial agriculturalists were also yeomen, but all but two of them were from Massachusetts and Rhode Island, where advancement procedures had some semblance of popular base and internal control before the Revolution. Overall, the difference was slight, except in the sense that seven states had freehold farmers in executive offices as compared to four colonies.[12] Thus there was some measurable increase in the level of opportunity for men of average occupational status, especially when the rise in the number of physicians is taken into consideration, to move into high offices after 1774. Even though differences were slight, some men of lesser occupational standing were realizing wider political opportunities in 1776 and 1777.

III

Quantitative change was minimal, but qualitative differences in executive occupational patterns were striking. Taking the merchant category, late colonial and loyalist merchants concentrated their economic activities more often in major commercial centers controlling the inflow and outflow of commerce on the provincial side of the British community. Great numbers of them involved themselves in imperial commerce. These old guard merchant executives lived in Portsmouth, Boston, Newport, New York, Philadelphia, and Charleston; their overseas connections gave them contacts with prominent men in England and deepened the imperial orientation of their daily lives. Revolutionary executives, by comparison, more often were local merchants located in less populous and central communities. They bought goods from wholesalers and retailers in large commercial centers and distributed such products to other citizens living in their communities. Such men perceived their commercial functions from the local vantage point. Whereas the orienta-

Table 3.1

Primary Occupations of the Executives Compared to the General Population

Primary Occupation	% of General Population	Combined Executive Elite (Number)	%	Late Colonial (Number)	%	Loyalist (Number)	%	Revolutionary (Number)	%
Agriculture	85–90	(168)	35.8	(72)	32.7	(32)	25.0	(108)	36.0
Professional	1–2	(155)	33.0	(73)	33.2	(46)	35.9	(105)	35.0
Mercantile	1–2	(98)	20.9	(52)	23.6	(33)	25.8	(60)	20.0
Manufacturing	1–2	(8)	1.7	(2)	1.0	(1)	0.8	(6)	2.0
Landholding	0–1	(39)	8.3	(21)	9.5	(16)	12.5	(20)	6.7
Artisans and Mechanics	2–5	(1)	0.3	(0)	0.0	(0)	0.0	(1)	0.3
TOTAL	Est. 100 *	(469)	100.0	(220)	100.0	(128)	100.0	(300)	100.0

Primary Occupations of the Executives Compared to the General Population

Primary Occupation	% of General Population	Combined Executive Elite (Number) %		Late Colonial (Number) %		Loyalist (Number) %		Revolutionary (Number) %	
Agricultural Subgroup									
Plantation	2–5	(113)	67.3	(52)	72.2	(30)	93.7	(63)	58.3
Commercial	10–15	(24)	14.3	(10)	13.9	(2)	6.3	(20)	18.5
Yeoman	40–55	(31)	18.4	(10)	13.9	(0)	0.0	(25)	23.2
Tenant	5–10	(0)	0.0	(0)	0.0	(0)	0.0	(0)	0.0
Slave	10–15	(0)	0.0	(0)	0.0	(0)	0.0	(0)	0.0
TOTAL	Est. 100 *	(168)	100.0	(72)	100.0	(32)	100.0	(108)	100.0
Professional Subgroup									
Lawyer	60–70	(136)	87.7	(67)	91.7	(44)	95.6	(91)	86.6
Doctor	15–25	(14)	9.0	(3)	4.1	(1)	2.2	(11)	10.5
Minister	2–5	(1)	0.7	(1)	1.4	(1)	2.2	(0)	0.0
Professor	0–1	(2)	1.3	(1)	1.4	(0)	0.0	(2)	1.9
Teacher	0–1	(2)	1.3	(1)	1.4	(0)	0.0	(1)	1.0
TOTAL	Est. 100 *	(155)	100.0	(73)	100.0	(46)	100.0	(105)	100.0

* Figures do not necessarily total to 100 per cent because they are only estimates.

tion of the colonial executives was generally outward toward the Atlantic community, the orientation of the revolutionary merchant insurgents was toward native soil. Here was a critical distinction between the two groups and a major reason why it was easier for the Revolutionaries to break all ties after 1774. Insurgents did not depend so heavily upon the British empire for personal economic (or political) aggrandizement. In fact, the empire often was at odds with their needs and expectations.

New York and its major trading entrepôt, New York City, had many such examples. Differences in occupational orientations may be shown by comparing the life of the loyalist councilor, John Watts (1758–1776), with that of the revolutionary senator, Isaac Paris (1777). John Watts began his life with incredible natural advantages. His father had been a successful New York merchant who had constructed a thriving network of imperial trading connections. Watts's father died a wealthy man, and that family wealth (and the social respectability it earned) helped John win the favor of Ann De Lancey, sister of the politically powerful brothers, James and Oliver De Lancey. Proper family connections and wealth gained Watts a council commission in 1758, a commission that he held for seventeen years until he left New York never to return in 1775. Watts's family connections, his councilorship, and his mercantile pursuits all had an imperial cast. The old order had been good to him; unable to accept the change, Watts became an avowed loyalist and died in Wales after the Revolution, but not before appearing before the Loyalists' Claims Commission and asking to be compensated for the loss of a personal fortune that he claimed amounted to £20,000 sterling.[13]

The outbreak of revolution cut short the political fortunes of John Watts. Ironically, the fighting Revolution also ended the plans that Isaac Paris had for developing the town of Palatine far up the Hudson River in Montgomery County, New York. Paris had migrated from Germany as a young man, arriving in New York almost penniless. But he was intelligent and industrious; by the early 1770s he had established himself as a grist-mill operator and frontier trader in the Palatine community. An activist in the local Reformed Church, the community recognized Paris's economic accomplishments by naming him to the local revolutionary committee of observation and safety; later Paris joined other insurgents in three of New York's five provincial congresses. In 1777 local voters elected him to the new New York state senate which replaced the old appointive council. Paris attained that office by a far different route than had John Watts; he had done so by earning a reputation as a socioeconomic leader in a small New York community. Gaining prominence, Paris took the military situation seriously by serving in the local revolutionary militia. He and one son died at the Battle of Oriskany in August 1777. Most likely slain by Indian allies of British regiments, Paris was trying to defend the frontier region that had given him the opportunity to use his economic and political talents. Unlike Watts, he owed little to the Crown and had no reason to take any other stand but that of insurgency.[14]

The pattern was essentially the same wherever merchant executives clashed. In New Hampshire the loyalist treasurer, George Jaffrey, Jr. (1749–1775), and the loyalist councilors, Daniel (1753–1775) and Jonathan Warner (1766–1775), worked through imperial trading connections. The insurgent state councilor Nathaniel Folsom (1776–1783), on the other hand, did not live in Portsmouth or conduct his commercial business with England; he rather traded from Exeter to Portsmouth. Folsom went to the first Continental Congress and a year later became major general of the New Hampshire militia. Meanwhile, Jaffrey and the Warners fell from grace and lost all the political favor which they had enjoyed under British sovereignty.[15]

In Pennsylvania Joseph Turner was typical in that he headed a Philadelphia-based commercial firm in conjunction with the provincial chief justice, William Allen. Turner sat on the governor's council from 1747 until the revolutionary insurgents took control of the government. The new Pennsylvania government in turn had a supreme executive council which served, at least in terms of making political appointments, as an upper house (it had no legislative powers). Wealthy, imperial-oriented merchants like Joseph Turner lost their places on the council to men like the local entrepreneur, John Bailey. Bailey was from the township of Donegal in Lancaster County and served just one year (1777–1778) before another superseded him through balloting on the executive council. Before the Revolution Bailey was operating a local grist mill and sawmill along with a tavern and a dry goods store. Bailey and others of local reputation found greater political opportunity for themselves with the adoption of the new Pennsylvania government, but such men would not have been considered for the old Penn council of gubernatorial advisers. They neither had the credentials nor the visibility that prospering merchants had.[16]

The general pattern held up throughout the colonies, even though exceptions existed. Not all imperial-oriented merchant executives remained inextricably tied to the mother country into the Revolution. One who violated the normal tendency was Thomas Willing, an associate justice of Pennsylvania from 1767 until the overthrow of proprietary government. Like John Watts, Willing began his life with several natural advantages. His father was a prospering Philadelphia merchant of English birth who made a fortune estimated at £20,000 sterling during twenty-six years of imperial trading. In 1748 he sent his son Thomas to London to read law at the Inns of Court. Thomas came back to Philadelphia, joined his father's firm, and later formed a business partnership with the revolutionary financier, Robert Morris. Given Willing's trading connections, his legal training, and his family standing, it is not surprising to find him involved in politics. Willing worked as the assistant secretary of the Pennsylvania delegation that attended the Albany Conference in 1754; in 1757 he assumed a chair on the Philadelphia common council; in 1764 he won election to the Assembly. Generally pro-British in politics (considering all of the imperial points of reference in his life), Willing went to the second Continental Congress and assisted other reconciliationists in delaying the independence question. He was one of the few Congressional delegates to vote against Richard Henry Lee's motion for independence. Even though evidencing loyalist sentiments in his actions, and even though he lost all of his political offices during the transition from proprietary to popular rule, Willing preferred to think of himself as a neutral. When the British army occupied Philadelphia, he refused to take the oath of allegiance to the King. In later years his neutralism paid off. Willing became the president of the Bank of North America in 1781, and a decade later President Washington appointed him to head the first Bank of the United States. Willing's neutrality eventually placed him on the winning side; as a result of his early benefits in life and postrevolutionary business enterprises, he died a millionaire in 1807. Perhaps he saw beyond his natural imperial orientation during the fighting war in the Revolution and sensed that even more far-flung and profitable trading adventures lay in the future. Perhaps, again, Willing was just pragmatic. But whatever his motive, his success within the imperial framework did not blind him to future opportunities.[17]

Thus there was a qualitative difference in orientations of executive merchants. Those in the late colonial group were more often located in large urban centers where they could readily develop imperial trading ties and readily come to the attention of royal and proprietary governors. Those in the revolutionary insurgent group more often resided in communities away from urban centers (where urban centers existed) and had fewer opportunities to construct trans-Atlantic connections. Yet they were men of substance in their local communities, but they were outside the favored inner group in the late colonial political elite. Even though men of substantial personal means (consult Table 3.3 ahead), their places of residence militated against acquiring the right qualifications for advancement into high offices.[18]

The same disparity in range of interests and contacts was there, though less dramatically, in other occupational groupings. The involvement of more freehold farmers in new revolutionary governments underscored the rise in the percentage of executives with no overarching imperial attachments, that is when small-scale farmers are compared to plantation owners who cultivated and harvested cash crops like rice, indigo, and tobacco for marketing directly to England. The freehold farmer did not look to the mother country for market outlets and supplies, but to local trading centers. Yeomen were more interested in what the John Baileys or the Nathaniel Folsoms were offering in return for excess crops than what the Joseph Turners or the George Jaffreys were about to import in the way of linens, rugs, glass, or other luxury trading goods. They were not as dependent upon the imperial system for their needs in life; it was easier for them to turn against the system which after 1763 looked more and more as if it was not cognizant of American community wants.

IV

Certain occupations by their nature will produce more income than other occupations. The author of *American Husbandry* as well as Cadwallader Colden recognized that one can make rough approximations of an individual's financial status by considering the income-generating aspects of his occupation. Wholesale merchants residing in Boston and engaging in overseas trade normally would have more potential for capital accumulation than would retail merchants bartering in local trading centers on the edge of the frontier. But local merchants had more income potential than did yeoman farmers or renters who were often lucky to have even the basics of life. Likewise, lawyers practicing before the various supreme or superior courts in the colonies and handling legal problems for a wealthy landholding and mercantile clientele certainly could earn more money from fees than could backcountry lawyers (many of whom were pettifoggers) who drafted deeds and wills and defended lawbreakers in county courts. Wealth in late colonial America tended to congregate in trading centers, on plantations, and in large commercial farming areas. Since substantial real and personal property holdings were a prerequisite to (and sometimes even the result of) officeholding, it is not hard to see why the vast majority of late colonial executives were plantation owners, commercial farmers, lawyers, and merchants.

As pointed out previously, the British ministry made it abundantly clear that it wanted only well-established and prosperous citizens in upper administrative, legislative, and judicial offices. Instructions sent with each royal governor insisted upon candidates who were "well affected to our government and of good estates and abilities and not necessitous persons or much in debt." [19] Governor Josiah Martin of North Carolina (1771–1775) demonstrated how the nomination process worked and what characteristics governors looked for when he recommended the following men for the North Carolina council in April 1774:

> Mr. Hugh Finlay at this time a member of the Council of Canada, a gentleman of education and good fortune, of an ex-

cellent character and great understanding. He is Surveyor of His Majesty's Post roads in America, and now fixing his residence in this Province.

Mr. Robert Munford, a gentleman of liberal education, of exceeding good understanding, very considerable fortune, and of a very amiable character, lately removed into this Province from Virginia.

Mr. Thomas Markwright, a gentleman of good education, who has made a large fortune in Trade, of liberal disposition, excellent understanding, and a very respectable character.

Mr. Robert Schard, a gentleman of exceeding good sense and amiable character, has lately retired from Trade with a good fortune, and is making great progress in the culture of rice.[20]

The candidate in each case was reputed to be of substantial means. The ministry demanded and was getting, on the whole, what it wanted in executive officers—upper-class citizens who were loyal and committed to the interests of the empire.

Thus the average colonial American with limited amounts of real and personal property had little hope for political advancement. The average citizen and more than average community leaders, moreover, did not have enough wealth or social status to stand out in the minds of royal and proprietary governors. We would predict, then, that a large proportion of late colonial executives, especially those coming from royal and proprietary colonies, were men who had earned or inherited high levels of wealth.

One historian of early American history, Jackson T. Main, has analyzed the amounts of property in the hands of revolutionary Americans and has concluded that approximately two-thirds of the population had less than £500 in assets. Of the other third, approximately two-thirds had holdings valued up to £2,000. These were men of *moderate* means. Those having property values between £2,000 and £5,000 were categorized as *well-to-do* while anyone with over £5,000 valuation of real and personal property was classified as *wealthy*. Roughly 10 per cent of all working Americans controlled enough personal wealth to be included in the *well-to-do* and *wealthy* categories.[21] To be in the highest 10 per cent most certainly made a citizen a member of the colonial and revolutionary propertied elite.

Trying to determine the overall wealth of any individual at any point in time is a nearly impossible task. Individual records are often nonexistent, and aggregate records, such as tax lists and probate inventories, usually are scattered, sometimes inaccurate, and often incomplete. Local variations in currency value, property value, and tax assessments, moreover, further complicate the problem of classification. When confronted with land records (acreage holdings), probate inventories, tax lists, and sometimes even slave holdings, one must consider the local context in estimating individual wealth. How does an individual's known property holdings compare with the holdings of others in the immediate vicinity? And how do these, in turn, compare with the size and amounts of holdings of others scattered throughout the colonies? If such questions are kept in mind, then it is possible to estimate, but only *estimate,* an individual's wealth and to assign it a place on a standardizing scale of measurement.[22]

Using the above criteria, it is possible to approximate the real and personal property holdings and overall personal wealth of 455 of the 487 executive leaders at the time of outbreaking revolution. Over 50 per cent of all of the executives could be categorized as *wealthy* while another 41 per cent fell into the *well-to-do* category. Some 9 per cent of the combined executive elite had only *average* amounts of property holdings, and none was classified as *below average.* Given the standards for advancement, it is not hard to understand the complete lack of below-average citizens in high public offices. Unskilled laborers, tenant farmers, indentured servants, and black slaves (those with little or no income potential) played no role in the decision-making process of late colonial and revolutionary governments. The executive elite, on the whole, was drawn from the *well-to-do* and *wealthy* 10 per cent of Americans, not the vast majority of the population (Table 3.2).

Striking variations, on the other hand, occurred among specific executive groupings. Of those who became loyalists, 78 per cent were of wealthy circumstances as were 65 per cent of the late colonial leaders. The revolutionary insurgents, however, numbered only

Table 3.2

Personal Wealth of the Executives Compared to the General Population

Level of Personal Wealth	% of General Population	Combined Executive Elite (Number)	%	Late Colonial (Number)	%	Loyalist (Number)	%	Revolutionary (Number)	%
Wealthy	2–5 Above £5,000	(230)	50.5	(138)	65.1	(96)	78.0	(108)	36.9
Well-to-do	2–5 £2,000–£5,000	(185)	40.7	(62)	29.2	(27)	22.0	(152)	51.8
Average	50–65 £200–£2,000	(40)	8.8	(12)	5.7	(0)	0.0	(33)	11.3
Below Average	20–30 Below £200	(0)	0.0	(0)	0.0	(0)	0.0	(0)	0.0
TOTAL	Est. 100 *	(455)	100.0	(212)	100.0	(123)	100.0	(293)	100.0

* Figures do not necessarily total to 100 per cent because they are only estimates.

37 per cent in the wealthy category; the majority fell into the well-to-do ranks (52 per cent). None of the loyalists was of average means or below (it is *probable* that some of the unknowns might have been), and only 6 per cent of the late colonial executives had average amounts of property. Again, these individuals came from colonies with some sort of internal, community-oriented procedures for advancement. Eleven per cent of the Revolutionaries were of average circumstances; they came from eight of the new American states. Men of average means, then, found more opportunity to hold executive offices once the state governments developed new advancement procedures.[23]

Comparing the late colonial and revolutionary executives, we observe a net downward shift in overall levels of wealth. Men of well-to-do circumstances found more opportunity to move into executive offices after the disruption of colonial governments, but the movement can hardly be labeled a democratizing trend in itself, as the influx of men of average means was numerically limited. The actual change in the transition from colonial to revolutionary governments seems to have been toward men of lesser financial standing (well-to-do circumstances) within the socioeconomic and political elite. Apparently, lesser officials before the Revolution were also lesser members of the late colonial socioeconomic elite. They were men like Nathanial Folsom and Isaac Paris, not like John Watts and Joseph Turner. They had earned enough personal wealth to become community leaders, but not enough to come to the attention of royal and proprietary governors. They had enough economic status to be elected to Assemblies, but not enough to gain access to upper-hierarchy offices. They were a cut above the general American population, but they were a cut below those with great wealth and imperial socioeconomic standing.

V

The leveling process in terms of elite wealth was true not only of merchants but of all general occupational categories. If we look more closely at the ranks of lawyers and agriculturalists, we find less imperial orientation and greater American community orientation among the revolutionary executive insurgents. We continue to discover two general kinds of individuals within the upper class prospering in two basically different orbits, at least prior to the Revolution. It becomes clear why the insurgent group within the upper class had less of a commitment to the empire and to high officials favored by the British imperial system.

Theodore Atkinson of New Hampshire, for example, was one of the most privileged late colonial elite lawyers benefiting from the British imperial system. His father had given him an exceptional start in life as a well-to-do landholder, leaving a personal family estate of £1,200. Young Theodore attended Harvard College, graduated in 1718, and returned to his native New Castle, New Hampshire, where be began to practice law. His father had been an officeholder, and Theodore took up where his father left off. In the 1720s the younger Atkinson became the provincial sheriff, and he served in the Assembly. He also married Hannah, sister of Benning and Mark Hunking Wentworth, thus allying himself with that politically powerful family. Atkinson further endeared himself to the Wentworths by helping them oppose their political rivals and aiding Benning Wentworth in his drive toward the royal governorship. Given a council commission in the 1730s, Atkinson's loyalty to Benning Wentworth paid off with more offices in the years ahead. By the early 1770s Atkinson was still working on the council (1734–1775), carrying out the duties of provincial secretary (1741–1762, 1769–1775), leading the provincial bar as chief justice of the superior court (1754–1775), and directing the militia as major general.[24]

Possessing many political offices obviously enhanced Atkinson's value as a practicing lawyer. Early in his career he moved his legal practice to the seat of government in Portsmouth and accumulated great personal wealth, enough to become one of the principal taxpayers in the colony.[25] His family carriage, which had the family coat of arms emblazoned on its doors, was the talk of Portsmouth, and he supposedly owned more silver plate than anyone else in the colony. When Atkinson died in 1779 at the advanced age of 82, he bequested £200 sterling to the local Anglican church for poor relief. That was about the only contact that this wealthy lawyer-politician had with the New Hampshire masses. He was far from representative of them.[26]

Atkinson used well his advantages—a prosperous father, a college education, and a Wentworth wife—and turned them into an extensive list of public offices and more silver plate than anyone needed in New Hampshire. As a supporter and defender of ministerial policies, he was "well affected" toward the British regime and sought to keep the imperial ties that had meant so much personal wealth, power, and prestige. When Governor John Wentworth fled New Hampshire in the summer of 1775, he left Secretary Atkinson behind as the one remaining symbol of British authority. The insurgent provincial congress, recognizing the significance of Atkinson's presence, sent a delegation to his office to take the official provincial records and remove them to Exeter where the congress was meeting. Atkinson prepared a formal protest, but could do little else. He pointed out that his oath of office "forbids my consent or even my connivance in such a Delivery. . . . Gentlemen—the Difficulties, I may say the Distresses in the Province, and indeed of the whole Continent are such that every cause of additional Perplexity need be avoided." Atkinson made it clear, however that he would not attempt "to maintain the security of the Records in my custody by force." [27] Token resistance ended, the committee took the provincial records, and the old man watched his public career come to an end. He no longer had the bodily energy or the basis of support to defend a collapsing system that had been more than good to him.

The old order providing the prop for Atkinson's success in life meant little or nothing to the revolutionary attorney general of New Jersey, William Paterson (1776–1783). Born in Antrim County, Ireland, Paterson migrated from Ireland while a boy and settled with his family in Princeton, New Jersey. His father began in the New World as a peddler and eventually became a land speculator and tin plate manufacturer. His economic efforts were enough to pay his son's way to the College of New Jersey (Princeton). William took his B.A. in 1763 and his M.A. in 1766; in the meantime he studied law in Richard Stockton's office. (Stockton was an eminent lawyer who numbered Elias Boudinot and Joseph Reed among his students; Stockton later signed the Declaration of Independence.) What Paterson lacked in family wealth and connections, he made up for with an excellent legal education. Yet he found it hard going as a young lawyer dependent upon county court business and sporadic fees for legal services. Just before the outbreak of the Revolution he opened up a country store to supplement his meager legal income.[28] Paterson attended the New Jersey provincial congress in May 1775 knowing that his legal career was floundering. He perhaps sensed that doing away with the old order and favored imperial lawyers would mean expanded legal and political opportunities for himself. Thus it was much easier for Paterson, young and struggling, to break with the past than it was for Theodore Atkinson.

Once the revolutionary New Jersey government got under way, Paterson received appointment to the attorney generalship. In 1783 he resumed his private law practice in New Brunswick, but with many more clients than he had had before the war. The next stage of his political career began at the Philadelphia constitutional convention in 1787. There he presented the New Jersey (small state) plan to his fellow delegates. Paterson went back to his home state, worked for ratification of the national constitution, and got himself elected to the United States Senate. When Governor William Livingston died in 1790, Paterson returned home and succeeded him. In 1793 President Washington selected Paterson for the United States Supreme Court. Paterson thus had gone far for a man who had been trying to make financial ends meet just two decades before under a different political regime. Although he never achieved great personal wealth, he could console himself with new-found power and fame.[29]

Comparisons between men like Atkinson and Paterson demonstrate the leveling process, in terms of wealth and status, which took place among executive legal practitioners. As the overall percentages indicate, however, not all wealthy lawyers backed off from the revolutionary effort. Many of them, although not the majority, found new career opportunities. Edmund Randolph of Virginia, the revolutionary attorney general (1776–1786), typified those who benefited from the transition from royal to popular sovereignty. Randolph was about as prestigious a name as one could hope to have in eighteenth-century Virginia; it meant almost automatic membership in the governing elite. Edmund's loyalist father, John Randolph, grew up thinking that he would someday fill political offices. Educated at William and Mary and at the Inns of Court, John opened a legal office in Williamsburg at the time when his older brother Peyton was Virginia's attorney general. John gained political experience, took a seat on the Williamsburg common council, and served as a clerk for the house of burgesses. When his older brother retired from the attorney generalship, John stepped in and kept the office in the family (1766–1776).[30]

Before the appointment he married Ariana Jenings from a Maryland planter family, and their son Edmund was born in 1753. Edmund too attended William and Mary, studied law in his father's office, and prepared for the time when he would have a place of public trust. He was just ripening into manhood when Governor Lord Dunmore (1771–1775) dissolved the Virginia Assembly in May 1774 because it called a day of fasting and prayer to protest the closing of the port of Boston. John Randolph could not face all severance of ties with Great Britain; he chose loyalism and left Virginia permanently. But his son Edmund stayed behind, lived with his Uncle Peyton, and had friends assist him in getting a commission as the aide-de-camp to the new Continental commander in chief, George Washington. Young Edmund joined Washington outside Boston in August 1775, but he soon learned that his Uncle Peyton had died while serving as president of the second Continental Congress. Edmund returned to Virginia to clear up his uncle's estate and to head the family. Even though he never officially practiced law, he had become personally wealthy because of his father's flight and because of some inheritance from Uncle Peyton. Within a year Edmund was elected the first attorney general of Virginia's revolutionary government. He thus began a public career which climaxed in terms of offices during 1794 when President Washington named him to replace Thomas Jefferson as Secretary of State.[31] Despite his father's disavowal of the revolutionary movement, Edmund put his family wealth and his name behind the insurgent cause; and his decision paid off in a notable public career. Such men, however, were no longer the dominant type in the executive elite. They had to make room in the new governments for rising local legal entrepreneurs like William Paterson.

The pattern of wealthy plantation owners among agriculturalists in executive offices was also modified with the coming Revolution.

Sir James Wright, the last royal governor of Georgia (1762–1775), exemplified the wealthy loyalist planter. James Wright's father had been a placeman chief justice and councilor in South Carolina and had acquired large landholdings which he passed on to his son. James read law at the Inns of Court and worked as South Carolina's colonial agent in England before securing an appointment as Georgia's lieutenant governor. Soon elevated to the governorship, Wright continued his involvement in large-scale planting operations. In the early 1770s his eleven plantations, consisting of over twenty-five thousand acres worked by five hundred slaves, were producing between two and three thousand barrels of rice per year. Wright had a large personal economic stake to protect in defending British policies as governor, but he was forced to leave Georgia in the spring of 1776. He sailed for England but returned in mid-1779 to reestablish royal government under British military occupation. Yet Wright was destined to fail and left Georgia and his plantations for the last time in 1782. He later filed a claim for property losses amounting to £33,000 sterling before the Loyalists' Claims Commission. It was small consolation when he received an annual pension of £500 sterling plus compensation for his property losses.[32]

General Griffith Rutherford of North Carolina, on the other hand, more nearly fit the agricultural norm of the new revolutionary executive elite. His property holdings were sparse in comparison to Wright's, but extensive relative to the average revolutionary agriculturalist. Rutherford took part in the general Scots-Irish migration into the North Carolina backcountry during the mid-eighteenth century. Born in Ireland just before his parents—his father was a Scottish political exile—embarked for New Jersey, Rutherford was taken into a relative's home after his parents died at sea. He had a roof over his head, yet little else. Griffith learned to use surveyor's instruments before migrating south and settling as a young man in Rowan County, North Carolina. There he acquired a farm, began a flour milling operation, and speculated in the lands that he surveyed. He prospered, bought a few slaves, and produced cash crops for local consumption. By 1790 and the first national census, he had over 2,000 acres and eight slaves, representing substantial acquisitions for a man who began life without a penny.[33]

Rutherford built a political career for himself on top of his local economic accomplishments. First he served as Rowan County justice of the peace. He went to the provincial Assembly for the first time in 1771 and later received an officer's commission in the local militia. When the Revolution led to fighting, he became brigadier general of state militia and was later elected to the new state senate (1777–1781, 1783–1787). Rutherford was wounded and captured in August 1780 at the Battle of Camden, and the British sent him to a dungeon cell at St. Augustine. Somehow he survived the ordeal of brutal imprisonment and later was exchanged for a high-ranking British officer. During the 1780s Rutherford continued his land speculation in conjunction with other notorious North Carolina speculators—William Blount, Richard Caswell, and John Sevier—in attempting to develop parts of Tennessee. The General spent the last few years of his life in Tennessee, able to live quite well off the sizable income which his small plantation and his speculative activities netted him.[34]

The difference in the kind of plantations operated by Sir James Wright and General Griffith Rutherford reflects the overall shift in executive agricultural wealth (Table 3.3). Whereas 84 per cent of all loyalist agriculturalists were wealthy, as were nearly 69 per cent of the late colonial group, the insurgents, representing a larger number of small planters, commercial farmers, and freeholders, had only 38 per cent identified as wealthy. The majority were now in the well-to-do and average categories (39 per cent and 23 per cent respectively). Similarly, 65 per cent of all loyalist lawyers were categorized as wealthy as were 54 per cent of the late colonial executive lawyers. But only 42 per cent of the revolutionary lawyers could be so classified; the shift was again toward well-to-do circumstances (nearly 57 per cent). The corresponding percentages for wealthy merchants were loyalist (88 per cent), late colonial (73 per cent) and revolutionary (42 per cent). Men of well-to-do economic standing came to dominate in each of the important occupational groupings. The shift was in the direction of men with less wealth within the late colonial and revolutionary upper class. The privileged 10 per cent still controlled most executive offices, though with some increase in the numbers of men of average means.

Table 3.3

Select Occupational Groupings of the Executives Compared by Wealth

Level of Personal Wealth	Agriculture					
	Late Colonial (Number)	%	Loyalist (Number)	%	Revolutionary (Number)	%
Wealthy	(46)	68.7	(26)	83.9	(38)	38.0
Well-to-do	(12)	17.9	(5)	16.1	(39)	39.0
Average	(9)	13.4	(0)	0.0	(23)	23.0
Below Average	(0)	0.0	(0)	0.0	(0)	0.0
TOTAL	(67)	100.0	(31)	100.0	(100)	100.0

Lawyers

Level of Personal Wealth	Late Colonial (Number)	%	Loyalist (Number)	%	Revolutionary (Number)	%
Wealthy	(34)	54.0	(26)	65.0	(38)	42.2
Well-to-do	(29)	46.0	(14)	35.0	(51)	56.7
Average	(0)	0.0	(0)	0.0	(1)	1.1
Below Average	(0)	0.0	(0)	0.0	(0)	0.0
TOTAL	(63)	100.0	(40)	100.0	(90)	100.0

Merchants

Level of Personal Wealth	Late Colonial (Number)	%	Loyalist (Number)	%	Revolutionary (Number)	%
Wealthy	(38)	73.1	(29)	87.9	(25)	41.7
Well-to-do	(13)	25.0	(4)	12.1	(31)	51.6
Average	(1)	1.9	(0)	0.0	(4)	6.7
Below Average	(0)	0.0	(0)	0.0	(0)	0.0
TOTAL	(52)	100.0	(33)	100.0	(60)	100.0

VI

Some men of average means worked their way into revolutionary executive offices, but most of the commonalty continued to defer in matters of state to their immediate socioeconomic superiors, men who have been identified as lesser officials before the Revolution. Community socioeconomic leaders were a cut above the population because of their wealth, but many of them remained a step below the privileged few who pursued their occupations within the larger imperial framework. Occupationally, community leaders did not fall that often on the British side of the community-imperial continuum. They congregated more on the provincial or local side. Lacking imperial economic ties, they found it difficult to gain admittance to higher offices, despite very respectable qualifications. Their credentials earned them local and county offices and even elections to the lower houses of Assemblies. In Assembly elections they had the favor of the people. Logically, then, when such insurgents wrote state constitutions, they expanded the political rights of these same citizens so that citizen voters or their representatives in both houses of Assemblies would have the power to select high officials. If they were striking a democratic note, they were doing so in one sense because they wanted to guarantee that men like themselves (community socioeconomic leaders) would not continue to experience political immobility beyond the Assembly level. They trusted in the proposition that the people would know "men of merit" when they voted for them.

But wealth and occupation represent too narrow a base to confirm serious tensions between the favored few and the immobile many making up the late colonial political elite. Turning our attention to the family backgrounds, social origins, and kinship connections of elite leaders, it is possible to clarify further the sources of discord making for revolution within the elite.

Chapter Three: Notes

[1] Local political training was an important factor in preparation for colony-wide offices. Consult Carl Bridenbaugh, *Seat of Empire: The Political Role of Eighteenth-Century Williamsburg* (Williamsburg, 1950); Charles S. Sydnor, *Gentlemen Freeholders: Political Practices in Washington's Virginia* (Chapel Hill, 1952); Benjamin W. Labaree, *Patriots and Partisans: The Merchants of Newburyport, 1764–1815* (Cambridge, 1962); Leonard W. Labaree, *Conservatism in Early American History*, pp. 1–31. For contradictory assessments, see Robert E. Brown, *Middle-Class Democracy and the Revolution in Massachusetts*, pp. 78–99, and Michael Zuckerman, *Peaceable Kingdoms*, pp. 187–219.

[2] The term "community-imperial continuum" is an adaptation of Samuel P. Hays's phrase "community-society continuum." See "Political Parties and the Community-Society Continuum," The *American Party Systems*, pp. 152–81.

[3] The terminology is that of Bernard Bailyn, "Communications and Trade: The Atlantic in the Seventeenth Century," *Journal of Economic History* 13 (1953), pp. 378–87.

[4] *American Husbandry, Containing an Account of the Soil, Climate, Production and Agriculture, of the British Colonies in North-America and the West-Indies* (2 vols., London, 1775), I, pp. 62–71. Recent investigations, however, dispute the findings of those who argue that opportunity to advance economically was abundant. See James A. Henretta, "Economic Development and Social Structure in Colonial Boston," *William and Mary Quarterly*, 3rd Sers. 22 (1965), pp. 75–92; Aubrey C. Land, "Economic Base and Social Structure: The Northern Chesapeake in the Eighteenth Century," *Journal of Economic History* 25 (1965), pp. 639–54; James T. Lemon and Gary B. Nash, "The Distribution of Wealth in Eighteenth-Century America: A Century of Change in Chester County, Pennsylvania, 1693–1802," *Journal of Social History* 2 (1968), pp. 1–24; Kenneth A. Lockridge, "Land, Population, and the Evolution of New England Society, 1630–1790," *Past and Present* 39 (1968), pp. 62–80.

[5] Sidney H. Aronson, *Status and Kinship in the Higher Civil Service: Standards of Selection in the Administrations of John Adams, Thomas Jefferson, and Andrew Jackson* (Cambridge, 1964), pp. 44–46, suggests that occupation is the most trustworthy variable to use in assessing the characteristics of leadership groups, if for no other reason than that information about individual occupations is more readily available than data about family wealth, personal wealth, or social position. For Aronson's comments, see pp. 33–34. Data collected by Jackson T. Main, *The Social Structure of Revolutionary America* (Princeton, 1965), p. 113, demonstrate the degree to which occupations reflect personal income and wealth, the latter being much more elusive to determine at any point in time. In the same study Main (p.

43) estimates those employed in agriculture in the North at 70 per cent, somewhat lower than other estimates. Merrill Jensen, "The American Revolution and American Agriculture," *Agricultural History* 43 (1969), p. 107, states that the agricultural force represented about 90 per cent of working Americans. No matter what the overall percentage, tilling the soil was the dominant occupational activity in eighteenth-century America.

[6] *The Colden Letter Books, 1765–1775,* Collections of the New-York Historical Society Vol. X (New York, 1878), pp. 68–69. For a full-scale treatment of the economic structure, see Main, *Social Structure,* pp. 7–67.

[7] Alice M. Keys, *Cadwallader Colden: A Representative Eighteenth-Century Official* (New York, 1906); *D. A. B.,* IV pp. 286–87.

[8] Aronson, *Status and Kinship,* pp. 45–46; Main, *Social Structure,* pp. 68–114.

[9] An older interpretation was that yeoman farmers had no interest in producing surplus crops for market. They were thought to have operated from the framework of self-sufficiency and on a subsistence level. See Percy N. Bidwell and John I. Falconer, *History of Agriculture in the Northern United States, 1620–1860,* 2nd ed. (New York, 1941). More recent materials suggest that farmers actively sought to produce enough for market. Yeomen wanted commercial status. See Jensen, "The American Revolution and American Agriculture," *Agricultural History* (1969), pp. 107–24. Main, *Social Structure,* pp. 7–67, concluded that agriculturalists in the South were generally more market-oriented and more prosperous than those in the North.

[10] We must include pettifoggers as well as trained attorneys in our definition of lawyers. James Otis, Sr., represented the former and John Adams the latter. See John M. Murrin, "The Legal Transformation," *Essays in Politics and Social Development,* pp. 415–49. Aronson, *Status and Kinship,* pp. 44–45, points out that the proportion of professional men in the work force was infinitesimal. He shows that there were less than one hundred attorneys practicing in Massachusetts when the Revolution broke out and that the *Charleston Directory* listed only eleven attorneys in 1782. Doctors represented less than one in every six hundred working individuals, and ministers were even fewer in number, representing perhaps three to four hundred men in Massachusetts, but only sixty in Virginia. Main, *Social Structure,* pp. 112–14, summarized his estimates of the occupational structure, but in less precise terms than Aronson. Main claimed that about one in five of the white laboring force were poor rural and urban dwellers, that there was a relatively large middle class, perhaps over 50 per cent of the whites, and that on top of the economic structure were those with the highest wealth potential—merchants, professional men, and landholders.

[11] Just over 84 per cent of the loyalist and late colonial merchant executives resided in northern colonies. The figure dropped to 61.7 per cent of the revolutionary group. Because of my own classification scheme, all of those labeled as planters lived in the southern colonies. I used the term

"planter" when I found evidence of slaveholding. The legal profession, on the other hand, showed more balance between the North and the South. Some 70 per cent of the late colonial and 63.6 per cent of the loyalist lawyers resided north of Delaware and Maryland. Yet only 46.2 per cent of the revolutionary executive lawyers did. Lawyers and merchants apparently filled the void left by so many planter-loyalists in the South.

[12] Before the Revolution five of the freehold farmers were from Massachusetts; three from Rhode Island; one from Pennsylvania; one from Delaware. The five in Massachusetts were men elected to the upper house by the lower house of the General Court. The three in Rhode Island were elected to the Board of Assistants by the voting citizenry. Thus only *two* were *appointed officials*. John Morton, as associate justice of the Pennsylvania supreme court (1774–1776), appeared to be a farmer. There is also some evidence that he was a surveyor and land speculator. Thus his primary income might not have come from farming. David Hall, an associate judge on the Delaware supreme court (1769–1776), likewise appeared to be a freehold farmer. Freehold farmers appeared in many more state governments. Seven were from Massachusetts; four from Rhode Island; three from New York; three from New Jersey; two from Pennsylvania; four from Delaware; two from North Carolina. The reason for the influx had a great deal to do with making state senatorial positions directly elective for the first time, thus giving such men the opportunity to compete for high offices as some had been able to do in Massachusetts and Rhode Island before the Revolution.

[13] *Letter Book of John Watts, Merchant and Councilor of New York, January 1, 1762–December 22, 1765,* Collections of the New-York Historical Society Vol. LXI (New York, 1928), pp. ix–xvi; Virginia D. Harrington, *The New York Merchant on the Eve of the Revolution,* Columbia University Studies in History, Economics, and Public Law no. 404 (New York, 1935), pp. 19, 36–41.

[14] Washington Frothingham, ed., *History of Montgomery County* (Syracuse, 1892), pp. 218, 225–26, 325–26; John J. Vrooman, *Forts and Firesides of the Mohawk Country New York* (Jamestown, 1951), pp. 211–12. Of the nineteen late colonial executives in New York, eight were merchants, including Abraham Lott, Charles Warde Apthorpe, William Axtell, John Harris Cruger, Oliver De Lancey, Hugh Wallace, John Watts, and Henry White. All eight lived in New York City and had various degrees of imperial trading connections. Of the thirty-one revolutionary executives six were merchants, including Peter V. B. Livingston, William Duer, Jellis Fonda, Philip Livingston, Jr., Rinier Mynderse, and Isaac Paris. The two Livingstons traded out of New York City. William Duer had imperial connections and was involved in supplying masts for the royal navy prior to the Revolution. Jellis Fonda and Rinier Mynderse were local merchants in the area of Schenectady, New York, and they lacked imperial connections. Along with Paris they fell on the local side of the community-imperial continuum of occupational interests.

[15] For Jaffrey, see John Wentworth, *The Wentworth Genealogy*, I, pp. 171–73, 304; Clifford K. Shipton, *Sibley's Harvard Graduates*, X, pp. 36–42. For the Warners, Wentworth, *Wentworth Genealogy*, I, pp. 171–87. For Nathaniel Folsom, *D. A. B.*, VI, pp. 494–95. Five of the seventeen New Hampshire late colonial executives were merchants, including Daniel Rindge and Mark Hunking Wentworth besides Jaffrey and the two Warners. All five resided in Portsmouth. Besides Folsom among the Revolutionaries, two others were merchants. Nicholas Gilman was both merchant and shipbuilder who lived in Exeter, and William Whipple resided in Portsmouth. Whipple seemingly had more than local trading connections.

[16] For Turner, consult Charles P. Keith, *The Provincial Councilors of Pennsylvania, Who Held Office between 1733 and 1776* (Philadelphia, 1883), pp. 220–21, 331. For John Bailey, *Lancaster Historical Society Proceedings* Vol. I (1896–1897), pp. 302–4, and Vol. XI (1907), pp. 30, 253–55. Turner, Thomas Willing, and William Logan were merchant higher officials among the late colonial group, and they worked and lived in Philadelphia. Timothy Matlack, George Bryan, and Thomas Wharton, Jr., besides Bailey, were merchants among the revolutionary group. They too resided in Philadelphia. Bryan, however, retired from his failing import business in the early 1770s, and Matlack loved to gamble and had constant problems with his finances. Neither was prospering on the eve of revolution.

[17] For a patronizing view, see Burton A. Konkle, *Thomas Willing and the First American Financial System* (Philadelphia, 1937); *D. A. B.*, XX, pp. 302–4.

[18] If we consider the four colonies which had urban centers of consequence (Massachusetts, New York, Pennsylvania, and South Carolina) and where higher offices were appointive, we find that all of the late colonial merchant executives resided in and centered their firms in the trading center (Boston, New York City, Philadelphia, and Charleston). Including the Massachusetts councilors elected by the lower house of the General Court, 82.1 per cent worked out of these four centers. With the revolutionary executives the figure dropped to 50 per cent. Half of the revolutionary merchant executives lived outside the major urban center of their respective four states. They were community entrepreneurs. In terms of appointive offices before the Revolution, then, merchants in urban centers had every advantage over merchants in outlying areas, but that was no longer the case once the Revolution began.

[19] Leonard W. Labaree, ed., *Royal Instructions to British Colonial Governors*, I, pp. 55–56.

[20] To Lord Dartmouth, New Bern, April 6, 1774, William L. Saunders, *et al.*, eds., *The Colonial [and State] Records of North Carolina* (30 vols., Raleigh, 1886–1914), IX, pp. 973–74.

[21]. Main, "Government by the People," *William and Mary Quarterly* (1966), pp. 392–93. For a general application of the scale, see Main, *Social Structure*, and *The Upper House in Revolutionary America*.

[22] In my estimation, Main's categories show a bias toward the top because two-thirds of the population are not represented in the highest three categories. In my own classification of leadership wealth, then, I have broadened out the *moderate* category and have included those families and individuals who had property holdings worth between £200 and £2,000, instead of between £500 and £2,000. Many freehold farmers would have been hard pressed to have come up with £500 worth of real and personal property, but they surely should not be classified in the lowest bracket of property holding along with indentured servants, desperate tenant farmers, day laborers, and slaves. Thus my use of the scale attempts to make the break at the bottom between those of generally *average* circumstances and those citizens who had little or no means to acquire personal wealth. It is my hope that the scale has more accuracy in making the division between *average* and *below average* rather than between *moderate* and the rest of the population.

[23] Seven of those with average amounts of wealth in the late colonial executive group came from Massachusetts; four were from Rhode Island; one was from Pennsylvania. Only one, John Morton of Pennsylvania, was an appointed official. The others were elected, either to the Massachusetts upper house or to the Rhode Island Board of Assistants. Generally, they were men of comfortable means whose primary source of income lay in farming. Typical was James Gowen of Kittery, Maine, who served in the Massachusetts upper house (1770–1774). Gowen's freehold estate was inventoried at £1,385 in 1781. The revolutionary executives of average personal means included seven from Massachusetts; four from Rhode Island; three from New York; three from New Jersey; seven from Pennsylvania; four from Delaware; two from Virginia; three from North Carolina. Most of these men were farmers like Councilor John Wetherill of New Jersey (1776–1777), a man who owned approximately five hundred acres when he died and had an inventoried estate of £411. Wetherill was not the type of individual whom royal governors turned to in nominating men for council commissions.

It should be pointed out, moreover, that age in no way affected levels of wealth among the three groups. Data in Chapter Six show that there was only a slight age differential among the late colonial, loyalist, and revolutionary higher officials. Furthermore, if we split each of the groups into two categories (comparing those who were forty and under, on the one hand, with those who were forty-one and older, on the other hand), we discover that younger leaders compared very favorably in terms of personal wealth with older officials, despite fewer years of adult earning power. Of those twelve men in the late colonial group who were of average means, eleven were over forty. The sole exception was John Congdon of Rhode Island, an elected councilor who was thirty-eight in 1774. There were thirty-three men of average financial standing among the revolutionary group. I was able to determine the ages of twenty-three of these leaders; all of them were over forty. Even if the other ten for whom ages are unknown were under forty, we could not conclude that age was somehow influencing comparative levels of wealth within the revolutionary group. There was no tendency, finally, for those under forty to fall more heavily in the well-to-do than the wealthy category. For the known cases in the late colonial group, twenty-two of those leaders who were under forty were personally wealthy as compared to two men under forty who were well-to-do. All of the loyalists who were under forty were wealthy while thirty of the sixty-three Revolutionaries under forty were wealthy. The other thirty-three men were well-to-do. If anything, the data suggest that younger men compensated for age disadvantages when entering the political arena through substantial personal wealth.

[24] Shipton, *Sibley's Harvard Graduates,* VI, pp. 221–31.

[25] Charles W. Brewster, *Rambles About Portsmouth: Sketches of Persons, Localities, and Incidents of Two Centuries* (2 vols., Portsmouth, 1859–1869), I, p. 163.

[26] *Ibid.,* I, pp. 105–6; Lorenzo Sabine, *Biographical Sketches of Loyalists,* I, p. 193.

[27] Quoted in Otis G. Hammond, *Tories of New Hampshire in the War of the Revolution* (Concord, 1917), pp. 42–43.

[28] Richard C. Haskett, "William Paterson, Attorney General of New Jersey," *William and Mary Quarterly,* 3rd Sers. 7 (1950), pp. 26–38. For a unique comparison of three different kinds of revolutionary elite lawyers, see Clement Eaton, "A Mirror of the Southern Colonial Lawyer: The Fee Books of Patrick Henry, Thomas Jefferson, and Waightstill Avery," *William and Mary Quarterly,* 3rd Sers. 8 (1951), pp. 520–34.

[29] Haskett, "William Paterson," *William and Mary Quarterly* (1950), pp. 26–38; See also *D. A. B.,* XIV, pp. 293–95.

[30] E. Alfred Jones, *American Members of the Inns of Court,* pp. 178–79; *D. A. B.,* XV, pp. 362–63.

[31] *D. A. B.,* XV, pp. 353–55. Jackson T. Main, "The One Hundred," *William and Mary Quarterly,* 3rd Sers. 11 (1954), p. 380, lists Edmund Randolph as owning 7,463 acres, 101 slaves, 19 horses, and 127 head of cattle in the 1780s. That was more than enough personal wealth to include Randolph *the lawyer* in the "one hundred" known wealthiest Virginia families.

[32] Kenneth Coleman, "James Wright," *Georgians in Profile: Historical Essays in Honor of Ellis Merton Coulter,* ed. Horace Montgomery (Athens, 1958), pp. 40–60; M. Eugene Sirmans, "The South Carolina Royal Council, 1720–1763," *William and Mary Quarterly,* 3rd Sers. 18 (1961), pp. 377, 383, 392. Consult also W. W. Abbot, *The Royal Governors of Georgia, 1754–1775* (Chapel Hill, 1959).

[33] William C. Pool, "An Economic Interpretation of the Ratification of the Federal Constitution in North Carolina, Part II: The Hillsboro Convention—The Economic Interests of the Anti-Federalists," *North Carolina Historical Review* 27 (1950), p. 308.

[34] Minnie R. H. Long, *General Griffith Rutherford and Allied Families* (Milwaukee, 1942), pp. 5–70.

CHAPTER FOUR

Breaking Ties in the Upper Class: Family Units and Political Tensions

I

THE FAMILY UNIT traditionally has been critical to the placement of young adults in socioeconomic structures. A wealthy family in the eighteenth century, as today, had the potential to pass property, status, and standing on to its progeny. By comparison, the poorer family could do little for its children. The wealthy family would be more willing to see that adolescents had the time and the financial support for formal educational experiences. Yet poorer families, swept up in the daily task of survival in the New World, hardly could afford to send offspring to the few schools of higher learning in the provinces, let alone to universities in England or Europe. Such children were fortunate if their parents allowed them the time to master the basic skills of reading and writing. Family status and wealth, moreover, brought children into contact with other expectant heirs in upper-class families. Marriages produced entangled family alliances among the better sort, often carrying over into politics. Younger adults within expanding upper-class family networks more easily came into contact with older and perhaps wiser family political leaders, helping them to an inside track in terms of connections when moving up the political ladder.

Perhaps most important before the Revolution, a wealthy family with established imperial contacts had the ultimate resource in setting offspring on the road to high offices. Children with imperial connections coming through families were less likely to experience political immobility in adulthood than were children from families with circumscribed financial, social, and political resources. Thus children from wealthy families more often found themselves embedded in the imperial end of the community-imperial continuum of interests, and normally that was to their political advantage. Children from average circumstances, on the other hand, usually knew only local community experiences before adulthood. It was more than probable that political immobility beyond the Assembly level was to be their fate in the provincial political arena.[1]

II

Many methods have been devised to measure changing social origins through time. Obviously family wealth, drawn primarily from estimates of the father's income, property, and occupational standing when the future political leader was in his youth, may serve as a common basis for comparisons. Family wealth may be aligned on the same scale that appeared in the last chapter in assessing levels of personal executive wealth (Table 4.1). On the whole, the families of late colonial and revolutionary executive leaders did not have as much wealth as did their ruling sons, but we must keep in mind a general rise in the standard of living among colonists during the eighteenth century.[2] Yet compared with norms in the population, executive families were well-off and generally members of the propertied upper class (defined as the privileged 10 per cent of well-to-do and wealthy citizens). Whereas 50 per cent of the combined executive elite officeholders were *personally* wealthy and over 40 per cent were well-to-do, only 34 per cent came from families categorized as wealthy and nearly 32 per cent as well-to-do. Indeed, the same number of executives (34 per cent) grew up in families of average means as families of wealthy circumstances.

When the combined executive elite percentages are broken down into subgroupings, we discover that a large proportion of those families in the average category produced revolutionary executives.[3] Those who became loyalists were more often from families of wealth (49.5 per cent) than were late colonial (40.3 per cent) or revolutionary leaders (26.4 per cent). Revolutionary insurgents most predominantly grew up in families with average amounts of property (40.7 per cent). Recalling that 89 per cent of the Revolutionaries had attained well-to-do or wealthy circumstances by the time of the outbreaking Revolution, the general pattern of upward economic mobility among the insurgent executives becomes clear.

Table 4.1

Comparative Family Wealth of the Executives

Level of Family Wealth	Combined Executive Elite (Number)	%	Late Colonial (Number)	%	Loyalist (Number)	%	Revolutionary (Number)	%
Wealthy	(140)	34.1	(81)	40.3	(57)	49.5	(68)	26.4
Well-to-do	(131)	31.8	(68)	33.8	(37)	32.2	(85)	32.9
Average	(140)	34.1	(52)	25.9	(21)	18.3	(105)	40.7
Below Average	(0)	0.0	(0)	0.0	(0)	0.0	(0)	0.0
TOTAL	(411)	100.0	(201)	100.0	(115)	100.0	(258)	100.0

Late colonial executives, on the whole from wealthier families, had greater family resources to rely upon in their advancement in society and government. They did not demonstrate as much upward economic mobility out of family circumstances as did the revolutionary insurgent leaders. But then again, great numbers of them had a better start in life. The revolutionary executives, by comparison, more often were men of personal initiative and drive—men with less of a start in life but individuals on the make who wanted to maximize their wealth and standing. Higher offices in government were one representation of maximum achievement for such men in the political realm, but for many of them their average family backgrounds were a disadvantage when officials controlling provincial executive appointments more willingly selected from among the sons of the most visible and prominent upper-class families. Family wealth was one factor that rising community leaders had to overcome if they wanted high offices before the Revolution.[4]

Many leaders had to struggle to gain socioeconomic status in the process of overcoming common family backgrounds, and such men found it much easier to obtain elective higher offices (Massachusetts, Rhode Island, and Connecticut) than appointive positions. Rather typical of those who were economically upwardly mobile was Samuel Huntington of Connecticut, who by the 1770s was a well-to-do lawyer, yet from yeoman stock. His ancestors were early settlers in the Puritan Massachusetts Bay colony, and his father Nathaniel was a freehold farmer and clothier residing in eastern Connecticut. Samuel grew to manhood working on the family farm and receiving only the bare rudiments of an education. At sixteen his father apprenticed him to a cooper, but while finishing his apprenticeship Samuel improved his reading and writing skills and began to study law. Soon admitted to the Connecticut bar, he opened a law office in Norwich, rapidly establishing himself as a community leader. In 1765 the local freemen elected him to the lower house of the Connecticut Assembly. Ten years later he became an assistant (councilor) before representing Connecticut in the Continental Congress and signing the Declaration of Independence. In the intervening years Huntington served as a justice of the peace and as a local King's attorney general. Enough assemblymen were impressed with his legal ability to appoint him in 1773 as an assistant judge of the Connecticut superior court. During the 1780s Samuel became successively chief justice of the superior court, lieutenant governor, and governor.[5] Huntington had advanced far beyond his freehold origins, and his rise to higher offices before 1776 had been easier in Connecticut because of the right that voters had to elect citizens to some high positions.

The case of Samuel Huntington also is instructive because he represented men from average family circumstances in both the late colonial and revolutionary executive groupings, most of whom in the late colonial group (thirty-three out of fifty-two or 64 per cent) lived in Massachusetts, Rhode Island, or Connecticut (provinces with varying types of internally controlled procedures for political advancement). Huntington had the opportunity to win high offices before the Revolution because the local populace or their elected leaders in the General Assembly, not ministers in England or royal and proprietary governors, controlled the power to make executive appointments. Huntington clearly lacked imperial connections. Voting citizens, however, cared more about his community socioeconomic standing and accomplishments within the localized context. Great family wealth did not mean as much as local prestige and whether one was "well affected" to the Jonathan Trumbull political faction. Thus community leaders, regardless of backgrounds, potentially could move into the highest offices in the "land of steady habits" before the Revolution; such men, even though upwardly mobile economically, generally lacked such opportunity in royal and proprietary provinces where appointment procedures were externally controlled.[6]

The importance of family wealth in the selection of higher officials varied according to the nature of advancement procedures in the provinces. Some 79 per cent of the parents of late colonial Maryland executives were classified as wealthy as were 65 per cent in Pennsylvania, 86 per cent in Virginia, and 64 per cent in South Carolina. Just over 58 per cent of all late colonial executives in the South were products of wealthy families, as compared to 31 per cent in the North where advancement procedures in Massachusetts, Rhode Island, and Connecticut held down the percentage. Personal success apparently had more meaning in movement into high offices where some semblance of popular control existed, but family wealth counted more heavily south of Pennsylvania where royal and proprietary appointment rules predominated (Table 4.2). Greater popular control over the selection of higher officials, more widespread after state constitution-making, seemingly reduced the importance of family credentials as a critical factor in personal po-

Table 4.2

Comparative Family Wealth of the Executives by Section *

	The North					
Level of	*Late Colonial*		*Loyalist*		*Revolutionary*	
Family Wealth	(Number)	%	(Number)	%	(Number)	%
Wealthy	(42)	31.3	(31)	42.5	(18)	12.6
Well-to-do	(49)	36.6	(26)	35.6	(50)	35.0
Average	(43)	32.1	(16)	21.9	(75)	52.4
Below Average	(0)	0.0	(0)	0.0	(0)	0.0
TOTAL	(134)	100.0	(73)	100.0	(143)	100.0
	The South					
Wealthy	(39)	58.2	(26)	61.9	(50)	43.5
Well-to-do	(19)	28.4	(11)	26.2	(35)	30.4
Average	(9)	13.4	(5)	11.9	(30)	26.1
Below Average	(0)	0.0	(0)	0.0	(0)	0.0
TOTAL	(67)	100.0	(42)	100.0	(115)	100.0

* The North includes New Hampshire, Massachusetts, Rhode Island, Connecticut, New York, New Jersey, and Pennsylvania. The South includes Delaware, Maryland, Virginia, North Carolina, South Carolina, and Georgia.

litical ascendancy. Political opportunities thus became more prevalent after 1776 for entrepreneurial community socioeconomic leaders.

In Maryland, to look at a proprietary colony, the executive appointive power before 1776 lay with the ruling Lord Baltimore, who normally confirmed the nominations of his provincial governor.[7] Social origins and proper family connections hence were more important than in Connecticut. The provincial governors naturally looked to well-established Maryland families for proprietary support in government. Thus the late colonial secretary, Daniel Dulany the Younger (1761–1774)—he also was a councilor (1757–1776)—had a wealthy father who came to Maryland as an immigrant, developed a profitable law practice, and ingratiated himself to the Calverts through service in a variety of offices ranging from attorney general to commissary general and admiralty judge.[8] The councilor Benedict Calvert (1748–1776) had even better connections, though slightly blemished. His wealth and standing came from his father, Charles Calvert, the fifth Lord Baltimore, who fathered him illegitimately. Charles achieved notoriety not because of his amours but because he was a member of Parliament, a lord of the Admiralty, and a fellow of the Royal Society. Benedict was an embarrassment, and thus Charles sent his bastard son to Maryland. First Benedict received a commission as collector of customs for Patuxent; then Charles approved him for the proprietary council. Just to keep the perquisites of the proprietorship in the family, Benedict married Elizabeth Calvert, daughter of the fifth Lord Baltimore's cousin. Besides political appointments, Benedict watched over Calvert family economic interests as well as his own plantation, Mount Airy. Even though illegitimate, his origins were both wealthy and critical to his political advancement.[9] Benedict Calvert and Daniel Dulany the Younger typify the kind of men who came from wealthy (79 per cent) and trusted families, men who filled executive offices for the proprietor in Maryland.

Provincial Virginia counted even more heavily upon great family wealth (86 per cent) than did Maryland. Councilor William Byrd III (1754–1776) was the son and heir of the wealthy tobacco magnate and land speculating diarist, William Byrd II. Secretary (1743–1782) and Councilor (1749–1776) Thomas Nelson was one of two prominent male heirs of the immigrant Thomas, a man who founded Yorktown in 1705 with the hope that it would become a trading center. The elder Thomas passed monetary distinctions to his sons after becoming quite wealthy in overseas commercial operations. Councilor Philip Ludwell Lee (1757–d.1775), the older brother of Richard Henry Lee, was the son of Thomas Lee, a wealthy tobacco planter who earlier in the eighteenth century held positions as naval officer, justice of the peace, militia colonel, burgess, councilor, and even for a short time acting governor (as head of the council). As eldest son Philip fell heir to the family fortune as well as to the "family place" on the council. Family wealth, one key to membership in the tobacco gentry elite, was a vital prerequisite for elite sons who found it possible to move into Virginia's late colonial executive offices.[10]

III

To this point our investigation of the family unit has been one-dimensional, but a second dimension may be included by looking at the value placed upon family names themselves. Some family names took on magic qualities as successive generations proved themselves capable of leadership in provincial America. One obvious example of a man with a "quality" name was the colonial and revolutionary Massachusetts councilor, John Winthrop IV (1773–1774, 1775–1777). John represented the fifth generation of a family that could trace its lineage directly back to the first Puritan governor of Massachusetts Bay, John Winthrop I. Councilor John IV's father, Adam, had not been one of the distinguished Winthrops. He speculated in land and engaged in commerce, but he never achieved great financial or political success. He was often in debt, yet he provided his progeny with the Winthrop name and comfortable financial circumstances.[11] Thus John IV had a family name that substituted for the prestige inherent in wealth. A brilliant man, John completed a Harvard B.A. in 1732 and took an M.A. in 1735. He demonstrated an uncanny ability to innovate in mathematics and the physical sciences; hence he replaced Isaac Greenwood as the Hollis Professor of Natural Philosophy at Harvard in 1738 when Greenwood was no longer able to control his drinking habits. From that time forward John stood out as one of colonial America's leading scientists, perhaps eclipsed only by Benjamin Franklin. Winthrop in 1746, for example, gave the first practical demonstration of electricity and magnetism in the provinces to his Harvard classes. He helped to formulate mathematical relationships which would assist in the development of integral and differential calculus. He also studied earthquakes, offering the hypothesis that they were caused by vibrations in the earth's surface, not by the wrath of God. (John Winthrop I would have been displeased with such speculation.) In 1765 through the intervention of Franklin, John IV gained membership in the exclusive Royal Society of London, an honor rarely bestowed upon "provincial" Americans.

Winthrop had a penetrating understanding of physics, mathematics, and astronomy, but his academic endeavors did not deter him from political involvement. He identified his interests with the Adams-Otis faction, opposed the policies of the Hutchinson-Oliver combination, and found himself elected to a position on the council in 1773. Winthrop hardly had time to get used to his office before the Boston Tea Party intervened and British authority collapsed; but Winthrop attended the first provincial congress of April 1774 and retained his council position when his fellow Revolutionaries restored the 1691 charter as the basis of government in 1775. He also became a justice of the peace as well as a probate judge for Middlesex County. Four years later John IV died, but the prominence of his family name lived on. Winthrop remained a name that would open doors in Massachusetts.[12]

Association with an old and distinguished family aided the standing of youthful family members in the deferential framework of provincial society. Indeed, over 59 per cent of the late colonial executives were descendants of old colonial families (defined as third generation or more). Some 73 per cent of the revolutionary insurgents, though, also came from old families, but family units that had not attained the high levels of wealth of colonial executive families. What is most interesting (Table 4.3) in the generational pattern is that loyalists came most rarely from old families (45.7 per cent) relative to the other two groups. Just under 28 per cent of the southern loyalist executives were from old families, yet over 64 per cent were immigrants, whereas in the North the figures were 59 per cent and 24 per cent respectively among loyalists. The difference points to the presence of placemen in many southern offices (North Carolina, South Carolina, and Georgia). By comparison only 17.5 per cent of the southern revolutionary executives were immigrants while 65.8 per cent were from old families. Men from old families led the surge into high southern offices after the collapse of British authority. Placemen and other nonnatives, on the other hand, did not have generations of commitment to the American provinces; it was easier (and perhaps necessary) for them to remain loyal to the

Table 4.3

Comparative Generational Pattern of Executive Families

Generation	Late Colonial (Number)	%	Loyalist (Number)	%	Revolutionary (Number)	%
Old Family *	(130)	59.3	(59)	45.7	(193)	73.1
New Family **	(31)	14.2	(17)	13.2	(38)	14.4
Immigrant	(58)	26.5	(53)	41.1	(33)	12.5
TOTAL	(219)	100.0	(129)	100.0	(264)	100.0

* The executive represents at least the third generation in the colonies. No less than his grandfather was the immigrant.

** The executive represents at least the second generation. No less than his father was the immigrant. The executive himself had to be born in the colonies.

mother country. Leaders from old families refused any longer to remain subordinate to placeman immigrants.[13]

Generations of family distinction, however, must also be understood in terms of the important part that a father played in establishing the socioeconomic prominence of sons. If the father was successful in developing a family reputation, then it really did not matter what grandfathers and great-grandfathers had done. The younger Daniel Dulany and Thomas Nelson constructed distinguished careers upon the socioeconomic accomplishments of their immigrant fathers. Governor John Wentworth of New Hampshire was able to tap the trading connections of his father Mark Hunking and the political connections of his uncle, Governor Benning, to gain the New Hampshire governorship. Philip Ludwell Lee watched over the tobacco-planting interests of his enterprising father Thomas. In none of these cases did the sons have to start and work up from next to nothing as had Samuel Huntington, despite a good Connecticut name. Their world had been made in good part by industrious fathers.

One of the best examples of a father working overtime to give his children every natural advantage in life relates to the case of the South Carolina immigrant physician, Dr. John Rutledge. Dr. John and his brother Andrew were the sons of an Irish tavernkeeper who managed to eke out enough income for Andrew to acquire the basics of a legal education. After the father died, Andrew turned over the small family patrimony for John's medical education; then he sailed to America looking for the opportunity to practice law. In 1733 Andrew married a young South Carolina widow, Sarah Boone Hext, whose uncle had been acting governor of the colony, and whose first husband had been a wealthy planter. It seemed that Andrew had found his way to substantial property, except for one small problem. Hugh Hext had bequeathed his estate to his widow only so long as she lived; then the total inheritance passed directly to their young daughter Sarah. Sarah was just nine years old when Andrew wrote to brother John suggesting that he might win the hand of the young girl. Andrew was trying to stop the Hext estate from passing through his own opportunistic hands. Dr. John at that time was serving as a physician in the East Indian service. It took him over two years to get to Charleston but only a few days to propose marriage. Realizing that his act was a bit premature, John waited and opened a medical office. Finally in December 1738, when Sarah had just celebrated her fourteenth birthday, she married the young doctor. He closed his medical office (never practicing again) and turned his attention to building up the Rutledge name to a place of social prominence in Charleston planter society.[14]

John also devoted much energy to propagating the Rutledge family. By the time Sarah was eighteen she had delivered four children, and another three would be born before her twenty-fifth birthday. The offspring included the first president (governor) of revolutionary South Carolina, John Rutledge (1776–1778, 1779–1782), and Edward Rutledge, a signer of the Declaration of Independence. Meantime, Dr. John became quite literally the "toast" of Charleston society. He concocted a drink known as "officers' punch," consisting of cognac with a touch of spice. The social elite took to his blend, but Dr. John overestimated his own capacity and died from what some have presumed was an overdose on Christmas day 1750.[15]

Dr. John had made use of the Hext estate for over a decade. He also had given the Rutledge name a certain kind of social respectability. Fortunately, there was more than enough money left from the estate to send young John, Jr., to the Inns of Court and to see him well established as a Charleston lawyer. A shrewd and hard-working man, John, Jr., quickly replenished the family coffers. Fifteen years later when he assumed the presidency of South Carolina, he was one of the richest lawyers in America. Among other assets he had five plantations, and his property was valued at £70,000 sterling with an annual cash income of £9,000.[16] He had become a central figure in the socioeconomic elite which rebelled in South Carolina, at least partially because they despised the superimposition of placemen of foreign birth in upper-hierarchy offices. Dr. John Rutledge had given his sons the opportunity to become leaders of insurgent resistance when he married many years before a wealthy fourteen-year-old heiress, and also by assiduously developing connections with the native socioeconomic elite. Between John Rutledge, Jr., the wealthy lawyer-planter, and his Irish tavernkeeping grandfather stood an opportunistic father.

Thus prominence came to family names in many ways. For Professor John Winthrop IV (before he demonstrated his scientific aptitude) it was an ancestry which had been instrumental in founding Puritan New England. For John Rutledge, Jr., the key had been a father who was unscrupulous enough to siphon off a family fortune for his own benefit. Good breeding helped, but an industrious, active, and socially and politically prominent father was a primary key to clearing channels to executive offices, especially before 1776. Unlike John Rutledge, though, many revolutionary insurgent executives did not have prominent (or notorious) fathers. Late colonial leaders depended more upon family energy in preparation for political ascendancy; revolutionary insurgents depended more upon their own drive and energy.

IV

Another way to summarize the change that occurred in family backgrounds would be to make comparisons on a scale devised by Sidney Aronson and designed to evaluate the social origins of political leaders. The scale analyzes the social standing, status, and prominence of one family unit relative to others. It takes into account the intrinsic value placed on family names (Winthrop, Livingston, or Byrd as compared to Henry, Dexter, or Paterson) based on the general socioeconomic and political accomplishments of fathers and previous generations. The function of the scale is to measure and rate the extent of family reputations.[17]

Thus sons with *Class I* origins were products of families with more than local reputations—the great families of colonial America. The Wentworths of New Hampshire, the Winthrops, Hutchinsons, and Olivers of Massachusetts, the Livingstons and De Lanceys of New York, the Penns and Logans of Pennsylvania, the Draytons, Bulls, and Pinckneys of South Carolina all had developed colony-wide and even intercolonial reputations by the mid-eighteenth century, if not before. Their children received recognition as coming from the best family stock on the American side of the imperial community. Royal and proprietary governors turned more readily to the scions of such families in nominating and selecting executive officials. The great families lent tradition and stability plus a sense of continuity to upper-hierarchy leadership; moreover, they had imperial attachments and connections and were usually more susceptible to carrying out the Crown's bidding.[18]

Directly below the great families were those clans of local prominence and reputation (*Class II*). This category refers to families of distinction in local settings who had not as yet earned colony-wide or intercolonial reputations. Usually the fathers or earlier generations in Class II families provided communities with lawyers, ministers, or merchants, men who also took noticeable roles in local political deliberations as town selectmen, justices of the peace, or militia officers. Class II families hence often led the grass-roots populace in economic, religious, and political matters. Their family trees had firm roots in years of community service, but the limbs had not been nurtured to the point where successive generations grew imperial branches, so vital to gaining upper-hierarchy political offices.

If approximately 2 to 5 per cent of all eighteenth-century families had attained Class I reputations and another estimated 5 to 15 per cent offered progeny respectable Class II origins, then a much larger portion of families, perhaps 40 to 55 per cent, were of relatively average *Class III* circumstances.[19] These were the families who were the backbone of American communities, families who toiled on farms as freeholders or who produced skilled and semi-skilled community artisans—fishermen, coopers, ropemakers, cobblers. They and their offspring represented the sturdy labor upon whose physical strength New World society emerged. Their sons had no special advantages of birth.

Finally, at the bottom of the scale and the bottom of society were the progeny of slave families, indentured servants, common day laborers, and destitute tenant farmers. They made up an estimated 20 to 30 per cent of all provincial American families, and they offered their sons little or nothing of a start in life, little more

Table 4.4

Social Origins of the Executives
Compared to the General Population

Social Origins of the Population	Late Colonial (Number)	%	Loyalist (Number)	%	Revolutionary (Number)	%
Class I 2 to 5%	(99)	49.3	(69)	60.0	(80)	31.0
Class II 5 to 15%	(68)	33.8	(33)	28.7	(100)	38.8
Class III 40 to 55%	(34)	16.9	(13)	11.3	(78)	30.2
Class IV 20 to 30%	(0)	0.0	(0)	0.0	(0)	0.0
TOTAL	(201)	100.0	(115)	100.0	(258)	100.0

that is than drudgery, misery, hard labor, scant economic rewards, and disdain from the better sort of citizens. Even the children of whites had to possess unique characteristics of intelligence and determination to rise out of the "mudsill" level of existence. None of the executive leaders with known backgrounds had *Class IV* social origins.[20]

The rating of executive leaders by family reputation and prominence confirms the general observation that revolutionary insurgents had more diverse and somewhat lower social origins than did late colonial and loyalist leaders (Table 4.4). Some 60 per cent of the loyalist, 49.3 per cent of the late colonial, but only 31 per cent of the revolutionary executives were products of Class I backgrounds.

While an estimated maximum of 20 per cent of all colonial and revolutionary American families gave sons Class I or Class II beginnings, 88.7 per cent of the loyalists and 83.1 per cent of the late colonial executives had such favorable backgrounds. Nearly 70 per cent of the Revolutionaries had similarly high origins, but the weight (38.8 per cent) was with Class II. Indeed, the most striking finding in the data is that the revolutionary executives were fairly evenly divided among the first three classes whereas the percentage distribution for the late colonial and loyalist leaders lay in the two highest categories with the brunt of their percentage in Class I. The revolutionary executives demonstrated a greater heterogeneity in family origins and less percentage family stature than did late colonial executives. More important, late colonial and loyalist executive families were more often of colony-wide and intercolonial reputations, a significant factor in passing imperial contacts to the emerging generation of office seekers.

In total, executive families ranked higher on the social origins scale than on the family wealth scale. John Winthrop IV again serves as an example to explain the discrepancy. His immediate family was not rated as wealthy, but his family name was of the highest quality, and therefore Winthrop fell into the Class I category. Samuel Huntington of Connecticut, likewise, had a long family tree, but his particular branch of the family were yeoman farmers. He had Class III origins. A distant relation of Huntington was Abraham Davenport who sat on the Connecticut council for eighteen years (1766–1784). His father was the Reverend John Davenport, a man who headed the local Congregational Church in Stamford. The very nature of John Davenport's occupation put his family in a position of high community status. Although Reverend John's property and income from his ministerial calling was not enough to include him in the well-to-do category, he was a central leader in the context of a local community and was able to pass that standing on to his son Abraham.[21]

The Class II family unit of Abraham Davenport was more common among revolutionary executives than was the Class III nexus of Samuel Huntington. The difference was important in that families like the Davenports usually had a broader range of contacts outside the local community, contacts which served to overcome family financial limitations. As a Congregational minister, the Reverend John Davenport had ties with Yale College. Abraham attended Yale, graduated in 1732, returned to Stamford, and then began to prove himself in community offices before being elected to the Assembly. His family's local prominence and his Yale education undoubtedly helped his burgeoning political career.[22]

Class II families had more to offer their children in the local context, that is as opposed to a colony-wide and intercolonial framework. Yet sons of Class II families, lacking imperial ties, still needed a burst of personal energy or a relatively open and internally directed political system if they aspired to holding high political offices, when compared to sons with Class I origins. Abraham Davenport had more to overcome in constructing a political career than did men like Daniel Dulany the Younger or Philip Ludwell Lee. Dulany and Lee grew up with greater access to high offices, but only as long as advancement procedures beyond the Assembly level remained in the hands of men who most readily had contact with Class I family units. Comparative percentages suggest that many men with local community stature resulting from birth or from economic achievements were unable to work their way to the top of the political hierarchy before the Revolution. They were on the local side of the community-imperial continuum, and their resentment about the political placement of the scions from the best families (those in the imperial orbit) was increasing.

V

An analysis of families would be incomplete without an investigation of family kinship ties, a critical factor in conceptualizing the insurgents' motivational pattern in the years of the coming Revolution. The late colonial executives had developed intricate networks of family kinship connections that became so entangled at times as almost to defy the power of genealogical explanation. Two brothers in one family, for example, would marry two sisters in another family, and then their children, as cousins, would intermarry. Wealthy Class I families preferred that their young marry among upper-class ranks.[23] By endorsing exclusionist attitudes toward less than well-to-do outsiders, upper-class families in prerevolutionary America tied themselves closer and closer together. In the years immediately preceding revolution, some family oligarchies had emerged and were dominating high offices in some provinces. Intricate family kinship ties underscored political combinations and added to the general pattern of political immobility faced by ambitious local community leaders without proper family ties (Table 4.5).

Table 4.5

Comparative Family Kinship Connections
of the Executives by Colony and State

Colony or State	Late Colonial (Number)	%	Loyalist (Number)	%	Revolutionary (Number)	%
New Hampshire	(13)	76.5	(11)	78.6	(5)	33.4
Massachusetts	(17)	50.0	(9)	64.3	(13)	38.2
Rhode Island	(3)	15.0	(0)	0.0	(3)	15.0
Connecticut	(8)	47.1	(0)	0.0	(7)	43.8
New York	(8)	42.1	(7)	38.9	(13)	41.9
New Jersey	(8)	47.1	(5)	41.7	(3)	14.3
Pennsylvania	(12)	70.6	(11)	84.6	(0)	0.0
Delaware	(0)	0.0	(0)	0.0	(0)	0.0
Maryland	(13)	68.4	(6)	60.0	(13)	44.8
Virginia	(13)	92.8	(7)	87.5	(20)	55.6
North Carolina	(4)	25.0	(2)	16.7	(7)	16.7
South Carolina	(8)	40.0	(5)	35.7	(17)	62.9
Georgia	(0)	0.0	(0)	0.0	(no data)	
AVERAGE TOTAL	(107)	46.3	(63)	47.0	(101)	32.8

In New Hampshire one family name, Wentworth, stood out above all others. The Wentworth oligarchy ruled over the northernmost of the revolting colonies for many decades before the Revolution. Over 76 per cent of the late colonial executives were interrelated to the Wentworths. The family traced its political origins back to Lieutenant Governor John Wentworth (1717–1730). The elder Wentworth held that office when it was the highest in the province. (Until 1741 New Hampshire and Massachusetts shared the same royal governor.) Before assuming the lieutenant governor's office, John worked as a sea captain and as a merchant, amassing a fortune of over £8,000. His eldest son was Benning, New Hampshire governor (1741–1767), and another son was Councilor Mark Hunking, father of the last royal governor John (1767–1775). Hannah, the eldest daughter of Lieutenant Governor John, married Theodore Atkinson, and Sarah, the second daughter, married George Jaffrey, Sr., father of the late colonial treasurer and councilor, George Jaffrey, Jr. The Wentworth family tree spread its branches outward as the eighteenth century progressed. Leverett Hubbard, a superior court judge (1763–1784), took as a wife a daughter of George Jaffrey, Jr., in 1769. Peter Gilman, councilor (1771–1775), married Dorothy Sherburne, whose mother was a sister of Lieutenant Governor John. Dorothy Sherburne's brother was John Sherburne, councilor (1774–1775). Daniel Warner, councilor (1753–1775), fathered Jonathan Warner, councilor (1766–1775), and the latter Warner married a granddaughter of Lieutenant Governor John in 1748 at the home of Theodore Atkinson. A citizen thus needed a twig on the rather confusing Wentworth family tree if he wanted political preferment in prerevolutionary New Hampshire.[24]

Family connections among New Hampshire executives became more intertwined as the British-American rift developed, yet even as early as the 1740s Wentworth opponents were voicing excited disapproval of family favoritism in leadership selection. The archenemy of Benning Wentworth, Richard Waldron, even took notes about Wentworth family ties which he hoped to use before the British ministry in pleading for Wentworth's removal from the governorship.[25] But Benning was able to ward off all opponents and to continue nominating and appointing his relatives to high New Hampshire offices. Only the Revolution cracked the pattern of family oligarchical domination. The early phase of the New Hampshire Revolution, in fact, represented a successful attempt on the part of lesser officials, scattered throughout the province, to oust the Wentworth clan from office and seize power for themselves.[26]

Upper-class family kinship ties in Massachusetts varied somewhat from those in New Hampshire. No one family was ascendant above all others, and family ties did not invariably follow court-country factional lines. Royal Governor Thomas Hutchinson's (1771–1774) wife was the sister of the wife of Lieutenant Governor Andrew Oliver (1771–1774). Andrew's brother was Peter

Oliver, who served as the last colonial chief justice of the Massachusetts superior court (1771–1774). One of Oliver's associate justices was Foster Hutchinson (1771–1774), brother of Governor Thomas. The Hutchinson-Oliver family nexus underpinned its pro-British political connections with family ties.[27] In some cases, though, family kinship ties cut across factional lines. The loyalist secretary, Thomas Flucker (1770–1774), married much earlier in life Judith Bowdoin, sister of James Bowdoin, councilor (1757–1769, 1770–1774, 1775–1777), and a revolutionary governor of Massachusetts during the 1780s. The Fluckers and Bowdoins probably were more interested in linking wealth gained through commercial activity than worrying about political factionalism. The loyalist treasurer, Harrison Gray (1753–1774), had a daughter who married Samuel A. Otis, brother of James Otis, Jr., in 1764. Gray fled to England when the Revolution struck while the Otises maintained their insurgent status. The marriage had originally been contracted with no reference to factional lines; its purpose was to unite the children of socioeconomic leaders.[28] Thus some marriages helped to undergird factional lines in Massachusetts whereas others, unlike those in New Hampshire, cut across these same lines.

Family kinship ties among New York executives involved the warring Livingston and De Lancey clans who fought to control political resources for years before the Revolution. Within the limits of the executive sample, the De Lanceys generally became tories while the Livingstons joined the revolutionary cause. The loyalist councilor, Oliver De Lancey (1760–1776), numbered among his relatives Lieutenant Governor Cadwallader Colden, whose daughter wed Oliver's brother Peter De Lancey. John Watts also became a member of the De Lancey family by marrying Ann, sister of Peter and Oliver De Lancey. Another councilor of loyalist persuasion, John Harris Cruger (1773–1776), married a daughter of Oliver De Lancey. Finally, Thomas Jones, an associate justice of the New York supreme court (1773–1776), joined the family by uniting with a daughter of James De Lancey, another brother of Oliver.[29] In many ways the De Lanceys typified late colonial elite families. They married among the most distinguished and wealthy citizens in the province. Their kinship ties gave form to the political faction that they represented in New York politics; moreover, leading family members turned loyalist with the coming Revolution. Unlike their Livingston family political rivals, they were controlling many New York offices at the wrong time and were caught defending ministerial schemes.[30]

It would be misleading to assume that all Livingstons were out of executive office when the Revolution came. Robert R. Livingston, the only son of Robert of Clermont, whose father was Robert, first lord of Livingston Manor, gained an appointment to the New York supreme court in 1763 long before he demonstrated opposition to British measures. He was serving in the Continental Congress and leaning in the direction of insurgency when he died in 1775.[31] Another prerevolutionary Livingston connection was William Smith, Jr., one of the acknowledged leaders of the Livingston coterie in late colonial New York. He married Janet Livingston before he accepted a council commission (1767–1776). Smith had a difficult time making a decision about which side to support in the Revolution, but after much thought and delay he became a loyalist, unlike most of his Livingston kin.[32]

Thus political leaders of the De Lancey family nexus did not survive the Revolution, but some from the Livingston unit did. In fact, the Livingstons linked up with rising community leaders in filling revolutionary New York offices. Lieutenant Governor Pierre Van Cortlandt (1777–1795) married Joanna Livingston in the late 1740s. She was the daughter of Gilbert, who was an indirect heir to family property left by Robert, first lord of the Manor. Peter Van Brugh Livingston, brother of Philip and William Livingston (governor of New Jersey, 1776–1790) served briefly as the revolutionary treasurer of New York (1776–1778). Philip, brother of Peter and William, held a New York state senate seat for only a few months (1777) before dying unexpectedly while attending the Continental Congress. Even John Jay, who served as New York's first state chief justice (1777–1779), was connected to the Livingstons through his wife. He married Sarah, daughter of William Livingston, in 1774. The Livingstons, then, were one of the few wealthy and well-placed colonial families to maintain themselves and to even gain offices in the internal upheaval of high leadership between 1774 and 1777.[33]

Prominent colonial families like the Livingstons often moved in larger orbits than the particular colony in which the family seat was located. William Livingston, for example, after providing leadership to the Livingston faction for years before the Revolution, retired to New Jersey in the early 1770s and laid out a pretentious country estate, later known as Liberty Hall. Tired of politics, he hoped to lead a quieter life and pursue the pleasures of semiretirement as a country gentleman. Because of his socioeconomic standing and political experience, however, Livingston found himself involved in the New Jersey Revolution and led his adopted state as governor through fourteen years of military and political conflict before dying in 1790.[34] Livingston could count among his New Jersey relatives William Alexander, the pretended Lord Stirling. Alexander had married William's sister Sarah before he set out for England in the 1750s to pursue his tenuous claim to the Stirling title. Embittered when the peers of the realm refused to award him peerage status, Alexander returned to New Jersey, lived in the style of a country gentleman, used the title Lord Stirling, and filled a position on the New Jersey council (1758–1775). Commissioned a general in the Continental service, Stirling developed a lackluster reputation as a military strategist and commander. Military reputation aside, he was a distinguished member of the Livingston family network who stood on the side of insurgency.[35]

Farther south in the tobacco-planting region of Maryland and Virginia a small number of upper-class families came to control most political offices. These families were extensively intertwined by the years of outbreaking revolution. Virginia ranked first (92.8 per cent) in terms of related late colonial executives and Maryland ranked fourth (68.4 per cent). Indeed, membership in one of the great tobacco-planting families was almost a requirement for holding almost any kind of political office. Class I family names included among others the Byrds, Carters, Fitzhughs, Lees, Pages, Tilghmans, Tayloes, and Wormeleys. Family kinship connections, moreover, represented intensive inbreeding among the great tobacco magnates. Robert "King" Carter and his Virginia progeny were most productive of genealogical confusion. Robert's first son was John (c.1690–1743) who married Elizabeth Hill. They had a daughter by the same name who wed William Byrd III of Westover, councilor (1754–1776). She died in 1761; Byrd looked around and eventually married a daughter of Thomas Willing of Pennsylvania. "King" Carter's eldest daughter, Elizabeth, married Nathaniel Burwell of Gloucester County, Virginia. By him she had Robert Carter Burwell of Isle of Wight County, councilor (1764–1776). When Nathaniel Burwell died Elizabeth took as a second husband Dr. George Nicholas and mothered Robert Carter Nicholas, the last colonial treasurer of Virginia (1764–1776) and member of the state chancery court until his death in 1780. "King" Carter married again later in life and had his fifth child, Robert of Nomini, father of Councilor Robert Carter (1758–1776). Another son of "King" Carter was Colonel Landon Carter of Sabine Hall, who married as his second wife a sister of William Byrd III and as his third wife, Elizabeth Wormeley of Rosegill, aunt of Ralph Wormeley III, councilor (1771–1776).[36]

By introducing the Page family tree, the pattern of family kinship ties in Virginia becomes even more complex. "King" Carter had a daughter, Judith, a young woman who like her brothers and sisters selected a mate from the sons and daughters of high ranking tobacco-planting families. Her husband was Mann Page of Rosewell. They had as one son Councilor John Page (1768–d.1774). John Page married Jane Byrd, sister of William Byrd III in 1746. Her nephew, John Page II, councilor (1773–1776), was the son of Mann, brother of Councilor John Page. Just to complete the circle, John Page II chose Frances Burwell as his bride in 1765; she was the daughter of Robert Carter Burwell, late colonial councilor from Isle of Wight County. Robert Carter Burwell was the son of John Page II's great aunt, Elizabeth Burwell Nicholas. The only summary that can be made is that the Virginia tobacco-planting families not only controlled political offices, but also inbred in a world unto themselves.[37]

Maryland family ties among the executives were not quite so entangled as those of the Virginians. The last proprietary governor, Robert Eden (1769–1776), was a descendant of a prominent Irish family. Both his father Robert and grandfather John attended sessions of Parliament. Robert, Jr., received an officer's commission, married Caroline Calvert, a legitimate daughter of the fifth Lord Baltimore (and therefore, half-sister of Benedict Calvert), and came to Maryland with governor's commission in hand during 1769.[38]

Another councilor, George Steuart (1769–1776), had a son who married a daughter of Benedict Calvert. A second Steuart daughter married James Tilghman in 1769, brother of Matthew Tilghman, a wealthy Eastern Shore tobacco planter who served as Maryland's speaker of the house in 1773 and 1774, presided over Maryland's revolutionary conventions, and attended the Continental Congress. Matthew sat in the new Maryland senate from 1777 to 1783.[39] Charles Carroll, known as the barrister, married Margaret, daughter of Matthew Tilghman, in 1763. He served in the senate (1777–1780) along with his Roman Catholic cousin, Charles Carroll of Carrollton, senator (1777–1801).[40] Great family kinship connections were so extensive in Virginia and Maryland that some family leaders—those who chose insurgent status—continued in authority even after the formation of revolutionary governments.

Only South Carolina had fewer interrelated late colonial executive leaders (40 per cent) than Revolutionary executives (nearly 63 per cent). This finding supports the point that native socioeconomic leaders shunned associations with placeman appointees in upper-hierarchy offices. The rule, however, was not ironclad. Not all upper-hierarchy officials were placemen—far from it. The Bull family had taken an active part in filling South Carolina executive offices for years. William Bull I had been lieutenant governor in the early eighteenth century, and his son William Bull II was the perennial lieutenant and acting governor in the years before the Revolution (1760–1761, 1764–1766, 1768, 1769–1771, 1773–1775). Well-educated members of the local planter elite, the Bulls were willing to associate with placemen. Other exceptions were John Drayton, councilor (1761–1775), who married as a second wife Charlotte, sister of William Bull II. Their son was William Henry Drayton, the man who became dissatisfied with his failure to get a permanent appointment to the circuit court and shortly thereafter became an active revolutionary insurgent. One of William Henry Drayton's cousins was Henrietta, daughter of William Bull II. She married Henry Middleton, councilor (1755–1775, 1776–1777), in 1762. The children of Henry Middleton wed sons and daughters of the Pinckney and Rutledge families.[41] When the Revolution came, the Bulls lost power, but the Draytons, Middletons, Pinckneys, and Rutledges did not. They led the native elite thrust.

On the whole, leaders from the great families were biding their time in the commons house of the South Carolina Assembly, looking for an opportunity to dispose of British placemen. They were storing up their wrath against outsiders like Edgerton Leigh. Leigh's father had been appointed as a placeman chief justice and councilor in the early 1750s. His son Edgerton, who was born and raised in England, took over the family enterprises in South Carolina from his father. He married into a distinguished native elite family when he wed Martha Breman, daughter of Henry Laurens's sister. It was not long until Leigh became one of the wealthiest lawyers and most successful plural officeholders in the province. In 1755 he took the post of surveyor general; in 1759 he received a council commission; in 1762 he became judge of the admiralty court; in 1765 he accepted the South Carolina attorney generalship. Leigh, moreover, actively supported new ministerial policies. Even though attached to the family of a local mercantile leader, an association rarely accorded placemen, Leigh was much too rigorous in condemning merchants' ships as admiralty judge—Henry Laurens's ships at that. Leigh became the butt of local elite abuse, and his private law practice fell apart. Not even a baronetcy awarded to him in 1772 could earn him the favor of native socioeconomic leaders. Leigh had been too willing to siphon off executive offices for himself and to carry out the controversial duties assigned to him. Then the final blow fell when he reputedly seduced his wife's younger sister while she was under his immediate family care. Leigh explained his fate in 1775 after he left South Carolina for the last time. He claimed that "from the year 1756 to the year 1766 he [Leigh] always made by his profession alone (Exclusive of his Employment) Ten or Twelve Hundred pounds sterling Per Annum, but since the last Mentioned Period he has never made more than One Hundred pounds sterling Per Annum, owing to the Successful Combinations of a powerful Faction, to whose Insults your Memorialist became Subject on the score of his public Stations." [42]

Leigh was both typical and atypical of South Carolina placemen. He had married into a noteworthy family; most had not. He also brought out the wrath and ill-treatment which only local socioeconomic elite leaders could hand out. Since most placemen were not intermarried with native elite families and the Revolution in South Carolina was directed by the leading families, there was a striking percentage increase in the numbers of interconnected executive leaders. The Laurens clan joined the Rutledges, Pinckneys, Hugers, Moultries, Draytons, and a few wealthy backcountry gentlemen in seizing upper administrative, legislative, and judicial offices. Like other late colonial scions of great families, they were intermarried; unlike them, they remained aloof from high offices until the Revolution cleansed the environment of placemen.

Table 4.6

Comparative Family Kinship Connections of the Executives

Extent of Connection	Late Colonial (Number)	%	Loyalist (Number)	%	Revolutionary (Number)	%
No Kinship Connections	(124)	53.7	(71)	53.0	(207)	67.2
Direct Kinship Connections *	(48)	20.8	(29)	21.6	(50)	16.2
Indirect Kinship Connections **	(59)	25.5	(34)	25.4	(51)	16.6
TOTAL	(231)	100.0	(134)	100.0	(308)	100.0

* Ties by blood, such as cousins, brothers, aunts, or uncles.
** Ties by marriage, representing an artificial link between the executives, such as brothers-in-law.

Whereas 47 per cent of the loyalist executives in the thirteen provinces were related in some way to one another as were 46.3 per cent of the whole late colonial group, the figure dropped to 32.8 per cent among the revolutionary insurgents (Table 4.6). No doubt the percentage difference would have been greater and the revolutionary figure lower had states like South Carolina not been included. Likewise, the revolutionary percentage would have been lower had states like New York and Maryland been eliminated. In these two cases some elite family leaders like the Livingstons continued in office. In qualitative terms the percentage difference was much sharper than the numbers indicate.

Another reason that change was of greater magnitude was that *fragmented* family ties replaced the elaborate family networks constructed during the eighteenth century. Instead of a relatively entangled web of kinship connections, ties among the Revolutionaries normally involved only an isolated number of individuals. Robert Sumner, a North Carolina senator (1777–1780, 1785–1788) and small plantation operator from Hertford County, for instance, was either the brother or first cousin of Luke Sumner, North Carolina senator (1777–1781) and planter from Chowan County. The Sumners, however, were not related to anyone else in the North Carolina revolutionary group.[43]   Robert Yates, a well-known New York Antifederalist opponent of the Constitution of 1787, became an associate justice of New York (1777–1790) and culminated his career as chief justice during the 1790s. His blood relative was Abraham Yates—Robert's grandfather was a brother of Abraham's father—who served the town of Albany for many years as councilman and sheriff before winning elections for the New York state senate (1777–1790). Abraham joined Robert in fighting state ratification of the Constitution of 1787. Neither man had any other kinship ties with New York revolutionary executive leaders.[44] The first state governor of Virginia, firebrand Patrick Henry (1776–1779, 1784–1786), numbered two other revolutionary upper-hierarchy leaders among his kin, but none of the Carter, Byrd, Page, Wormeley tobacco-gentry type. Henry's mother was Sarah Winston, and she had a brother William who fathered Edmund Winston, a locally prominent frontier lawyer and revolutionary senator (1776–1784). Edmund was not only Henry's cousin, but close friend; he even married Patrick's widow. Like Henry, Winston was interested in frontier land speculation. So was William Christian, a man of local economic stature who married Henry's sister Anne. Christian had Scots-Irish parents who started a general store in westernmost Augusta County. Despite undistinguished parentage, Christian studied law briefly in Henry's office, speculated in lands, and fought Indians during the Revolution. About as close as he came to the great families before the Revolution was during the 1760s when he served as a captain in William Byrd III's militia regiment. New governmental relationships, however, permitted him to establish himself on an equal plane with scions of the great tobacco families as a state senator (1776–1777, 1780–1784). Christian could not possibly have earned that distinction before the upheaval of 1776.[45]

Even though kinship ties remained among some revolutionary leaders, they were connections that meant little or nothing in terms of political advancement. Most relationships were too fragmented. Kinship ties were no longer of the entwined Wentworth, De Lancey, Carter type, ties which served to bring children up within the imperial framework and which supported privileged sons in their entrance into high offices. Some family units (the Livingstons and the South Carolina insurgents) did survive the onslaught of revolution, but domination of high offices by the children of intermarried elite families became more of the exception than the rule.

VI

A sound hypothesis, after investigating the family unit, would be that the constitutional relationships endorsed in new state governments during 1776 and 1777 effectively downgraded (but did not eliminate) the value of family wealth, status, and kinship connections as variables which previously supported patterns of political immobility for many who were not from families of imperial stature and reputation. Lesser officials, a surprising number of whom had risen out of middling family backgrounds, made it possible in writing the constitutions for greater numbers of citizens of demonstrated socioeconomic talent to move up the political ladder, so long as such citizens had earned some status in their home communities. The Patrick Henrys replaced the Lord Dunmores in high offices. David Ramsay was not that inaccurate when he stated that "all offices [now] lie open to *men of merit,* of whatever rank or condition; and that even the reins of state may be held by the *son of the poorest man,* if possessed of abilities equal to the important station." [46]

We have seen that poor men and their sons did not gain the opportunity to compete in the political arena on the highest office-holding levels, yet we have observed that greater numbers of individuals appeared who had shown that they were "men of merit" through personal economic accomplishments, even though from common family backgrounds. Such men had experienced the unfettered opportunity to advance in the economic structure. But compare the economic to the political structure. Mobility generally ceased for such men when they reached the Assembly level. There were still visible levels to conquer but few chances for advancement before 1774. Community entrepreneurs had not known barriers to mobility in the provincial economic structure, but they were experiencing them first hand in the political structure. Such men already had demonstrated their achievement orientation in the economic realm, but there was a gap between expectations and achievements in the political realm, a gap that was further enhanced by untrammeled economic success. That gap produced pent-up frustrations, frustrations that became one catalyst resulting in revolutionary behavior among men of lesser standing in the late colonial political elite.

Chapter Four: Notes

[1] It was not always an advantage for younger sons to be born into the best families. Consider the plight of Richard Henry Lee who desperately wanted a Virginia council appointment in the early 1760s but was blocked because of the presence of his older brother on the council (Philip Ludwell Lee, 1757–1775). Consult James C. Ballagh, ed., *The Letters of Richard Henry Lee* (2 vols., New York, 1911–1914), I, pp. 1–4.

[2] Aubrey C. Land, "Economic Base and Social Structure," *Journal of Economic History* (1965), pp. 639–54, demonstrates the rising standard through Chesapeake Bay area probate records.

[3] No doubt a few of the sons were from below average families, especially among those unknown cases in the revolutionary group. General Griffith Rutherford's parents apparently had no property or visible means of support when they migrated from Ireland. But there was no record that would prove poverty. Thus families like Rutherford's could not be classified. It is a safe assumption that some correlation exists between family poverty and lack of extant records.

[4] Sidney H. Aronson, *Status and Kinship in the Higher Civil Service,* pp. 67–76, lays stress upon the importance of families in the development of late colonial leadership elites.

[5] *The Huntington Family in America* (Hartford, 1915), pp. 419–21, 447–48, 535–50; *D. A. B.,* IX, pp. 418–19.

[6] Thirty-one of the thirty-three men from Massachusetts, Rhode Island, and Connecticut who grew up in average families were either directly or indirectly elected to office. If we subtract these thirty-one from the late colonial group, we have twenty-one men in high appointive office in all the thirteen colonies in 1773 and/or 1774 who were from average family backgrounds. These twenty-one represent 12.4 per cent of late colonial executives who were in appointive office, based on known cases.

[7] Consult Donnell M. Owings, *His Lordship's Patronage,* one of the few studies of prerevolutionary officeholding patterns and practices. Also of interest is Beverly McAnear, *The Income of the Colonial Governors of British North America* (New York, 1967).

[8] Aubrey C. Land, *The Dulanys of Maryland,* Studies in Maryland History no. 3 (Baltimore, 1955); *D. A. B.,* V, pp. 499–500.

[9] George N. Mackenzie, *et al.,* eds., *Colonial Families of the United States of America* (7 vols., New York and Baltimore, 1907–1920), II, pp. 165–66; George A. Hanson, *Old Kent: The Eastern Shore of Maryland* (Baltimore, 1876), p. 267.

[10] For Byrd, see Thomas A. Glenn, *Some Colonial Mansions and Those Who Lived in Them,* pp. 17–58; *Virginia Magazine of History and Biography* 9 (1901–1902), pp. 80–88. For Thomas Nelson, Lyon G. Tyler, *Encyclopedia of Virginia Biography* (5 vols., New York, 1915), I, pp. 157–58;

Virginia Magazine of History and Biography 9 (1901–1902), p. 356, and 16 (1908), pp. 23–24, and 33 (1925), pp. 192–93. For Lee, Burton J. Hendrick, *The Lees of Virginia: Biography of a Family* (New York, 1935), pp. 87–90; Cazenove Lee, *Lee Chronicle: Studies of the Early Generations of the Lees of Virginia* (New York, 1957), pp. 70–72.

[11] Clifford K. Shipton, *Sibley's Harvard Graduates,* IV, pp. 209–14.

[12] Lawrence S. Mayo, *The Winthrop Family in America* (Boston, 1948), pp. 167–93; Shipton, *Sibley's Harvard Graduates,* IX, pp. 240–64; *D. A. B.,* XX, pp. 414–16.

[13] In the North there was also an increase in the number of executive leaders from old families in the revolutionary group. Whereas 70.6 per cent of the northern late colonial executives were from old families, 79.2 per cent of the Revolutionaries were also products of old families. Thus there was only a slight percentage drop in the number of immigrants, specifically from 13.2 per cent in the late colonial group to 8.3 per cent in the revolutionary group. The percentage differences seem too slight to have meaning, but they should be placed in juxtaposition to the southern figures. See Chapter Six for more information.

[14] Richard H. Barry, *Mr. Rutledge of South Carolina* (New York, 1942), pp. 1–14.

[15] Joseph I. Waring, *A History of Medicine in South Carolina, 1670–1825* (Columbia, 1964), p. 303.

[16] *D. A. B.,* XVI, pp. 258–60; Forrest McDonald, *We the People: The Economic Origins of the Constitution* (Chicago, 1958), pp. 79–80.

[17] Aronson included those families of state, national, and international reputations in *Class I.* He also placed those families who had earned high status in local communities in that category. It is my feeling, though, that there was a difference in late colonial America between those families who had colony-wide and intercolonial reputations (those already known to officials with the power of executive appointment), and those families with more localized reputations (those who could hardly be known). Such families worked within the context of local institutions and perceived politics from the vantage point of American communities. They had not established contacts in the larger orbit of empire on the community-imperial continuum. Thus local families of prominence made up the bulk of my *Class II* grouping. Aronson's *Class III* and *Class IV* categories are for all practical purposes identical with my use of them. As with Professor Jackson Main, I am most indebted to Professor Aronson for his conceptualization of this scale. See *Status and Kinship,* pp. 67–76.

[18] For other data about social origins and patterns of upper-class family rule in prerevolutionary America, see Leonard W. Labaree, *Conservatism in Early American History,* pp. 1–31; Jackson T. Main, "Social Origins of a Political Elite: The Upper House in Revolutionary America," *Huntington Library Quarterly* 27 (1964), pp. 147–58; P. M. G. Harris, "The Social Origins of American Leaders: The Demographic Foundations," *Perspectives in*

American History, Vol. III, ed. Donald Fleming and Bernard Bailyn (Cambridge, 1969), pp. 159–344, has analyzed the social backgrounds of all kinds of American leaders which he applies to a cyclical theory of opportunity covering the span of American history.

[19] Whereas up to 10 per cent of the population fell into the upper class of property and wealth (well-to-do and wealthy), up to 20 per cent of all families could be included in the Class I and Class II categories. Community standing, especially on the local level, was much easier to earn than was wealth, as the example of Abraham Davenport's family demonstrates. More families had potential to earn community status and pass that on to their progeny than could earn and pass on significant wealth.

[20] Professor Main estimates that approximately one in five white adult males belonged to the class of dependent laborers. With the addition of blacks, it is possible that one-third of all eighteenth-century Americans fell into the lowest group on the eve of revolution, a much higher proportion than proponents of rampant middle-class democracy admit. See *The Social Structure of Revolutionary America,* pp. 66–67.

[21] Franklin B. Dexter, *Biographical Sketches of the Graduates of Yale College with Annals of the College History, 1701–1815* (6 vols., New York and New Haven, 1885–1912), I, pp. 444–46; E. B. Huntington, *The History of Stamford, Connecticut* (Stamford, 1868), pp. 381–83.

[22] *Idem;* Lucy Ann Carhart, *Genealogy of the Morris Family: Descendants of Thomas Morris of Connecticut* (New Haven, 1911), p. 143.

[23] Although class lines were fluid in early America, upper-class families did want their children to marry among the better sort. Children of planter families in Virginia, for example, did not have sustained contact with the lower sort. The general upper-class attitude is portrayed vividly in the family of Councilor Robert Carter of Nomini Hall, as recorded by Philip V. Fithian, *Journal and Letters of Philip Vickers Fithian, 1773–1774: A Plantation Tutor of the Old Dominion,* ed. Hunter D. Farish (Williamsburg, 1957).

[24] John Wentworth, *The Wentworth Genealogy,* I, pp. 95–101, 105–7, 171–87.

[25] *Ibid.,* I, p. 160; For correspondence dealing with Waldron's attempted move to oust Benning Wentworth and his family, consult Nathaniel Bouton, *et al.,* eds., *Documents and Records Relating to the Province, Towns, and State of New Hampshire* (40 vols., Manchester and Concord, 1867–1943), VI, pp. 38–68.

[26] James Kirby Martin, "A Model for the Coming American Revolution," *Journal of Social History* (1970), pp. 41–60.

[27] For Andrew Oliver, consult *D. A. B.,* XIV, pp. 14–15; Shipton, *Sibley's Harvard Graduates,* VII, pp. 383–413. For Peter Oliver, besides his published history of Massachusetts, see *D. A. B.,* XIV, pp. 22–23; Shipton, *Sibley's Harvard Graduates,* VIII, pp. 737–63. For Foster Hutchinson, Shipton, *Sibley's Harvard Graduates,* XI, pp. 237–43.

[28] For Flucker-Bowdoin kinship ties, see Temple Prime, *Some Account of*

the Bowdoin Family (New York, 1894), p. 7; Edmund J. and Horace G. Cleveland, *The Genealogy of the Cleveland and Cleaveland Families* (3 vols., Hartford, 1899), II, p. 1722. For Gray-Otis, M. D. Raymond, *Gray Genealogy* (Tarrytown, 1887), pp. 191–92.

[29] Margherita A. Hamm, *Famous Families of New York* (2 vols., New York, 1902), I, pp. 89–98; *Letter Book of John Watts,* Collections of the New-York Historical Society Vol. LXI, pp. ix–xvi.

[30] Carl Lotus Becker, *The History of Political Parties in the Province of New York,* pp. 253–76; Patricia U. Bonomi, *A Factious People: Politics and Society in Colonial New York* (New York, 1971), pp. 229–78.

[31] *D. A. B.,* XI, pp. 319–20.

[32] L. F. S. Upton, *The Loyal Whig: William Smith of New York and Quebec* (Toronto, 1969); William A. Benton, *Whig-Loyalism,* pp. 22–28, 182–89, 197–202; *D. A. B.,* XVII, pp. 357–58.

[33] Edwin B. Livingston, *The Livingstons of Livingston Manor* (New York, 1910), pp. 158–307.

[34] *Idem; D. A. B.,* XI, pp. 325–27.

[35] Alan Valentine, *Lord Stirling* (New York, 1969); Ludwig Schumacher, *Major-General the Earl of Stirling* (New York, 1897); *D. A. B.,* I, pp. 175–76.

[36] Glenn, *Some Colonial Mansions,* pp. 288–89; See also the relevant biographies in the *D. A. B.* and in Tyler, *Encyclopedia of Virginia Biography.*

[37] Richard C. M. Page, *Genealogy of the Page Family in America,* 2nd ed. (New York, 1893), pp. 71–81; *D. A. B.,* XIV, pp. 137–39; Tyler, *Encyclopedia of Virginia Biography,* I, p. 164; *Virginia Magazine of History and Biography* 34 (1926), pp. 275–77.

[38] Bernard C. Steiner, *Life and Administration of Sir Robert Eden,* Johns Hopkins Studies in Historical and Political Science [16 series] nos. 7–9 (Baltimore 1898), pp. 341–476; *D. A. B.,* VI, pp. 16–17.

[39] For Steuart, consult Hanson, *Old Kent,* pp. 239–40, 262–66, 383; Hester D. Richardson, *Side-Lights of Maryland History, with Sketches of Early Maryland Families* (2 vols., Baltimore, 1913), II, pp. 225–28. For Tilghman, Oswald Tilghman, *History of Talbot County Maryland, 1661–1861* (2 vols., Baltimore, 1915), I, pp. 423–32; *D. A. B.,* XVIII, pp. 543–44.

[40] For Charles the barrister, see E. Alfred Jones, *American Members of the Inns of Court,* pp. 39–40; *Maryland Historical Magazine* 9 (1914), pp. 336–47; Hanson, *Old Kent,* p. 149. For Charles of Carrollton, Kate M. Rowland, *The Life of Charles Carroll of Carrollton, 1737–1832* (2 vols., New York, 1898); *D. A. B.,* III, pp. 522–23.

[41] M. Eugene Sirmans, "The South Carolina Royal Council," *William and Mary Quarterly* (1961), pp. 373–92; For William Bull II, see *South Carolina Historical and Genealogical Magazine* 1 (1900), pp. 76–90; *D. A. B.,* III, pp. 252–53. For the Draytons, Emily H. D. Taylor, "The Draytons of South Carolina and Philadelphia," *Publications of the Genealogical Society of Pennsylvania* 8 (1921), pp. 1–26. For Middleton, Langdon Cheves, "Mid-

dleton of South Carolina," *South Carolina Historical and Genealogical Magazine* 1 (1900), pp. 230–32, 239–42; *D. A. B.,* XII, p. 600.

[42] Dated London, March 1775, quoted in H. Hale Bellot, "The Leighs in South Carolina," *Royal Historical Society Transactions,* 5th Sers. 6 (1956), pp. 183–84; Robert M. Calhoun and Robert M. Weir, "The Scandalous History of Sir Edgerton Leigh," *William and Mary Quarterly,* 3rd Sers. 26 (1969), pp. 47–74.

[43] Bryan Grimes, *Abstract of North Carolina Wills* (Raleigh, 1910), p. 365; Benjamin B. Winborne, *The Colonial and State History of Hertford County, N.C.* (n. p., 1906), pp. 24–36.

[44] For Robert Yates, see *D. A. B.,* XX, pp. 601–2. For Abraham Yates, Jr., *D. A. B.,* XX, pp. 597–98.

[45] For Henry, consult Robert D. Meade, *Patrick Henry: Patriot in the Making* (Philadelphia, 1957), pp. 66–67, 104–5, 235–36; *D. A. B.,* VIII, pp. 554–59. For Winston, Tyler, *Encyclopedia of Virginia Biography,* V, pp. 206–7; Clayton Torrence, *Winston of Virginia and Allied Families* (Richmond, 1927), pp. 18–24. For Christian, Robert D. Stoner, *A Seed-Bed of the Republic: A Study of the Pioneers in the Upper (Southern) Valley of Virginia* (Roanoke, 1962), pp. 165, 247, 285–89, 433–34; *D. A. B.,* IV, p. 96.

[46] "An Oration on the Advantages of American Independence," Hezekiah Niles, *Principle and Acts of the Revolution in America,* p. 375. *Italics mine.*

CHAPTER FIVE

Deferred Expectations: Educational and Religious Distinctions

I

PARENTS have an impact on the lives of their children not only by raising offspring in differing socioeconomic settings, but also by instilling attitudes and associations. The better sort in provincial America presumed that it was their right to guide decision-making in state and society, and they conveyed such attitudes to their children. Parents from upper-class families were aware that formal schooling would benefit their sons in preparation for leadership roles, given the assumption that only the most qualified and fit should rule. We would expect to discover from the data, then, that numbers of higher officials, unlike the masses of common citizens, had gone far in educational accomplishments, far enough to have graduated from the small number of colonial colleges and English and European universities open to them. Normal behavior would be that elite sons would take advantage of a gentleman's education with the prospect in view that they must be intellectually qualified for the acquisition of social and political authority in the years ahead.[1]

Another form of exposure with the potential to affect the formation of attitudes and behavior, especially in the eighteenth century, was religious identification. The youngster who grew up within the Anglican fold, representing the transplanted Church of England in the provinces, was more likely to be aware of and accept theories about indivisible British authority in the empire. In Anglicanism the late colonial higher official might reinforce other positive imperial associations.

Some eighteenth-century religious sects, by comparison, did not feel so well disposed toward the empire. Evangelical groups which had molded the Great Awakening of the late 1730s and early 1740s often fell into that category. "New Light" Congregation-alists, Baptists, and "New Side" Presbyterians among other groups emphasized personal confrontation with God through grace and the conversion experience. Such groups rejected the almost lifeless, good works, Arminian theology of Anglicanism. Some members in these sects came to believe that it was their duty to prepare the American wilderness for the coming millenium. Such people viewed imperial associations as more of a hindrance than a help in the construction of the pure society in which Jesus Christ would reappear.[2] Even in conjunction with "Old Lights" and anti-Awak-ening divines, believers outside the Anglican Church feared the in-troduction of Anglican bishops into the American community. Bishops smacked of tyranny and suppression of non-Anglican groups, whether essentially evangelical or rational in theological orientation.[3] Thus images of Anglicanism produced neutral, if not negative, responses from large numbers of colonists. The data should suggest that Anglicanism, especially in the northern colonies where it was not the established church, was more prevalent among late colonial and loyalist leaders, and that other religious groups, especially those viewing imperial ties with disdain, held greater sway over the religious orientation of revolutionary leaders.

II

Education in eighteenth-century America had not as yet taken on its formalized, hierarchical character. Schools and academies were few in number, and children did not pass through one grade after another studying toward the day when diplomas and degrees would imply to others the extent of their formal knowledge and in-telligence. Most education was informal and took place within the family circle. Children could consider themselves privileged if their parents permitted them to learn to read and write before adult-hood. A high, although undetermined proportion of colonists were anywhere from illiterate to semiliterate to functionally literate. Ed-ucation for many young citizens amounted to listening to parents and to mastering the art of reading or memorizing passages from the family Bible.[4]

Fewer children yet became vocational specialists. Parents apprenticed them to coopers, silversmiths, cobblers, clockmakers, and printers for a term of years so that the techniques of particular crafts would become the basis of livelihoods in the adult years. Some sons gained the equivalent of a formal legal or medical education by training with established medical or legal practitioners. An aspiring pettifogger might only read the basic law manuals before seeking out clients. Those who became doctors studied primitive medical treatises and then sought patients who were sick enough to take their chances about better health or death.[5] Some children learned the intricacies of mercantile activity by working in counting houses. Very few had family tutors like Philip V. Fithian, the young man from New Jersey who supervised the training of Councilor Robert Carter's children at Nomini Hall in Virginia.[6] Such education, formal or otherwise, had as its purpose the preparation of individuals for specific economic functions and roles in adulthood.

The rarest sort of individual in prerevolutionary America was the college-educated man. There were only a few colonial colleges, but wealthy families had the option to send children abroad for training at Oxford, Cambridge, the Inns of Court, the University of Edinburgh, or to one or more major European university. A safe estimate is that there were three thousand living college graduates in the thirteen provinces on the eve of revolution, a figure which must be set in contrast to a total population base of over two million.[7] Approximately one in every six hundred Americans had the chance to matriculate at or graduate from a college. Indeed, the college-trained student was a privileged person in a society which emphasized informal as opposed to formal schooling.

Although college-trained men were uncommon in the general population, they were more common among higher officials (Table 5.1). Thirty-one per cent of the combined executive elite attended or graduated from some college. The loyalists had the highest proportion of college men (just over 40 per cent) followed by the late colonial group (38 per cent). Revolutionary insurgents were not as favored with college training (27.5 per cent) but definitely were more exposed to classrooms than were the masses of citizens. With so few college-educated men in the population, the percentage dif-

Table 5.1

Comparative Formal Educational Experience of the Executives

Formal Educational Level	Late Colonial (Number)	%	Loyalist (Number)	%	Revolutionary (Number)	%
No Formal Education *	(108)	46.7	(58)	43.3	(166)	53.9
Some College-Attended	(9)	3.9	(7)	5.2	(6)	1.9
College Graduate	(79)	34.2	(47)	35.1	(79)	25.6
Equivalent in Law or Medicine **	(35)	15.2	(22)	16.4	(57)	18.6
TOTAL	(231)	100.0	(134)	100.0	(308)	100.0

* No formal education is here defined as not having attended or graduated from college, or not having studied in a legal or medical office. This definition does not preclude the possibility that the individual received other types of informal education, such as training in basic verbal and mathematical skills or such as clerking in a counting house or serving out an apprenticeship.

** Oftentimes, elite sons were educated in college and then studied in legal or medical offices. If so, they were counted as college graduates and not counted in this column. A surprising number of executive leaders who did not attend or graduate from college received legal and in a few cases medical training. Therefore, those percentages are treated here as equivalency training.

ference between the late colonial and revolutionary groups was slight.

When the War for American Independence began, colonial families had nine functioning colleges open to their children. The schools represented various levels of academic sophistication and standing. Harvard had been in operation for well over a century while Queen's College (later Rutgers) in New Jersey graduated its first young scholar at the 1774 commencement.[8] Only three of the colleges—Harvard (1636), William and Mary (1693), and Yale (1701)—had lengthy heritages. It was not until a second wave of college founding occurred, resulting on one hand from new levels in secular learning as part of the Enlightenment and from renewed religious enthusiasm and the concern for an educated and conversion-oriented ministry, somewhat ironically on the other hand, that families had multiple options in the selection of institutions of higher learning. Six new colleges appeared in the three decades before revolution: The College of Philadelphia (1740), later Pennsylvania; the College of New Jersey (1746), later Princeton; King's College (1754), later Columbia; the College of Rhode Island (1764), later Brown; Queen's College (1766), later Rutgers; and Dartmouth College (1769).[9]

Eight of the nine colleges were in the northern colonies. The geographical imbalance meant that numbers of executive leaders with college exposure varied from region to region. New England, having four institutions as well as two of the oldest, had the highest number of college men in the combined elite (39 per cent), and the middle colonies—New York through Delaware—had 27 per cent. Even though four colleges were located in the central region, they were relatively new institutions. Some had not been open long enough to have been available to older executive leaders. Twenty-eight per cent of the southern executive group, by comparison, attended or graduated from college, despite the presence of only one school, William and Mary, in that region. Because of the institutional void, southern elite parents sent their sons to northern schools or abroad. Indeed, it may have been this habit among the best families that made it difficult to plant new colleges on southern soil.

The data suggest that where it was possible future executive leaders matriculated at colleges in the immediate vicinity of their homes. Hence six of New Hampshire's seven combined elite college graduates attended Harvard. All of the Massachusetts college-educated leaders did likewise. Only Governor Jonathan Trumbull (1769–1784) and assistant William Williams (1776–1780, 1784–1803) of the Connecticut group went to Harvard; the others matriculated at Yale. New York executives split between Yale and the College of New Jersey, and a small number attended King's, the youngest of the three schools. Some southern executives traveled north to the College of New Jersey or the College of Philadelphia, but the majority either went to William and Mary or gained their training in England and/or on the European continent. Southern elite planting families most often were willing to send their children abroad for study. Thus approximately two-thirds of the native American provincials who read law at the Inns of Court in London before 1800 were from southern homes.[10]

Those late colonial and revolutionary higher officials who studied at the Inns of Court normally grew up in the most prominent, wealthy, and prestigious southern family units. The Inns of Court, consisting of the Middle Temple, the Inner Temple, Gray's Inn, and Lincoln's Inn, first began to control the educational standards of English legal practitioners during the fourteenth century. Started as voluntary guilds, the Inns gained in prestige and recognition; eventually, only those Englishmen who were trained there could achieve the highest legal ranking, that of barrister.[11] Representative of southerners who went to London to study law at the Inns was Maryland's secretary (1761–1774) and councilor (1757–1776), Daniel Dulany the Younger. Maryland's councilor Philip Thomas Lee (1773–1776) and revolutionary senator Robert Goldsborough (1777–1783) worked at the Middle Temple while another Maryland senator, William Paca (1777–1779), entered the Inner Temple in 1762 after graduating from the College of Philadelphia. Virginia councilors Robert Carter (1758–1776) and Philip Ludwell Lee (1757–d.1775) both were admitted to the Inner Temple in 1749, and William Byrd III, councilor (1754–1776), began legal studies at the Middle Temple in 1747. The revolutionary governor of South Carolina, John Rutledge (1776–1778, 1779–1782), entered the Middle Temple in 1754 as did Daniel Horry, legislative councilor (1776–1777, 1778–1780), in 1758. Southern higher officials of all political persuasions—loyalist, neutral, insurgent—went to the Inns of Court, became experts by the highest provincial legal standards, and led other colonists at the bar. Lack of southern colleges abetted such a distinguished outflow of upper-class sons.[12]

Southern higher officials, moreover, more often enjoyed broader educational experiences in English and European universities relative to northern leaders. The wealthy Maryland senator, Charles Carroll of Carrollton (1777–1801), perhaps had the most extensive European training among the executives. First taught by Jesuits, Carroll's Roman Catholic parents sent him to study at the College of St. Omer in French Flanders during the late 1740s. Young Charles also attended classes at the University of Rheims and the

College of Louis the Grand in Paris before traveling to England for many years of legal and bookkeeping training. Much of Carroll's youth involved learning abroad, at least until the 1760s when he returned to Maryland and began the development of a ten-thousand-acre plantation, drawn from the family patrimony in Frederick County.[13] Another southerner, Ralph Wormeley III, Virginia councilor (1771–1776), studied at Cambridge; William Bull II, South Carolina's last acting royal governor (1760–1761, 1764–1766, 1768, 1769–1771, 1773–1775), learned about medicine in his youth at the University of Leyden.[14] Such examples indicate that wealthy southern families put a premium upon education abroad as a prime factor in preparing their sons for leadership duties.

The opportunity for executive leaders to matriculate at colleges or universities, both in the North and the South, varied directly with levels of family income. Sons from wealthy and well-to-do backgrounds more often attended and graduated from colleges than did sons from average homes, unless the family was of the Abraham Davenport type. Families with great wealth apparently understood that college training was a valuable asset for socioeconomic and political advancement. Academic study set the advantaged few apart from the unlettered masses. Of those college graduates among executive leaders, 82.1 per cent of the late colonial, 84.8 per cent of the loyalist, and 77.6 per cent of the revolutionary group grew up in wealthy or well-to-do family units. At the same time there was some opportunity for sons from meager family backgrounds to attend colleges (Table 5.2).

A few families of average means and Class III community standing did get their sons into college. But unusual circumstances usually surrounded the case, and the family unit was likely to live within close proximity of the college. Jedidiah Foster of Massachusetts was such a person, a man who despite common origins received a Harvard degree. Foster was born and raised in Andover, where his father, Ephraim, was a blacksmith. Ephraim died when Jedidiah was young, and his mother married Lieutenant Nathaniel Frie. Frie recognized the intellectual powers of Jedidiah and encouraged friends and neighbors to subscribe to a fund which would support his stepson at Harvard. Graduating in 1744, Jedidiah settled in Brookfield in the employ of a distinguished local merchant, Joseph Dwight. Dwight saw merit in Foster, enough to let him marry his daughter and become part heir to the Dwight estate. With a Harvard degree and a locally prominent father-in-law, Jedidiah metamorphosed into a man of local stature and prominence. He became successively a deacon in the Congregational Church, a justice of the peace, a militia officer, and in 1761 an assemblymen for the first time. Foster attached his interests in the General Court to the

Table 5.2

Comparative Family Wealth of the Executive College Graduates

Level of Family Wealth	Late Colonial Graduates (Number)	%	Loyalist Graduates (Number)	%	Revolutionary Graduates (Number)	%
Wealthy Family	(36)	46.2	(26)	56.5	(30)	39.0
Well-to-do Family	(28)	35.9	(13)	28.3	(29)	37.6
Average Family	(14)	17.9	(7)	15.2	(18)	23.4
Below Average Family	(0)	0.0	(0)	0.0	(0)	0.0
TOTAL	(78)	100.0	(46)	100.0	(77)	100.0

Adams-Otis faction; he attended the Massachusetts provincial congress which returned to the 1691 charter as a temporary basis for revolutionary government; then he accepted appointment to the revolutionary upper house (1775–1776). In 1776 Foster became an associate justice on the state superior court circuit until his death in 1779. Judge Foster, despite common origins, fortunately had grown up in the vicinity of Harvard, where as a student he was able to develop personal poise and intelligence. These qualities more than likely brought him to Joseph Dwight's attention. Lacking family wealth but with family support and personal energy, Foster moved beyond his origins to take a leadership role in community affairs, and later (after the outbreak of revolution) in the state. Education was a critical factor in his socioeconomic and political mobility.[15]

In a few instances the family origins of college-trained higher officials were so obscure (an indication that the family had little wealth or prominence) that family economic circumstances could not be ascertained. Samuel Spencer, a revolutionary supreme court judge in North Carolina (1777–1794), was the product of such hidden and presumably humble origins. Available records indicate that Spencer grew to manhood in the vicinity of Princeton, New Jersey, where he graduated from the College of New Jersey in 1759. Spencer then migrated to Anson County, North Carolina, became a local lawyer of dubious reputation, and ultimately earned the wrath of North Carolina Regulators because he abused the privileges of his county clerkship. The office had fees attached to it, and Spencer purchased the right to hold the clerkship in the early 1760s. One Regulator petition complained about Spencer in 1768, maintaining that "his extortions are burdensome to all that fall in his power as he takes double and sometimes treble his due [in fees for services]—And though it is true he purchased his Office from Colonel Frohock and gave to the amount of £150 for it yet it's unreasonable we should bear the expense by way of extortion."[16]

Spencer more than likely had scrounged in his youth to make ends meet, and he had no inhibitions about overcharging for his services as clerk. Spencer was able to buy the clerkship because his law practice provided him with a tidy income. His legal ability no doubt depended upon the mental sagacity he developed as a student. Spencer's education was paying off but in a corrupt way. Despite Regulator complaints and eventual violence, Spencer retained his county office and allied himself with the North Carolina revolutionary movement. Once the new state constitution gained acceptance, Spencer willingly took the position as state associate justice, a position he held for the remainder of his life. As supreme court judge, he earned a reputation for honesty, fairness, and legal intelligence. Spencer became so respectable that his alma mater awarded him an honorary doctorate in the mid-1780s. If there was retributive justice, though, for his earlier chicanery, it came at the time of his death—and caused it. One day Spencer, old and tired, was out in his yard sunning himself when a large wild turkey emerged from the woods, spotted the Judge, and attacked him. Within a few hours

Spencer succumbed to the wounds inflicted by the crazed turkey![17]

The educational backgrounds of Jedidiah Foster and Samuel Spencer were not typical for men coming from their stations in life, but college training assisted them in their political ascendancy. Only 18 per cent of the late colonial executives (5 per cent with Class III origins) and 23 per cent of the Revolutionaries (12 per cent with Class III origins) who graduated from college had common backgrounds.

Extensive education correlated more strikingly with high levels of personal wealth. Of the combined executive group 57 per cent had accumulated at least £5,000 in real and personal property by

Table 5.3

Comparative Personal Wealth of the Executive College Graduates

Level of Personal Wealth	Late Colonial (Number)	%	Loyalist (Number)	%	Revolutionary (Number)	%
Wealthy	(47)	61.0	(32)	71.1	(38)	48.7
Well-to-do	(29)	37.7	(13)	28.9	(38)	48.7
Average	(1)	1.3	(0)	0.0	(2)	2.6
Below Average	(0)	0.0	(0)	0.0	(0)	0.0
TOTAL	(77)	100.0	(45)	100.0	(78)	100.0

the eve of revolution. Broken into subgroups, 61 per cent of the late colonial and 71 per cent of the loyalist executives with college degrees were wealthy relative to 48.7 per cent of the revolutionary insurgents (Table 5.3). Indeed, only three executive college graduates, one late colonial and two revolutionary leaders, were men of average financial means, despite the fact that 17.9 per cent and 23.4 per cent of their families respectively were in the same middling category. Formal education enhanced opportunities for economic mobility, resulting in a stronger platform for political office-holding. A formal education prepared the advantaged, relative to the uneducated, for the acquisition of other criteria (community standing and prestige) necessary for political mobility. Education was valuable and essential for those future higher officials who began life in average family circumstances.

III

It would be normal to assume that the academic interchange inherent in formal education affected the behavior of high officials in personal decisions about loyalty, neutrality, or revolutionary insurgency. The last royal governor of North Carolina, Josiah Martin (1771–1775), thought so. Martin explained his reasoning in commenting about Samuel Johnston, a late colonial deputy naval officer in North Carolina who served briefly as state treasurer (1777) before becoming governor and eventually a United States senator. Martin wrote to George Germain that "This Gentleman, my Lord, was educated in New England, where, as in the other case I mentioned, it may be supposed he received that bent to Democracy which he has manifested upon all occasions." Despite Johnston's "good private character," Governor Martin lamented that the former's New England experience caused him to take the "part of Moderator of a Provincial Congress" and to accept "from that illegal Assembly the Office of Treasurer of the Colony." [18]

Unfortunately, Martin's explanation for Johnston's insurgent behavior breaks down when we recall that leading loyalists like Thomas and Foster Hutchinson, Andrew and Peter Oliver, and John Wentworth also were products of New England's educational institutions. Andrew Allen, the loyalist attorney general of Pennsylvania (1769–1776), graduated in the same class (1759) from the College of Philadelphia as did William Paca, revolutionary senator from Maryland (1777–1779).[19] James Jauncey, Jr., loyalist councilor of New York (1775–1776)—he replaced the deceased Indian agent and councilor Sir William Johnson—was the college classmate of William Paterson, New Jersey's revolutionary attorney general (1776–1783).[20] Samuel Adams, secretary (1775–1780) and councilor (1775–1776, 1779–1780, 1781–1787) from Massachusetts, took his Harvard degree in 1740, three years before Foster Hutchinson, younger brother of Thomas and associate justice of Massachusetts (1771–1774), finished his Harvard education. Both men took many of the same subjects from the same teachers, but Adams turned into a rabid revolutionary while Hutchinson fled to England in 1775.[21] If the values instilled through education varied from region to region, they apparently did not directly affect decisions about insurgency as opposed to loyalty to the Crown.

Indeed, the content of college curriculums was in flux by the mid-eighteenth century, but not because of regional differences in educational values. Enlightenment, rationalist thought was taking its toll upon traditional course offerings. Deductive logic and syllogistic reasoning were losing out to inductive logic and scientific inquiry. The change epitomized the dawning of the shift away from theological to secular study. Students and teachers wanted to know more about this world and less about that to come. The new and burgeoning discipline was natural philosophy (the physical sciences) taught by intellectuals such as John Winthrop IV. Increasingly, advanced mathematics became a part of curriculums, even though Latin, Greek, and Hebrew were holding their own, as was moral philosophy, the general subject area in which students explored matters ranging from personal ethics to the conceptual foundations of political thought.[22]

No matter what the curricular emphasis, colleges sought to train their students in the arts of abstract reasoning and expression, valuable skills to have when political factions crossed swords in the political arena. The well-educated political leader used such skills in relating ideas to political situations, that is before projecting thoughts into political actions. Yet what ideas leaders preferred usually reflected the socioeconomic and political standing (level of officeholding) at that point in time when decisions became actions. The ideological content of political behavior correlated with the leader's sense of position in provincial social and political systems. Content also mirrored the leader's sense of what he might gain or lose if insurgent activity resulted in overt political revolution. No doubt college training benefited leaders in thinking about a wider range of ideas, but there was no relationship between exposure to ideas in college classrooms and any form of pro- or antirevolutionary behavior.[23]

The real significance of the educational variable as it pertained to the lives of the executives was the role that it played in provoking tensions between lesser and higher officials. Formal education, whether college training or some form of equivalent experience, placed men in the educated elite. College education marked men for leadership positions. Education produced high expectations in men who as youngsters had not enjoyed more than their share of scarce socioeconomic rewards. Such men, especially those from average family backgrounds, relished success, and with each new economic or political accomplishment they expected more success and recognition. Yet the pattern of prerevolutionary political immobility cut such men off from the highest offices and the greatest chances for colony-wide and intercolonial political standing. As a group of social scientists has recently hypothesized, education increases "social expectations" and the need for "social achievement." But lack of opportunity to advance may be productive of "systemic frustration" and violent behavior by such men in modernizing societies. Education compounds the sense of frustration when the educated do not realize their expectations.[24] Thus well-educated and highly motivated lesser officials looked at the handful of late colonial executive leaders who were as a group no better-educated than themselves. The crisis in empire set off by Parliament's approval of new imperial programs gave educated lesser officials the chance to release their frustrations by eventually sweeping the more favored old guard with imperial connections out of office.

IV

A son's opportunity to acquire formal education varied with parental attitudes and financial standing. The same two factors contributed to the construction of religious associations. Families exposed children to any one of a variety of religious sects ranging in theological content from the good works formalism of the Anglican Church to the firebrand, conversion-oriented ministrations of the Baptist Church. Generally, the Congregational Church had the greatest number of parishioners in New England, although Anglicans, Baptists, and Quakers were not insignificant numbers before the Revolution. The established Anglican Church prevailed in the South, but Presbyterians were enjoying greater freedom in frontier regions. No one religious sect controlled the middle colonies. Many groups—Anglicans, Baptists, Lutherans, Presbyterians, Quakers, and Roman Catholics plus Reformed and Pietist sects—flourished in New York, New Jersey, Pennsylvania, Delaware, and even into Maryland.[25]

For purposes of analysis, the assumption is that Anglicanism, representing the official Church of England, had the potential to affect the attitudes of its parishioners in a pro-British direction. Anglican preachers, especially in areas where other sects were numerically dominant, could always use their pulpits to preach allegiance to the mother country. David Ramsay commented in his history of the Revolution that "Presbyterians and Independents were almost universally attached to the measures of [the Continental] Congress," but that Anglicans, especially in the North, were not. Ramsay claimed that northern Anglican ministers were typically "pensioners on the bounty of the British government." Hence "the greatest part of their clergy, and many of their laity in these provinces, were therefore disposed to support a connection with Great Britain." Southern Anglicans, by comparison, "being under no such bias, were often among the warmest Whigs. Some of them foreseeing the downfall of religious establishments from the success of the Americans, were less active: but in general, where their church was able to support itself, their clergy and laity zealously espoused the cause of independence." [26]

The pattern discerned by Ramsay applied directly to the executive political elite. In New England where there were approximately ten Congregational parishes for every Anglican parish on the eve of revolution, 19.3 per cent of the late colonial and 8.2 per cent of the revolutionary executives identified with Anglicanism, compared to 47.1 per cent of the loyalists. In the South where Anglicanism prevailed and received official state support (perhaps 75 to 85 per cent of the southern population was Anglican), high percentages of late colonial (86.9 per cent), loyalist (89.1 per cent), and revolutionary leaders (77.7 per cent) demonstrated at least nominal Anglican tendencies. Among New England executives, Anglicanism more often characterized loyalists relative to nonloyalists. In the South it apparently made little percentage difference, except that the Revolutionaries tended more toward general population characteristics and more often worshiped in nonestablished churches (Tables 5.4 and 5.5).[27]

The data illustrate the mixed influence that established churches

Table 5.4

Religious Affiliations of the Executives

Affiliation or Sect	Late Colonial (Number)	%	Loyalist (Number)	%	Revolutionary (Number)	%
Congregational	(54)	23.4	(17)	12.7	(65)	21.2
Anglican	(133)	57.6	(99)	73.9	(134)	43.6
Presbyterian	(5)	2.2	(3)	2.2	(46)	14.9
Quaker	(7)	3.0	(2)	1.5	(5)	1.6
Baptist	(4)	1.7	(0)	0.0	(6)	1.9
Dutch Reformed	(1)	0.4	(1)	0.7	(10)	3.2
Lutheran	(0)	0.0	(0)	0.0	(1)	0.3
Roman Catholic	(0)	0.0	(0)	0.0	(1)	0.3
Unknown or No Association	(27)	11.7	(12)	9.0	(40)	13.0
TOTAL	(231)	100.0	(134)	100.0	(308)	100.0

Table 5.5

Select Religious Affiliations of the Executives by Region *

Affiliation or Sect	Late Colonial (Number)	%	Loyalist (Number)	%	Revolutionary (Number)	%
	New England					
Congregational	(52)	59.1	(15)	44.1	(64)	75.3
Anglican	(17)	19.3	(16)	47.1	(7)	8.2
Presbyterian	(0)	0.0	(0)	0.0	(1)	1.2
	The South					
Congregational	(1)	1.2	(1)	1.8	(0)	0.0
Anglican	(73)	86.9	(49)	89.1	(104)	77.7
Presbyterian	(1)	1.2	(0)	0.0	(10)	7.5

* The New England region includes New Hampshire, Massachusetts, Rhode Island, and Connecticut. The southern colonies include Maryland, Virginia, North Carolina, South Carolina, and Georgia. Figures do not total to 100 per cent because the percentages are based upon all religious groupings within the particular region.

had upon the religious affiliations of higher officials. Anglicanism dominated where it was established—in the South. There were only a handful of Congregational churches in the South, and they were scattered around Charleston. But in New England where Congregationalism enjoyed government-sponsored support, 59.1 per cent of the late colonial, 75.3 per cent of the revolutionary, and 44.1 per cent of the loyalist leaders were Congregationalists. Available evidence does not reveal the degree of commitment to theological positions (New Light and evangelical as opposed to Old Light and rational), but it does indicate that almost as many New England loyalists were members of the Congregational establishment as were members of the Anglican Church. The pull of regional religious norms was as powerful as were the reinforcing imperial effects of the Anglican Church.[28]

We may grasp better the importance of the religious variable as it influenced executive political behavior by looking at specific colonies. The ruling Wentworth oligarchy in New Hampshire was predominantly Anglican in religious orientation. Anglicanism was just one more factor which set off the Wentworth family as a distinct ruling group. Seventy-one per cent of New Hampshire's loyalist elite —tantamount to being a Wentworth—was Anglican. Yet only 20 per cent of the revolutionary leaders were; they were more heavily (67 per cent) Congregationalists. The Wentworth clan met on Sundays at Queen's Chapel in Portsmouth, one of two Anglican meeting houses in the province. The Wentworths, perhaps unwisely, had different religious values from the masses of citizens and many lesser official insurgents. Anglicanism may have abetted their downfall from power.[29]

In Massachusetts, on the other hand, late colonial executives were prone to worship within the dominant Congregational fold. Fully 91 per cent of the Massachusetts late colonial higher officials were Congregationalists as were 86 per cent and 97 per cent of the loyalists and Revolutionaries respectively. Individual executives may have become targets of insurgent wrath because of Anglicanism; another likelihood is that Anglicanism reinforced other imperial ties among the late colonial executives. In this context it is worth mentioning that Congregational revolutionary leaders also became the targets of Isaac Backus and other backcountry Baptists who publicly accused the revolutionary leaders of hypocrisy when the latter spoke of "liberty" in relation to imperial policies, but at the same time refused Baptists and other non-Congregational groups the freedom to pursue their own faith unfettered by laws forcing them to support Congregational parishes. The revolutionary leadership was weighted toward Congregationalism, and that Church remained established by the state into the nineteenth century.[30]

Connecticut higher officials, likewise, normally supported the Congregational Church. All but one of Connecticut's late colonial executives were Congregationalists. The lone exception was William Samuel Johnson, reputed to have been the first Anglican to be elected to the Connecticut Board of Assistants (1766–1776, 1786–1789). Born in Stratford, Connecticut, he was the son of Samuel Johnson, an Anglican clergyman who rebelled earlier in life against Congregational training and who later became the first president of King's College. William's upbringing was thoroughly Anglican, yet he gained admission to Yale, graduating in 1744. (Anglican beliefs were not that different from "Old Light" Congregational doctrines taught at Yale. Neither theology was evangelical or conversion-oriented.) Johnson completed his education by studying law and became a practicing attorney. After winning several Assembly elections, he joined many other Connecticut leaders in throwing Governor Thomas Fitch's faction out of office for supporting the Stamp Act. His reward was election to the upper house. While serving on the Board Johnson went to England as Connecticut's colonial agent; after returning he briefly filled in as associate supreme court judge (1772–1773). Johnson at best was moderate in his views about impending rebellion; he thus refused to go to the Continental Congress when elected in 1774. Johnson feared a permanent split with England; his Anglican background no doubt was one basis for his equivocation about American rights. His personal stand led to his purge from the Connecticut upper house in 1776. Although he sought privacy and remained unobtrusive, local insurgents arrested him once during the war on the charge of collusion with the enemy. Despite Johnson's own confusion in allegiance, he weathered the years of military action and revived his political career during the 1780s by first attending the Continental Congress and then participating in the deliberations at Philadelphia which produced the Constitution of 1787. Before retiring from public life, Johnson became the first president of Columbia College (formerly King's) and served as Connecticut's United States senator. Successful in the end, Johnson's family and personal association with the Anglican Church had not made the vicissitudes of revolution any easier for him.[31]

Johnson may well not have become a target of insurgent censure if he had practiced law and pursued his political aspirations in Anglican strongholds like Maryland, Virginia, and the other southern provinces. In the South the socioeconomic elite adhered with high frequency to the ways of the established Anglican Church. Seventy-nine per cent of the late colonial executives in Maryland, 81 per cent in North Carolina, 80 per cent in South Carolina, and 100 per cent in Virginia and Georgia maintained Anglican affiliations. Among revolutionary executives the figures dropped off to 83 per cent in Virginia and 50 per cent in North Carolina. The percentages of Anglicans, however, actually increased by small margins in Maryland and South Carolina.

The decline in Virginia and North Carolina indicates that backcountry Presbyterians found greater opportunity to earn high offices in revolutionary governments. Patrick Henry's brother-in-law, William Christian, Virginia senator (1776–1777, 1780–1784), was one example of a frontier leader raised by Scots-Irish parents according to Presbyterian tenets. The same may have been true about Sampson Mathews, another backcountry Virginia senator (1776–1782, 1790–1792), who emigrated from Ireland in his youth and joined other Scots-Irish settlers in sweeping south through Pennsylvania to the Great Valley of Virginia. Sampson won local recognition by running a tavern and general store in Staunton, Virginia. Even though he publicly supported the local Anglican parish, he retained his Presbyterian identifications and expressed them later in life once religious toleration became law in Virginia. Charles McLean represented those North Carolina Presbyterians among revolutionary leaders who found more opportunity after 1776 to hold high office. McLean migrated to North Carolina either from Ireland or Scotland and set up a modest freehold farm in frontier Tryon County. He became a militia officer, served successively against Indians and Regulators, and then sat only briefly in the North Carolina state senate (1776–1777) before continuing his military exploits. In later life McLean moved to Kentucky where one of his sons led in the organization of the Cumberland Presbyterian Church.[32] Greater sectarian diversity characterized leadership change in Virginia and North Carolina, reflecting direct frontier representation in upper houses for the first time.

The observations of David Ramsay were essentially correct as they apply to the religious affiliations of the higher officials. Anglicans in the North were out of alignment with the established Congregational Church. Anglicans represented definable cultural minorities in many areas. They could quite easily become focal points of insurgent hatred when Anglican executives stood out as visibly as they did. New Englanders, especially dedicated Congregationalists, feared ministerial plans to set up Anglican bishops in the provinces, potentially threatening long-standing Congregational authority as the normal Way in New England. It made sense to exorcise visible Anglicans from high office when insurgents argued that plans for American bishops were another ramification of the general ministerial conspiracy to destroy American liberties. In the South, on the other hand, Anglicanism was the pervasive, established way, especially among the socioeconomic elite. Leaders followed the accepted norm in worship. They did not stand out as religious deviants and potential corruptors of liberties. Late colonial executives did not feel threatened by those who adhered to the established norm, and therefore their Anglican associations did not strengthen other imperial ties and so often produce loyalist responses to revolution.[33]

V

Provincial Americans, especially those well-educated citizens making up the socioeconomic and political elites, were putting greater stress upon human reason and rationalism and less weight upon an omnipresent God in coping with the problems of their world. Theological hair-splitting no longer fascinated the typical elite leader to the extent that it excited ministers. Even those inspired men who carried on in the evangelical tradition of the Great

Awakening and emphasized the conversion experience as the basis for reaching the grace of God became more abstruse and dull as the Revolution neared.[34] Yet most elite leaders kept up at least nominal church affiliations, identifying with a particular sect. The individual's sense of religious association had some potential to be a powerful force in affecting loyalist, neutral, or revolutionary behavior, depending on how strongly the individual identified with his church. It appears from the data that it was easier for Congregationalists and Presbyterians to take the path of rebellion than it was for Anglican higher officials. A sense of imperial association arose more easily from Anglicanism, in many cases reinforcing extended webs of imperial ties.

The family was the prime agent in religious socialization. Consistently among all groups wealthy and well-to-do families more often directed sons to Anglicanism when compared to other religious groups (Table 5.6). Eighty-one per cent of the combined political elite Anglicans grew up in well-to-do or wealthy families. On the other hand, slightly over 50 per cent of the combined Congregational group came from average backgrounds as did 65 per cent of the Presbyterians. Anglicanism more often characterized the religious preference of sons from wealthy families, and wealthy families in turn more often had loyalist and/or imperial-oriented children. Anglicanism, relative to other groups, was the favored religious norm among socioeconomic and political elite leaders.

Local Anglican churches provided common meeting grounds for late colonial upper-class families. The Wentworths came together at Queen's Chapel in Portsmouth; the De Lanceys worshiped with other socioeconomic peers at Trinity Church in New York City; the leading Virginia tobacco-planting families mingled with each other at local parish churches. In Virginia elite families gathered both to worship and to socialize, but usually put greater emphasis upon the latter expression of group fellowship. Philip Fithian, tutor of Robert Carter's children at Nomini Hall, left a vivid portrait of Virginia Anglicans on Sunday mornings:

> . . . the three grand divisions of time at the Church on Sundays, [include] Viz. before Service giving and receiving letters of business, reading Advertisements, consulting about the

Table 5.6

Comparative Family Wealth of the Executives by Religious Affiliation

Anglican Executives

Level of Family Wealth	Combined Executive Elite		Late Colonial		Loyalist		Revolutionary	
	(Number)	%	(Number)	%	(Number)	%	(Number)	%
Wealthy	(108)	49.1	(60)	51.3	(43)	50.0	(53)	45.3
Well-to-do	(69)	31.4	(38)	32.5	(28)	32.6	(37)	31.6
Average	(43)	19.5	(19)	16.2	(15)	17.4	(27)	23.1
Below Average	(0)	0.0	(0)	0.0	(0)	0.0	(0)	0.0
TOTAL	(220)	100.0	(117)	100.0	(86)	100.0	(117)	100.0

Congregational Executives

Level of Family Wealth	Combined Executive Elite		Late Colonial		Loyalist		Revolutionary	
	(Number)	%	(Number)	%	(Number)	%	(Number)	%
Wealthy	(12)	13.2	(12)	22.2	(8)	47.1	(3)	4.8
Well-to-do	(33)	36.3	(19)	35.2	(5)	29.4	(26)	41.9
Average	(46)	50.5	(23)	42.6	(4)	23.5	(33)	53.3
Below Average	(0)	0.0	(0)	0.0	(0)	0.0	(0)	0.0
TOTAL	(91)	100.0	(54)	100.0	(17)	100.0	(62)	100.0

Presbyterian Executives

Level of Family Wealth	Combined Executive Elite		Late Colonial		Loyalist		Revolutionary	
	(Number)	%	(Number)	%	(Number)	%	(Number)	%
Wealthy	(7)	16.7	(2)	66.7	(2)	100.0	(5)	12.5
Well-to-do	(8)	19.0	(1)	33.3	(0)	0.0	(8)	20.0
Average	(27)	64.3	(0)	0.0	(0)	0.0	(27)	67.5
Below Average	(0)	0.0	(0)	0.0	(0)	0.0	(0)	0.0
TOTAL	(42)	100.0	(3)	100.0	(2)	100.0	(40)	100.0

price of Tobacco, Grain, etc. and settling either the lineage, Age, or qualities of favorite Horses. 2. In the Church at Service, prayers read over in haste, a Sermon seldom under and never over twenty minutes, but always made up of sound morality, or deep studied Metaphysics. 3. After Service is over three quarters of an hour spent in strolling around the Church among the Crowd, in which time you will be invited by several Gentlemen home with them to dinner.[35]

Fithian's description makes the point that planters were not so concerned with sharp theological caveats as they were with enjoying a leisurely and graceful life style. Tobacco planters and their families went to church in the fashion befitting their station in society. Intense and devoted worship of God was not their life calling, but once a week they did come into contact with ritual symbolizing ties with Great Britain.

Congregational and Presbyterian leaders, by comparison, did not attend religious services containing imperial symbols; their faith, no matter how varied in intensity of feeling from individual to individual, was devoid of British overtones. Their religious associations, as in the case of New Light and even Old Light groups fearing bishops, could even be anti-imperial in content. Given the lesser socioeconomic and political standing of many revolutionary Congregational and Presbyterian insurgents, their religious identifications did not act as counterforces to local community orientations. Indeed, in a region like New England such religious affiliations potentially became another reason for the movement against upper-hierarchy leaders. Congregational and Presbyterian insurgents lacked religious ties with the power to defer high expectations of political advancement.

Chapter Five: Notes

[1] Louis B. Wright, *The First Gentlemen of Virginia*, pp. 95–154; Robert M. Weir, "'The Harmony We Were Famous For': An Interpretation of Pre-Revolutionary South Carolina Politics," *William and Mary Quarterly*, 3rd Sers. 26 (1969), pp. 473–501. For upper-class attitudes about the importance of education for leadership, see representative editorials in *The Maryland Gazette*, December 3, 1767; *The Pennsylvania Chronicle, and Universal Advertiser*, August 29, 1768; *The Providence Gazette; and Country Journal*, October 26, 1768; the *South Carolina Gazette*, September 21, 1769, and October 5, 1769; *The New York Gazette; and the Weekly Mercury*, April 23, 1770. Generally these editorials lament the decline in standards.

[2] Alan Heimert, *Religion and the American Mind: From the Great Awakening to the Revolution* (Cambridge, 1966); Perry Miller, "From the Covenant to the Revival," *The Shaping of American Religion*, ed. James W. Smith and A. Leland Jamison (Princeton, 1961), pp. 322–68.

[3] Carl Bridenbaugh, *Mitre and Sceptre: Transatlantic Faiths, Ideas, Personalities, and Politics, 1689–1775* (New York, 1962), pp. 207–29; Arthur L. Cross, *The Anglican Episcopate and the American Colonies* (New York, 1902).

[4] Bernard Bailyn, *Education in the Forming of American Society: Needs and Opportunities for Study* (Chapel Hill, 1960), pp. 5–49; for a more detailed analysis largely predicated on Bailyn's model, consult Lawrence A. Cremin, *American Education: The Colonial Experience, 1607–1783* (New York, 1970).

[5] Daniel J. Boorstin, *The Americans: The Colonial Experience* (New York, 1958), pp. 191–239; Clement Eaton, "A Mirror of the Southern Colonial Lawyer," *William and Mary Quarterly* (1951), pp. 520–34.

[6] Not all colonial elite families approved of the quality of education in American colleges. According to Philip Fithian, the tutor of Robert Carter's children, that planter said the following about the College of William and Mary in 1774: "He informed me that it is in such confusion at present, and so badly directed, that he cannot send his Children with propriety there for Improvement and useful Education—That he has known the Professors to play all Night at Cards in public Houses in the City, and has often seen them drunken in the street!" See *Journal and Letters of Philip Vickers Fithian*, ed. Hunter D. Farish, pp. 64–65.

[7] Frederick Rudolph, *The American College and University: A History* (New York, 1962), p. 22; Figures are based on those of Walter C. Eells, *Baccalaureate Degrees Conferred by American Colleges in the 17th and 18th Centuries* (Washington, 1958). Eell's estimates come close to my own calculated from the biographical catalogues of the colonial colleges.

[8] Richard P. McCormick, *Rutgers: A Bicentennial History* (New Brunswick, 1966), pp. 14–16.

[9] Rudolph, *American College and University*, pp. 3–22; McCormick, *Rutgers*, pp. 1–6; For a summary statement, consult Beverly McAnear, "College Founding in the American Colonies, 1745–1775," *Mississippi Valley Historical Review* 42 (1955), pp. 24–44.

[10] J. G. de Roulhac Hamilton, "Southern Members of the Inns of Court," *North Carolina Historical Review* 10 (1933), pp. 273–86.

[11] *Ibid.*, p. 275.

[12] *Ibid.*, pp. 277–86; For a listing with biographical data of the select group of Americans studying at the Inns, see E. Alfred Jones, *American Members of the Inns of Court.* An important question has to do with why those elite sons educated at the Inns did not consistently choose loyalism. Education in England should have been a powerful force in forming imperial attitudes and ties. But we must keep in mind that educational experiences for many executives lay buried twenty to thirty years in the past. Other, more important intervening experiences affected decision-making at the time of revolution. For instance, if the leader was educated in England, traded in the empire, had strong Anglican ties, had held an upper-hierarchy office before the Revolution, then a safe prediction would be that such a man, having so many strong imperial ties, would find it difficult not to remain loyal to England. Yet a person like President John Rutledge, even though studying law at the Inns, made his fortune by providing legal services to native South Carolinians, local elite leaders who were upset with the inundation of placemen in high offices. Rutledge had not become part of the royal establishment and stood outside it, despite his educational experience. More immediate factors turned Rutledge in the direction of revolution. Indeed, in Rutledge's case as in those of other provincial leaders who studied at the Inns but had no high office later in life, their exceptional educational qualifications may have fed their rancor with those who were more favored than they within the political elite.

[13] Kate M. Rowland, *The Life of Charles Carroll of Carrollton*, I, pp. 18–69; *D. A. B.*, III, pp. 522–23.

[14] For William Bull II, see *South Carolina Historical and Genealogical Magazine* I (1900), pp. 76–90; *D. A. B.*, III, pp. 252–53. For Wormeley, Lyon G. Tyler, *Encyclopedia of Virginia Biography*, I, pp. 164–65; *Virginia Magazine of History and Biography* 16 (1908), pp. 16–17.

[15] Clifford K. Shipton, *Sibley's Harvard Graduates*, XI, pp. 395–98; Charles J. Adams, *Quabaug, 1660–1910* (Worcester, 1915), pp. 80–102.

[16] Solomon Crofts and others to Governor William Tryon, Anson County [1768], William L. Saunders, *et al.*, eds., *The Colonial [and State] Records of North Carolina*, VII, p. 808.

[17] John H. Wheeler, *Historical Sketches of North Carolina from 1584 to 1851* (2 vols., Philadelphia, 1851), I, pp. 64, 73, 77, II, pp. 24–25; John W.

Moore, *History of North Carolina* (2 vols., Raleigh, 1880), I, pp. 159, 240, 348, 415.

[18] New York, May 17, 1777, Saunders, ed., *Colonial Records of North Carolina*, X, pp. 401–2. For Samuel Johnston, see *D. A. B.*, X, pp. 150–51.

[19] For Andrew Allen, consult Jones, *American Members of the Inns of Court*, pp. 3–5; William A. Benton, *Whig-Loyalism*, pp. 31–33, 201–3; *D. A. B.*, I, pp. 184–85. For Paca, Oswald Tilghman, *History of Talbot County Maryland*, II, pp. 542–55; *D. A. B.*, XIV, pp. 123–124.

[20] For James Jauncey, Jr., see Lorenzo Sabine, *Biographical Sketches of Loyalists*, I, pp. 572–73; David McAdam, *et al.*, eds., *History of the Bench and Bar of New York* (2 vols., New York, 1897), I, p. 93. For Paterson, Richard C. Haskett, "William Paterson," *William and Mary Quarterly* (1950), pp. 26–38; *D. A. B.*, XIV, pp. 293–95.

[21] Samuel Adams was secretary of Massachusetts only in name. He had an assistant who did the work. The appointment amounted to a sinecure to provide Adams with necessary income so that he could support himself while attending the Continental Congress. See Shipton, *Sibley's Harvard Graduates*, X, pp. 419–65. For Adams and the provocation of rebellion, see John C. Miller, *Sam Adams*. For Foster Hutchinson, Shipton, *Sibley's Harvard Graduates*, XI, pp. 237–43.

[22] Rudolph, *American College and University*, pp. 25–26.

[23] Among those actually enrolled in colonial colleges during the outbreaking Revolution, however, the likelihood was that high percentages devoted themselves to rebellious activity. My statement presumes that the higher officials were no longer in college environments.

[24] Ivo K. Feierabend, *et al.*, "Social Change and Political Violence: Cross-National Patterns," *The History of Violence in America: A Report to the National Commission on the Causes and Prevention of Violence*, ed. Hugh D. Graham and Ted R. Gurr (New York, 1969), pp. 632–87.

[25] Edwin Scott Gaustad, *Historical Atlas of Religion in America* (New York, 1962), pp. 6–36. See especially Figure 7 on p. 5 for comparative estimates of the number of churches in the various colonies on the eve of revolution. Bridenbaugh, *Mitre and Sceptre*, p. 12. For general background information on the rise of various religious groups, consult William Warren Sweet, *Religion in Colonial America* (New York, 1942).

[26] *The History of the American Revolution* (2 vols., London, 1793), II, pp. 312–13. Most historians have concluded that loyalists had a greater penchant for Anglicanism than did nonloyalists. See Claude H. Van Tyne, *The Loyalists in the American Revolution* (New York, 1929), pp. 108–15; Wallace Brown, *The King's Friends: The Composition and Motives of the American Loyalist Claimants* (Providence, 1965), pp. 267–68.

[27] According to Gaustad, *Historical Atlas of Religion*, p. 9, there were seventy-one Anglican meeting houses in New England on the eve of revolution, compared to over seven hundred Congregational churches. Anglican-

ism was still predominant in the South, but many Presbyterian groups were forming on the frontier. Consult pp. 19–21.

[28] Heimert, *Religion and the American Mind,* makes the sharp distinction between evangelical and rational types in conflict after the Great Awakening. The former, according to Heimert, were instrumental in paving the way to revolution.

[29] Richard F. Upton, *Revolutionary New Hampshire,* pp. 59–60, 208. The breakdown of Congregational control is the subject of Charles B. Kinney, Jr., *Church and State: The Struggle for Separation in New Hampshire, 1630–1900* (New York, 1955).

[30] William G. McLouglin, *Isaac Backus and the American Pietistic Tradition* (Boston, 1967), pp. 110–92.

[31] George C. Groce, Jr., *William Samuel Johnson: A Maker of the Constitution* (New York, 1937); Benton, *Whig-Loyalism,* pp. 27–30, 114–17, 190–94; *D. A. B.,* X, pp. 131–34.

[32] For Christian, see Robert D. Stoner, *A Seed-Bed of the Republic,* pp. 165, 247, 285–89, 433–34; *D. A. B.,* IV, p. 96. For Mathews, Joseph A. Waddell, *Annals of Augusta County, Virginia, 1726–1781,* 2nd ed. (Staunton, 1902), pp. 278–79, 309–11; Howard M. Wilson, *The Tinkling Spring: Headwater of Freedom* (Fishersville, 1954), pp. 183–89, 205. For McLean, Clarence W. Griffin, *History of Old Tryon and Rutherford Counties, North Carolina, 1730–1936* (Asheville, 1937), pp. 20–21; Wheeler, *Historical Sketches of North Carolina,* I, p. 75.

[33] Bridenbaugh, *Mitre and Sceptre,* pp. 207–340. William Warren Sweet, "The Role of Anglicanism in the American Revolution," *Huntington Library Quarterly* 11 (1947), pp. 51–70, argued that loyalist tendencies among Anglicans varied directly with their dominance in particular regions. Where Anglicanism was the norm, it did not lead to as much loyalist behavior as where it set men apart as distinct (and perhaps unwelcome) religious minorities. For a similar, though generalized statement, consult William H. Nelson, *The American Tory* (New York, 1961).

[34] Edmund S. Morgan, "The American Revolution Considered as an Intellectual Movement," *Paths of American Thought,* ed. Arthur M. Schlesinger, Jr. and Morton White (New York, 1963), pp. 11–33.

[35] Fithian to John Peck, Nomini Hall, Virginia, August 12, 1774, *Journal and Letters of Philip Vickers Fithian,* ed. Hunter D. Farish, p. 167.

CHAPTER SIX

Middle-Aged Men of the Revolution: Factors of Age and Origin

I

AMONG THE MANY variables used by historians to explain revolutionary as opposed to loyalist behavior has been that of age. The eighteenth-century observer Dr. David Ramsay reasoned that "the age and temperament of individuals had often an influence in fixing their political character. Old men were seldom warm Whigs: they could not relish the great changes which were daily taking place; attached to ancient forms and habits, they could not readily accommodate themselves to new systems." [1] More recently Stanley Elkins and Eric McKitrick have argued that age was one critical factor in understanding why the Federalist Founding Fathers met in Philadelphia to write the Constitution of 1787. The Fathers were younger men; they possessed determination and driving energy in their campaign for a stronger national government; therefore, they were more willing to make the necessary leap of faith that they could implement a more powerful national government through the Constitution of 1787. The Founding Fathers had the right quantity of youthful vigor and energy which older Antifederalist Revolutionaries lacked.[2] Youth traditionally has been equated with freshness and vibrancy in life. It has been associated with movements for innovation and change in politics whereas age has been relegated to the unfortunate role of stuffiness, lack of driving dynamism, and general unwillingness to tolerate anything but the status quo.

Unfortunately for stereotypes, though, the available data about ages of executive leaders on the eve of revolution do not reveal a serious generation gap between colonial higher officials and revolutionary insurgents. The tendency is there, but it is not significant enough to become the basis for arguments that older and younger men were fighting for the power and privileges of office in the mid-1770s. Whereas 24 per cent of the late colonial executives and loyalists were over sixty years of age, only 12 per cent of the revolutionary leaders fell into the elderly category (Table 6.1). At the same time 25 per cent of the revolutionary group was under forty years old, but only 15 per cent of the late colonial executives and 17 per cent of the loyalists were.

On the surface these figures indicate that revolutionary leaders were somethat younger than executives under British sovereignty. But another standard measurement must be taken. The combined political elite averaged forty-nine years of age (median forty-eight). Both the loyalist and late colonial groups were slightly older. The loyalists averaged fifty-two years (median fifty) as did the late colonial executives (median fifty-two). The revolutionary insurgents were slightly younger, averaging almost forty-eight years of age (median forty-eight). Indeed, the net difference is only a few years, hardly great enough to assert a wide generation gap. Men bursting with youthful vigor had not taken over the highest offices of state governments in 1776 and 1777. It is doubtful, moreover, that men in their late forties have all that much more bodily energy than do men in their early fifties. The point of real interest is that the age differential was so slight (Table 6.2).

The oldest late colonial officeholder was Cadwallader Colden, councilor (1721–1776) and lieutenant governor (1761–1776) of New York. Colden was eighty-seven in 1775 when he decided to retire to his Long Island estate, Spring Hill, rather than continue to resist the revolutionary movement. Almost as old was Chief Justice Daniel Horsmanden of New York (1763–1776), born in 1694. His father Daniel was the Anglican rector of Purleigh, Essex County, England, and was a brother-in-law of William Byrd I. Horsmanden studied law at the Middle Temple and Inner Temple before migrating to New York in search of offices and profits. Horsmanden's career was both long and flamboyant. He worked closely with the De Lancey faction, becoming successively a councilor in 1733 and associate judge of the supreme court in 1735, only to be stripped of his offices a decade later when he supported the De Lanceys in

Table 6.1

Comparative Age Distribution of the Executives

Group	Age Range													
	21–25	26–30	31–35	36–40	41–45	46–50	51–55	56–60	61–65	66–70	71–75	76–80	81–85	86–90
Combined Executives	5	10	28	43	66	73	53	48	28	21	8	4	1	1
Late Colonial Executives	1	1	7	19	30	34	26	27	21	15	6	4	0	1
Loyalist Executives	1	1	4	12	17	20	12	14	7	10	4	4	0	1
Revolutionary Executives	4	9	22	28	44	47	36	28	13	11	4	0	1	0

Combined Executives = 389   Loyalist Executives = 107
Late Colonial Executives = 192   Revolutionary Executives = 247

Table 6.2

Comparative Average Age of the Executives by Colony and State

Colony or State	Late Colonial (Number)	Average	Loyalist (Number)	Average	Revolutionary (Number)	Average
New Hampshire	(15)	55.8	(12)	55.2	(14)	51.3
Massachusetts	(34)	56.8	(14)	60.4	(34)	51.6
Rhode Island	(19)	54.4	(5)	57.0	(19)	51.2
Connecticut	(17)	55.8	(1)	47.0	(16)	56.8
New York	(14)	52.8	(13)	52.5	(27)	46.1
New Jersey	(16)	48.6	(11)	50.4	(19)	45.8
Pennsylvania	(17)	53.4	(13)	53.4	(15)	46.0
Delaware	(3)	41.7	(1)	37.0	(11)	43.3
Maryland	(14)	46.1	(9)	45.7	(25)	42.9
Virginia	(13)	47.3	(8)	47.5	(26)	43.6
North Carolina	(11)	46.7	(7)	46.6	(17)	45.8
South Carolina	(11)	47.1	(6)	48.2	(24)	45.8
Georgia	(8)	55.6	(7)	54.4	(no data collected)	46.9
TOTAL AVERAGE	(192)	52.3	(107)	52.3	(247)	47.6
MEDIAN		52		50		48

Average and median ages are based on the year of sampling. For the late colonial and loyalist executives that year was 1774 (Massachusetts 1773). Thus columns one and two represent average and median ages as of 1774, except for the Massachusetts leaders. The calculations for the revolutionary executives (column three) are based on their entry to office after revolutionary governments began to function. For Massachusetts leaders that year was 1775; for New York, Delaware, Maryland, and North Carolina it was 1777; for the other seven states average and median ages are calculated as of the year 1776.

their opposition to Governor George Clinton. Eventually, though, with the removal of Clinton he won back his councilorship (1733–1747, 1755–1776) and moved into the chief justiceship. For over four decades Horsmanden stood out as a leading figure in New York politics. He was too committed to old ways to join the revolutionary cause.[3]

Benjamin Ogle of Maryland, on the other end of the age spectrum, was the youngest late colonial executive leader. Born in 1749, he accepted an appointment to the Maryland council in 1773, when he was just twenty-four years old. Ogle would never have been named to the council at such a young age if he had not had critical family connections with the Calverts. Ogle's father had served in an earlier decade as Maryland's resident governor, and the Ogles had kinship connections with other ruling planting families. Benjamin helped his own cause by studying at Oxford University. Thus Calvert favoritism descended quite naturally from a chosen and trustworthy father to his son. Benjamin could not mentally adjust to revolution, and he retired quietly from Maryland politics with the collapse of Calvert authority. Sitting out the war as a neutral, Ogle avoided the taint of loyalism placed upon many others and reemerged in the Maryland political arena to serve as state governor during the 1790s.[4]

Ogle and Colden had their insurgent counterparts in William Reed of Massachusetts and James Booth of Delaware. Reed nominally held an associate justiceship for one year after Massachusetts returned to its 1691 charter as the temporary basis of government. He had had a long career in the Massachusetts General Court, first being elected in 1742. He was eighty-two when the Massachusetts Revolutionaries selected him for the superior court. James Booth was born eleven years after the local Lexington, Massachusetts, freemen first elected Reed to represent them in the General Court. He was twenty-three years old when the revolutionary faction in Delaware drew him out of their ranks and named him the secretary of the convention that drafted Delaware's first state constitution. Booth lacked the vital family connections of a Benjamin Ogle, but he happened to be in the right place at a critical time because of his prorevolutionary sentiments. Booth's continued rapport with Delaware's revolutionary insurgents led to his lengthy term as state secretary (1778–1799).[5]

Thus men of all ages found their way into the ranks of the executive groupings. Stereotypes about youthful dynamism or elderly conservatism do not fit any of the groups. As an alternative hypothesis, then, it is possible that the lack of a significant age differential played an important part in generating revolutionary behavior. Many insurgent lesser officials, rapidly passing beyond the prime years of life, sensed either consciously or unconsciously that they were running out of time if they wanted to acquire upper-hierarchy offices in colonial governments. Upwardly mobile by measures of family wealth, community standing, and personal educational achievements, they had lived long enough to establish themselves as prominent local leaders. By all quantitative measures the revolutionary executives were industrious and ambitious men, but as lesser officials in the early 1770s they still confronted the tension-producing gap between their political expectations and achievements. For those who were at least middle-aged or older, the coming Revolution gave them the chance to close that gap before all opportunity was lost.

William Cabell of Union Hall, Amherst County, Virginia, was one of many revolutionary leaders who fitted the pattern. Cabell was forty-seven years old in 1776 when he assisted in drafting the Virginia state constitution. His father had migrated to the Chesapeake Bay area many years before, and as an Indian fighter, surveyor, deputy sheriff, surgeon, and tobacco planter, had taken an active role in opening up the Piedmont region to cultivation. Cabell's father used his surveying ability to select the best available lands for the family plantation. Within a generation his son William was living in the comfortable style of prominent tidewater planters. William quite naturally assumed a role in Amherst County politics. A vestryman and sheriff during the 1750s, the local freeholders first elected Cabell to the house of burgesses in the 1760s. By the time of revolution William was an active lesser official who had acquired title to over 15,000 acres of land and who owned an estimated ninety slaves. In terms of property and slaves, he had built upon his father's efforts and had become one of the leading planters in Piedmont Virginia.[6]

But William had not married into the select circle of great planting families—the Byrds, Carters, Lees, Randolphs, Pages, and Wormeleys—who dominated Virginia's upper-hierarchy offices. It

was unlikely, moreover, that he could acquire the prominence, contacts, or influence to be appointed to high office. He was simply not
a member of the old and established tidewater gentry. His grandfather was not "King" Carter; his father had been only an aggressive frontiersman and planter. William could hope at best to keep his
peripheral and subordinate status in relation to tidewater planters
and higher officials. Not surprisingly, then, Cabell was a dedicated
opponent to British policies among the burgesses. He attended all
of Virginia's revolutionary conventions and signed the insurgent
Declaration of Rights. He became the first elected state senator
from his district (1776–1781). The Revolution thus gave this middle-aged and upwardly mobile Virginian the opportunity to move
into higher offices. Cabell was not getting any younger in 1776.[7]

Neither was Azor Orne, a Massachusetts insurgent who was for-
ty-four years old when he was elevated to the revolutionary upper
house (1775–1777, 1780–1782, 1788–1796). Azor was the son of
Deacon Joshua Orne, a Marblehead merchant of well-to-do means.
The younger Orne learned the details of the family trading business
from his father and eventually took over the firm. He also involved
himself in community affairs, rose to the rank of militia colonel,
became a justice of the peace and a judge on the county court of
common pleas. In 1773 the Marblehead freemen elected him to the
General Court. This was his first colony-wide post, and he had
achieved it at the age of forty-two. From that point forward Orne
took an active part in leading the local revolutionary forces and in
ousting the Hutchinson-Oliver faction from power. Besides lengthy
service on the revolutionary council, Orne attended the 1779 Massachusetts constitutional convention. In 1788 he voted for adoption
of the new national Constitution of 1787 in representing Marblehead at the Massachusetts ratifying convention. Before his death
Orne even had the opportunity to vote for George Washington as a
presidential elector in the 1792 election. Despite the elective nature
of the prerevolutionary Massachusetts upper house which made it
theoretically possible for Orne to gain an upper-hierarchy office
(that was hardly William Cabell's situation), the coming Revolution
undoubtedly speeded up Orne's upward political mobility. It gave
the middle-aged Marblehead merchant the chance to expand upon
his localized accomplishments, once he won election to the General
Court and demonstrated his opposition to pro-British leaders.[8]

Azor Orne at least had the opportunity of election to the General Court before the disruption of colonial governments. Joseph Kershaw of South Carolina had not been so fortunate. Kershaw migrated to Charleston in the 1750s and clerked in a local retail store. He was nearly thirty years old (born in 1728) when another Charleston firm sought his labor and sent him into the South Carolina backcountry to open flour mills. Soon the ambitious Kershaw struck out for himself and built up one of the largest trading firms in the backcountry areas of Camden and Cheraw. Even though he served as the local sheriff after 1772, he was not able to gain election to the commons house of the Assembly—there was no provision for backcountry representation. Yet when William Henry Drayton and the Reverend William Tennent toured the Carolina backlands in 1775 to gain support for Charleston's stand against British policies and placemen, Kershaw, unlike many other local leaders, helped them. He was forty-seven years old when he threw the weight of his community standing into the revolutionary camp. He attended the provincial congresses, sat only briefly on the legislative council (1776–1777), but then took a large role as a military commander in defending South Carolina from British invasion. His military efforts, indeed, hampered full-blown development of his political career. The invading British captured Kershaw at the Battle of Camden in August 1780 and sent him out of the province rather than let him continue to influence the populace from jail. The British commanders even used Kershaw's home, since known as the Cornwallis House, as their headquarters. It was the most spacious and elegant house in the district. Kershaw eventually gained his freedom, returned to the Camden area in the 1780s, rebuilt his fortune, and won electoral contests for the Assembly. He died a wealthy entrepreneur in 1790, having served briefly (and probably longer if it had not been for his active military career) in the upper hierarchy of South Carolina government.[9]

Middle-aged men like Joseph Kershaw, Azor Orne, and William Cabell made the Revolution work just as much as did younger men with fiery, exuberant, and radical temperaments like Thomas Paine. Their age may have given a sense of urgency to their activity. Perhaps they saw in the revolution, subconsciously if in no other way, the opportunity to give added momentum to their personal socioeconomic and political mobility, as many were no longer young men. It took a lot more than youthful dynamism to build the American Revolution. Most of all it took political sagacity and experience, characteristics which came through the seasoning and maturity that middle-aged lesser officials had already gained in late colonial politics.

II

Age potentially affected loyalist or revolutionary behavior; so too did the place of birth of political elite leaders. The normal assumption would be that men born in the colonies would have stronger attachments to their native soil, especially if they were

Table 6.3

Places of Birth of the Executives

Place of Birth	Late Colonial (Number)	%	Loyalist (Number)	%	Revolutionary (Number)	%
Same Colony as Holding Office	(137)	61.2	(63)	47.7	(206)	76.1
Different Colony From Holding Office	(26)	11.6	(13)	9.9	(31)	11.4
Outside the Thirteen Colonies	(61)	27.2	(56)	42.4	(34)	12.5
TOTAL	(224)	100.0	(132)	100.0	(271)	100.0

from families with generations of commitment in colonial America. In a general sense the data confirm this observation. Only slightly over 20 per cent of the combined executive elite were born outside the thirteen colonies. Seventy-three per cent of the late colonial and 88 per cent of the revolutionary leaders were native to the American provinces. The Revolutionaries, moreover, tended more often to hold executive offices in their native provinces (76 per cent) relative to late colonial leaders (61 per cent). Loyalists, by comparison, were most often nonnatives (42 per cent) and tended least often to hold their executive office in the colony in which they were born (48 per cent). Place of birth, then, apparently did affect individual decisions either to work for or against the revolutionary cause (Table 6.3).

Table 6.4

Places of Birth of the Executives by Section

	The North					
	Late Colonial		Loyalist		Revolutionary	
Place of Birth	(Number)	%	(Number)	%	(Number)	%
Same Colony as Holding Office	(102)	73.4	(47)	61.0	(116)	79.0
Different Colony From Holding Office	(16)	11.5	(9)	11.7	(18)	12.2
Outside the Thirteen Colonies	(21)	15.1	(21)	27.3	(13)	8.8
TOTAL	(139)	100.0	(77)	100.0	(147)	100.0

	The South					
	Late Colonial		Loyalist		Revolutionary	
Place of Birth	(Number)	%	(Number)	%	(Number)	%
Same Colony as Holding Office	(35)	41.2	(16)	29.1	(90)	72.6
Different Colony From Holding Office	(10)	11.7	(4)	7.3	(13)	10.5
Outside the Thirteen Colonies	(40)	47.1	(35)	63.6	(21)	16.9
TOTAL	(85)	100.0	(55)	100.0	(124)	100.0

The difference in percentages suggests the degree to which non-native placemen participated in late colonial governments. Ministers in England were most fond of appointing placemen to southern offices. Approximately two out of every three non-Americans were to be found in southern colonial governments. Nonnatives, moreover, were interspersed throughout the upper-hierarchy structure. Many times English ministers awarded placemen more than one position so as to expand official and unofficial income. This practice only further compounded the problem of political immobility in late colonial America. Nonnative placemen were never popular with the native political elite, and the former found an unpleasant life awaiting them when they began official duties in the colonies (Table 6.4).[10]

Governor John Murray, Lord Dunmore, had better social credentials than did the average nonnative officeholder. He was of the Scottish peerage. As the eldest son of William Murray, the third Earl of Dunmore, the younger Murray succeeded his father to the family title and estate when the latter died in the 1750s. In the next decade Dunmore became one of the sixteen Scottish peers elected to Parliament. He spent much of his time in London cavorting with women of low reputation. Either he had become dissatisfied with his London life, had bankrupted himself, or was looking for different kinds of conquests when he accepted the governorship of New York in 1770. Dunmore arrived in New York City and quickly won the favor of the local landed, legal, and mercantile elite (many of whom longed for peerage status). Within a few months, however, the Board of Trade transferred Dunmore to Virginia where he served with slightly less favor as governor until his forced retirement to a British man-of-war during the summer of 1775. He had never been successful in earning the loyal respect of the great tobacco planters, perhaps because he maintained British policy with an iron hand, much to the ire of local insurgents like Patrick Henry, his revolutionary replacement in the governorship. Dunmore did not have the resources to stem the tide. One of his last acts before abdicating authority was the emancipation of Virginia slaves. He was not a permanent resident trying to develop a plantation in the New World. His Scottish and British background allowed for no other possible alternative except loyalism and consequent loss of power.[11]

More typical of the general run of placemen—few had peerage standing—were those men appointed to the late colonial South Carolina circuit court after it became a colony-wide institution in 1769. The chief justice, Thomas Knox Gordon, and three of the four assistant judges were not living in South Carolina when named to their offices. Gordon came from Dublin, Ireland, where he practiced law. One South Carolina historian claimed that Gordon's elevation to the chief justiceship and council (1771–1775) represented "the appointment of a vulgar, ignorant bully . . . for the gratification of a mistress of the secretary [Lord Hillsborough]."[12] Gordon's four assistants included John Fewtrell, Matthews Gosslett, Edward Savage, and John Murray. Little information has survived about them. John Fewtrell studied at the Inner

Temple, became an English barrister, and held his Carolina assistant judgeship until the insurgent provincial congress ordered the confinement of all the circuit court judges in 1775. Two years later Fewtrell left the state permanently. He and the other judges ostensibly were thrown out because they refused to take the oath of allegiance to the revolutionary government.[13]

Only John Murray could have objected to the placeman label. He had acquired medical training before migrating to Charleston in the early 1740s. He operated a drug business in Charleston to complement his medical practice. Murray won election to the commons house of Assembly, served as a justice of the peace, and worked as a private secretary to the governor. He married the third daughter of the Earl of Cromartie, Lady Anne Atkins. His appointment, then, to the assistant judgeship (1771–d.1774) presumably came through English peerage connections. Murray remained a popular and trusted figure among the local socioeconomic elite. Unlike many doctors, he had a solid reputation as a medical practitioner. It was his circuit court position which William Henry Drayton temporarily filled in 1774 after the doctor died, and which led Drayton, when the judgeship passed to another nonnative placeman, to attack placemanship in South Carolina as being exemplary of British tyranny.[14]

Not all placemen were born in England, Scotland, Ireland, or other parts of the empire. Occasionally they were native Americans, and they usually held office in colonies other than those in which they were born. (Men of the Thomas Hutchinson type were not really placemen; they were from old, native families. Their political enemies, however, to cast aspersions on them often referred to them as placemen. It was a political term full of derision.) Martin Howard of Rhode Island and North Carolina represented those who fitted the role of native American placemen. The date of Martin Howard's birth is unknown, but the Rhode Island Assembly admitted his father to freemanship status in 1726. Howard grew up in Newport, established himself as a lawyer, and associated with a group known as the Newport Junto, holding strongly pro-British views in the early years of imperial crisis. In 1765 Howard wrote a pamphlet which defended the Stamp Act. Before the year was out the local insurgent mob destroyed much of his and the Junto's personal property. With his reputation, legal career, and property holdings ruined, Howard went to England to seek reparations because of his loyalty on the Stamp Act issue. The Board of Trade responded in 1766 by naming him to the North Carolina chief justiceship, a post that Martin held along with a councilorship until the outbreak of revolutionary warfare. To local leaders his specific place of birth did not matter. Howard was just another placeman outsider, to be treated as such.[15]

After the suspension of North Carolina's colonial courts, Howard retired to his homestead in Craven County—his principal income came from his offices—and lived quietly until revolutionary insurgents confronted him with the state loyalty oath. Howard refused to swear allegiance and retired with his family to British-occupied New York City. He soon sailed for England and died before the peace settlement. Like other placemen in colonial governments, his life ended in the country which no longer had the legitimacy or the strength to sustain him in power.[16]

For late colonial leaders, then, birthplaces outside the colonies usually indicated that they were placemen. It was otherwise with revolutionary executives. Most of the revolutionary nonnatives (12 per cent) were of the Griffith Rutherford and Sampson Mathews type, men who had come to the colonies with parents hoping to improve upon their Old World position in life. Their sons led in developing frontier regions and became local political elite leaders. Yet they were a relative minority of the revolutionary group. They were certainly less numerous than were nonnative placemen in late colonial and loyalist ranks.

Over 76 per cent of the revolutionary executives were native to their colonies, and over 73 per cent were from old families (third generation or more in America). They had long been associated with and identified with their local communities. Only 59 per cent of the late colonial and 46 per cent of the loyalist executives, on the other hand, came from old families. Relative to the revolutionary insurgents, their roots did not run so deep in American soil. Fewer could trace their family lineages back into the colonial past. Fewer were born in the colonies. Their American ties and feelings thus were commensurately weaker. Late colonial and loyalist leaders more often looked through the imperial lens and found it colored by their place of birth and non-American family heritage. It made sense for them to cling tenaciously to the vanishing authority of the mother country.

III

Various factors combined differently in the lives of late colonial and revolutionary higher officials to determine whether they resisted or joined the revolutionary cause. Indeed, what side to take was the fundamental question that all political leaders (and most colonists) had to resolve between 1774 and 1777. Primary decision-making factors were those variables affecting the range of contacts, interests, and perceptions of individuals on the eve of revolution. Past experiences and associations likewise mattered, but not with the same intensity as immediate factors. Few men of standing had the chance to make completely rational decisions based solely on the context of widespread political argumentation and ideology. Individual placement in the socioeconomic and political structures narrowed the possibility for detached reasoning. But placement did have an impact upon the development of supporting ideas in decision-making.[17]

Each individual had the potential to act and to be acted upon as the Revolution neared. Cumulative life experiences affected and often forced men to select from among unresolvable alternatives. Some life experiences, normally those closest in time to the point of decision-making, played the most important part in responses to individual dilemmas. This study has attempted to isolate and quantify a wide range of those variables (occupation, wealth, family status, kinship ties, education, religious affiliation, age, and place of birth) which influenced behavior. Each political elite leader represented a unique blending of such characteristics, yet patterns emerged from the data indicating differences in the collected lives of late colonial and revolutionary executives. The patterns suggest reasons why some became loyalists while others became dedicated insurgents. Behavioral motivation for or against revolution was the end product of conflicting human experiences.[18]

William Tryon, for example, who served as the last royal governor of New York (1771–1775) after holding the governorship in North Carolina, was so much a product of the British empire that it would have been nearly impossible for him to throw off his allegiance to the mother country. The son of an English landed gentry family, Tryon married a wealthy heiress in 1757 and took a commission in a British regiment of Foot Guards before sailing to North Carolina. The placeman Tryon lived on the income which his wife and his governorships provided. He was an outsider, a symbol of British authority when the Revolution turned to open warfare in New York. Tryon had little alternative but to retreat to a British war vessel in New York harbor. His life had too much of an imperial orientation to permit anything but dedicated loyalism.[19]

David Ogden of New Jersey, like Tryon, became a loyalist; but unlike Tryon, he was native to the provinces and New Jersey. Both a prerevolutionary councilor (1751–1775) and an associate justice of the colony's highest court (1772–1775), Ogden's ancestors had settled in Elizabethtown over a century before his time of decision. Ogden's father was one founder of the Newark Anglican Church, and his son early identified with the Church of England. A Yale graduate of 1728, Ogden studied law in New York City; by the time of his elevation to the council, he enjoyed wealth and status as a practicing attorney. He benefited immeasurably under the New Jersey royal regime and had no reason to desire governmental upheaval. Religious training, monetary success at the bar (the Loyalists' Claims Commission granted him over £9,000 sterling for property losses), age (he was sixty-seven in 1774), and his high offices all outweighed his lengthy New Jersey ancestry and pushed him toward loyalism. Less than two years later he fled for his personal safety behind British lines in New York, spending much of the remainder of his life as an exile in England. Ogden did not reject the system which for so many years had supported him in acquiring great wealth, power, prestige, and privilege. His cumulative experiences before 1776 deflected him from even token revolutionary behavior.[20]

Thomas Collins, revolutionary councilor from Delaware (1776–1782), had life experiences which should be juxtaposed to those of David Ogden. Little in Collins's life had an imperial cast, except for his Anglicanism. Even though the parentage of Collins is obscure, he prospered as a commercial farmer; his home, known as

Belmont Hall, was one of the finest residences in Delaware. An economic success, Collins held some local offices, but none higher than county sheriff in the 1760s. He was not linked to the Penn family proprietary establishment. As a local socioeconomic leader, though, he won the favor of fellow citizens and went to the Delaware constitutional convention of 1776. From 1777 to 1783 he served as a brigadier general of state militia and after that time as state president (governor). Collins had prospered before the Revolution in a localized context. He owed little to the mother country. There were few factors in Collins's life with the power to turn him in the direction of loyalism. If Collins kept up with the debate about representation and taxation, about the nature of British sovereignty, and about the impending destruction of American liberties, no doubt such argumentation reinforced his predilection, based on his life experiences, to defend the American position. Unlike Tryon and Ogden, Collins had no basis for socioeconomic, political, or emotional ties to what must have seemed a distant and tyrannical mother country.[21]

In 1774 Collins was prospering within the confines of his community whereas Tryon and Ogden were deriving benefits from imperial associations. To Collins British authority had no great advantage, but to the latter it supported their life styles. To Collins the coming of the Revolution meant opportunity, but to Tryon and Ogden it suggested social and political anarchy, and worse yet, loss of status and power. The Revolution thus came to be viewed in positive or negative terms, depending upon the sum total of individual experiences as they fitted on the community-imperial continuum of perceptions, contacts, and interests.

Each factor had its own ability to influence behavior, but each also worked in conjunction with other explanatory variables. Thus the religious affiliation of Thomas Collins lacked meaning because it supported no other imperial connections. But Anglicanism reinforced the imperial ties of loyalists like the Wentworths. The Hutchinsons and Olivers in Massachusetts, by comparison, were nominal Congregationalists but became loyalists. Religious affiliation normally was not primary to individual decision-making patterns, but it may have tipped the balance one way or the other. The general rule seemed to be that the greater the number of imperial associations, the greater was the likelihood that individuals would choose the loyalist as opposed to the revolutionary behavioral alternative.

Education worked in contradistinction to religious affiliation in that formal education among the executives was often an experience deep in the past, at least for middle-aged and older higher officials. If the executive leader, for instance, studied at the Inns of Court and was also a councilor in 1774, as were Philip Thomas Lee of Maryland (1773–1776), William Byrd III of Virginia (1754–1776), and Thomas McGuire of North Carolina (1774–1775), then that English educational exposure strengthened the more immediate imperial ties of high office and abetted loyalism.[22] Yet both Robert Goldsborough, Maryland senator (1777–1783), and John Mathews, South Carolina assistant judge (1776–c.1778), read law at the Inns of Court, but neither man received appointments to upper-hierarchy offices before 1776.[23] In their cases other factors did not strengthen imperial educational ties. The proper blending of variables had not been obtained. Each characteristic carried weight in life experiences relative to time and also relative to the number and intensity of other associations.

The family unit, moreover, should not be neglected. Parents and relatives had a powerful impact upon patterns of behavior. Parents could offer children high socioeconomic circumstances; they could have family connections resulting in upper-class marriages; they might insist upon and pay for formal education; they might identify strongly with one of a variety of religious groups; they could have imperial contacts in terms of political advancement. The data show that late colonial and loyalist executive families more often provided children with family wealth, prestige, social standing, and imperial connections. Revolutionary leaders, by comparison, did not come so often from well-placed families. They had to depend upon personal initiative, energy, and drive to move beyond their family origins. As a result, many revolutionary insurgents were upwardly mobile from relatively common family backgrounds. They were men who knew success, but they were men who in time became frustrated by the pattern of political immobility characterizing the provincial political systems.

Thus the variables affecting an individual's life experience gave the final determination about loyalist or insurgent behavior a personal historical context. If the higher official pursued an occupation which netted him great income within the imperial framework, if he came from a wealthy family intermarried with other favored family units, if his family raised him according to Anglican tenets and sent him to the Inns of Court for legal education, then it would have been much harder for that person to have joined the Revolution. It would have been harder yet had that person been a higher official. But if the individual was a local leader, a man who had gone far beyond humble origins in socioeconomic accomplishments, a man who had Congregational or Presbyterian ties, a man who had been well-educated at Harvard or Yale, but a man who was middle-aged, the predictable likelihood would be that such a man would encourage insurgency and rebellion. The former type of provincial leader, caught in a web of imperial influences, saw his world and all that it represented as coming apart in the early 1770s. Yet the latter type, standing high in his local community, sensed new horizons of opportunity. A successful revolution held the potential for the resolution of frustrations and complete political ascendancy. In the end that view depended upon personal life experiences as they fell on the community-imperial continuum and placed leaders on different levels of late colonial socioeconomic and political structures.

Chapter Six: Notes

[1] *The History of the American Revolution,* II, p. 314.

[2] "The Founding Fathers," *Political Science Quarterly* 76 (1961), pp. 201–16. For contrary comments, see Jackson T. Main, *The Antifederalists: Critics of the Constitution, 1781–1788* (Chapel Hill, 1961), p. 259.

[3] For Colden, consult Alice M. Keys, *Cadwallader Colden; D. A. B.,* IV, pp. 286–87. For Horsmanden, E. Alfred Jones, *American Members of the Inns of Court,* pp. 100–101; *D. A. B.,* IX, pp. 237–38.

[4] George N. Mackenzie, ed., *Colonial Families of the United States of America,* III, pp. 351–52; Ewald B. Heinrich, *Governors of Maryland: From the Revolution to the Year 1908,* 2nd ed. (Baltimore, 1908), pp. 46–50; Hester D. Richardson, *Side-Lights of Maryland History,* II, pp. 190–94.

[5] For William Reed, see Charles Hudson, *History of the Town of Lexington* (2 vols., Boston, 1913), I, pp. 76, 357, 413, 457, 463, II, pp. 558–59. For James Booth, J. Thomas Scharf, *History of Delaware, 1609–1888* (2 vols., Philadelphia, 1888), I, pp. 527–28; Thomas Holcomb, *Sketch of Early Ecclesiastical Affairs in New Castle, Delaware* (Wilmington, 1890), p. 254.

[6] Jackson T. Main, "The One Hundred," *William and Mary Quarterly* (1954), p. 371.

[7] *Idem.;* Alexander Brown, *The Cabells and Their Kin* (Boston, 1895), pp. 75–130, 145–77, 204–7; *D. A. B.,* III, pp. 389–90.

[8] Samuel Roads, Jr., *The History and Traditions of Marblehead* (Boston, 1880), pp. 217, 343–46; *Essex Institute Historical Collections* Vol. LX (1924), pp. 219–27.

[9] Thomas J. Kirkland and Robert M. Kennedy, *Historic Camden, Part One: Colonial and Revolutionary* (Columbia, 1905), pp. 375–83; Emily B. Reynolds and Joan R. Raunt, eds., *Biographical Directory of the Senate of the State of South Carolina, 1776–1964* (Columbia, 1964), p. 251.

[10] For further information about placemen, consult Chapter Two, and Jackson T. Main, *The Upper House in Revolutionary America,* pp. 3–42. For derogatory comments by those who felt frustrated by the presence of placemen in political offices, see Bernard Bailyn, *The Ideological Origins of the American Revolution,* pp. 94–143.

[11] *D. A. B.,* V, pp. 519–20.

[12] Quoted in Edward McCrady, *The History of South Carolina under the Royal Government, 1719–1776* (New York, 1899), p. 470; W. Roy Smith, *South Carolina as a Royal Province,* pp. 392–93; Lorenzo Sabine, *Biographical Sketches of Loyalists,* I, pp. 482–83.

[13] Information about Gosslett's life apparently is nonexistent, but some material about Savage is in Sabine, *Biographical Sketches of Loyalists,* II, p. 259. For Fewtrell, Jones, *American Members of the Inns of Court,* p. 77.

Jones asserts that all nonnative circuit court judges were confined by the South Carolina provincial congress in August 1775.

[14] Joseph I. Waring, *A History of Medicine in South Carolina,* pp. 82, 89, 180, 198, 272; *South Carolina Historical and Genealogical Magazine* 20 (1919), p. 206, and 38 (1937), p. 126.

[15] *Publications of the Colonial Society of Massachusetts* Vol. VI (1899–1900), pp. 385–94; Wilkins Updike, *A History of the Episcopal Church in Narragansett,* I, pp. 249–51, 567–71.

[16] *Idem;* Samuel A. Ashe, ed., *Biographical History of North Carolina, from Colonial Times to the Present,* III (Greensboro, 1905), pp. 210–15.

[17] Despite recent trends in revolutionary historiography emphasizing the importance of ideas, we must not forget that ideologies develop out of actual historical situations. There are many variables influencing individual lives which permit us to understand why ideologies had meaning for people at different points in time, and why individuals favored one ideological framework as opposed to others.

[18] Too often historians limit themselves to the exploration of one rather than a whole series of variables in attempting to explain behavior. Most popular has been the study of individual wealth. There are no better examples of endless historical debating emerging out of a monovariable approach than the books and articles attacking and defending Charles A. Beard, *An Economic Interpretation of the Constitution of the United States* (New York, 1913). We must consider a wide range of variables if we are to assess patterns of behavior in changing historical situations.

[19] Marshall D. Haywood, *Governor William Tryon and his Administration in the Province of North Carolina* (Raleigh, 1903); *D. A. B.,* XIX, pp. 25–27.

[20] E. Alfred Jones, *The Loyalists of New Jersey,* New Jersey Historical Society Collections Vol. X (Newark, 1927), pp. 157–60; Edward W. Keasbey, *The Courts and Lawyers of New Jersey, 1661–1912* (3 vols., New York, 1912), I, pp. 305–7; *D. A. B.,* XIII, pp. 637–38.

[21] Henry C. Conrad, *History of the State of Delaware* (3 vols., Wilmington, 1908), I, pp. 115, 270, II, p. 609, III, p. 825; Scharf, *History of Delaware,* I, p. 563, II, p. 1094.

[22] For Philip Thomas Lee, see Jones, *American Members of the Inns of Court,* pp. 125–26; Ethel R. Hayden, "The Lees of Blenheim," *Maryland Historical Magazine* 37 (1942), pp. 199–207. For Byrd, Jones, *American Members of the Inns of Court,* pp. 36–37; *Virginia Magazine of History and Biography* 9 (1901–1902), pp. 80–88; Thomas A. Glenn, *Some Colonial Mansions and Those Whoe Lived in Them,* pp. 17–58; For McGuire, Jones, *American Members of the Inns of Court,* pp. 147–48; *South Carolina Historical and Genealogical Magazine* 19 (1918), pp. 60–64, and 20 (1919), pp. 47–48.

[23] For Robert Goldsborough, consult Jones, *American Members of the*

Inns of Court, pp. 87–88; Richard H. Spencer, *Thomas Family of Talbot County, Maryland* (Baltimore, 1914), p. 82; *D. A. B.,* VII, pp. 366–67. For Mathews, Jones, *American Members of the Inns of Court,* pp. 157–58; *South Carolina Historical and Genealogical Magazine* 8 (1907), pp. 36–39; *D. A. B.,* XII, pp. 404–5.

CHAPTER SEVEN

The Decline of Deferential Politics:
Some Hypotheses in Conclusion

I

THE GRAND QUESTION facing political activists at any point in time is that of who should rule on what level of the political structure. The failure to resolve that question set the stage for the outbreak of the American Revolution. American community leaders, able to aspire to seats in lower houses of Assemblies, insisted upon Assembly autonomy in internal political matters. By 1763 legislators held the balance of power in decision-making.[1] Yet after nearly a century of ministerial indifference about the increasing authority of lower houses, Parliament began to approve new imperial programs following the Seven Years' War and threatened the de facto autonomy that community socioeconomic leaders had acquired as assemblymen. Lesser officials in lower houses refused to concede prerogatives. With no prospect for political mobility above the Assembly level, many of them saw no reason to hand back what they had taken from their opponents in higher offices. Instead, community leaders reacted to political tensions and personal frustrations by depersonalizing the problem and issuing statements to the effect that British appointees in the provinces were partakers in a ministerial conspiracy to destroy American liberties. Higher officials became noxious tools in the plot. They were agents of the ministry and corrupted by the lure of official favor and high office. They were about to corrupt in turn the known liberties of all provincial citizens.[2]

Higher officials had been losing the factional contest over prerogatives and authority for many years. No doubt they were willing to regain lost powers. But implementation of imperial plans was no easy task. Whether higher officials liked it or not, they had to attempt to make imperial programs work, that is if they wanted to keep their offices and the respect that they felt was due them as men of high official standing. Some of them as a result became the selected victims of group protest and intimidation; roving mobs of irate colonists destroyed their property and prized personal possessions.[3] An even greater number of executives felt the barbed sting of insurgent charges about corruption. They became the most hated men in the provinces. When the Crown and Parliament in the early 1770s finally refused to concede the American position, higher officials found themselves not only the victims of insurgent words but also of growing rebellion. Tensions, hatred, and frustrations boiled over into irreconciliation; political consensus about the importance of British sovereignty gave way to armed conflict. A power vacuum developed as governments collapsed. American community leaders, many of whom had gained years of political experience as lesser officials, took charge of the revolutionary cause.

The power vacuum did not last long. The end of British and the beginning of popular sovereignty came through the state constitutions of 1776 and 1777. Many of the lesser officials and future revolutionary leaders studied here (62.3 per cent) attended one or more of the provincial congresses which capped resistance to imperial authority by producing new constitutional frameworks for state governments. A new political environment emerged out of the destruction of royal authority in America.

The men who wrote the new constitutions, if at all typical of those participants under investigation here, had needs and expectations which they hoped would be realized in the revolutionary political arena. Many no doubt sought political preferment in high offices. After all, the men who became revolutionary executives were not politically inexperienced, but they had been active as lesser officials before the Revolution. Given the frustrations as well as the expectations of such men, the hypothesis is that insurgent leaders purged their political frustrations by writing constitutions which permitted men like themselves, men of community socioeconomic accomplishments, to compete for high offices. The new constitutions became the vehicles through which political immobility ceased to be an irritating phenomenon for those not favored by Crown procedures of advancement before the Revolution.

This is not to say that political theory had no meaning or importance to the constitution-makers. There is overwhelming evidence that leaders in constitutional conventions had read widely in ancient and modern political treatises. Yet men also came to the conventions with a lifetime of experiences and specific personal goals. Many such men wanted and took high offices when the opportunity presented itself in 1776 and 1777. The experiential dimension must not be neglected for those who wrote constitutions and desired high office. Their political expectations were about to become achievements.

There was both uniformity and variety in the theoretical foundations of the state constitutions. Many leaders spoke and thought in terms of "republicanism"; citizens had to be virtuous; governments could be effective and stable only if the commonalty did not abuse the public trust for immediate personal gain.[4] Yet within the context of republicanism there was no consistent pattern in relocating the balance among the three traditional orders in government. There was no rush to level the orders and to put all power in the hands of common citizens, despite expressions of popular sovereignty. On one side the Pennsylvania constitution-makers were least concerned with preserving balance. The first state constitution collapsed the traditional orders into one by eliminating the chief executive and by placing legislative authority in a popularly elected unicameral Assembly. Virtuous Pennsylvanians won the right to rule themselves through their annually elected representatives without upper-hierarchy restraints. But Pennsylvania was not typical; it was a real experiment in republicanism. The constitutional environments created in several other states emphasized hierarchical balance and placed checks upon the democracy of citizens. In Maryland, one of the most restrictive constitutions, the leaders (men of planter and commercial wealth) retained a sense of balance by approving among other provisions high property-holding qualifications for those in high offices. The presumption was that governors or state senators with substantial personal wealth would be less tempted by the possible corruptions of office; they would be less likely to ignore public needs for petty personal interests; they would be more willing to stand against unreasonable popular pressures from below and potential democratic excesses in decision-making.[5]

Few of the delegates to the constitutional conventions were social or political levelers. They were men of community standing. They believed in order and balance. They did not doubt their own talents or proven character, but they were not committed to the notion that common citizens had the ability to rule themselves in intelligence and wisdom.[6] Yet they were willing, as a second hypothesis, to expand the political rights of common citizens in the political arena so as to guarantee that men like themselves would have open access to offices on all levels of government. Cautiously making popular sovereignty something more than a hollow phrase, this extension of political rights proved to be a major step forward toward the decline of deferential politics in the eighteenth century.

II

To gain political hegemony as well as to end the pattern of political immobility, insurgent leaders employed several constitutional devices. First of all they saw to it that executive offices which formerly had been appointive became either directly or indirectly elective. Delegates adopted a variety of procedures to insure that the diffusion of the power to appoint shifted downward into the hands of voting citizens or their elected representatives in lower and upper houses of Assemblies. The norm was to grant enfranchised voters the right to elect state senators (formerly Crown-appointed councilors). Elected assemblymen and senators, meeting in state capitals, would fill other executive offices through joint balloting of both houses. Indeed, there was no more striking way to break apart the control that a handful of Crown and proprietary officials had exercised over executive appointments. There was no more potent means to assure that community socioeconomic leaders would have the opportunity to compete for high offices. Now voting citizens (white adult men who long had been accustomed within the deferential framework to electing local men of standing to community offices and to lower houses of Assemblies) rather than distant British officials would determine which prominent local elite gentleman would serve in elective high offices. Community leaders then would gather in Assemblies and determine what other men of ability, talent, and merit would carry out the duties of the remaining offices.

There were few exceptions to the new provisions for the selection of higher officials. Joint balloting of both houses usually extended to secretaries and attorneys general, and in fewer cases to supreme court judges. In New Jersey, Delaware, Virginia, North Carolina, and South Carolina, lower and upper houses voted each year to fill governorships. In Delaware the president (governor) met with the two houses of Assembly to name supreme court judges; the president with the advice of his privy council selected the secretary and attorney general. New York was an exception in another direction because the constitution-makers provided for direct, popular election of the governor and lieutenant governor. The New Yorkers also established a council of appointment, made up of four senators and the governor, who were to name all other nonelective officers in government, that is with the exception of the treasurer. The lower house had the prerogative to appoint the treasurer, since all financial matters were to originate in and be controlled by that body.

The only state constitution that modified the emerging pattern of direct election of senators was Maryland.[7] There the upper-class citizens who controlled the convention consciously kept the election of state senators one step removed from popular ratification. The enfranchised voters in the state would ballot on election day for electors who in turn would gather an Annapolis to pick state senators, chosen either from their own number or from the general population. Given property-holding qualifications for senators, Maryland constitution-makers sought to guarantee that men of wealth (proven ability or high birth) would check leveling influences rising from the lower house.

In conjunction with the direct or indirect election of higher officials, the constitution-makers, second, shattered the old appointive mechanism by establishing fixed election districts for offices not statewide in scope and authority. Indeed, representation based upon population distribution had its first application in some revolutionary governments. State senators were to be chosen from specific geographic districts, thereby presenting at least in name definite constituencies in the body politic. New Hampshire assigned each county councilors (senators) according to the number of residents in the county. This provision actually infuriated citizens in the more remote and less populous western Connecticut Valley region. Western community leaders understood that easterners would dominate in actual numbers in the Assembly. They knew that equity in legislation and governmental appropriations would not be their lot. Proportional representation in New Hampshire became one argument to stir a western secessionist movement occurring before the War for Independence had ended.[8] New Yorkers avoided upstate ire by establishing a septennial census, to commence after the war. First, the constitution-makers sectioned off four senatorial election districts; each district had a quota of senators according to the number of freeholders in the respective district.[9] If census-takers found at the end of seven years that population shifts had taken place, then a redistribution of seats was to follow. That way southern and eastern areas would be unable to retain a disproportionate share of senators as population spread north and west. If the census-takers discovered, moreover, that freeholders in any district had increased relative to all electors in the state by one twenty-fourth, then the senatorial district would get an additional seat. New York planned to expand the number of senators as population grew, but Virginia constitution-makers did not take future population shifts into consideration in mapping out twenty-four senatorial districts. The eastern planters in the convention thus guaranteed that they would have more senatorial power than their constituent numbers deserved, since population already was building in the west.[10] North Carolinians, by comparison, assigned each county a senator regardless of population. Western settlements were favored and would continue to be as new counties were set off, counties which were unlikely at first to have the same number of freeholders as those in the east.

No matter what the constitutional device and what part of the population (eastern or western) favored, the impact of spreading out senatorial election districts was profound in terms of changing leadership patterns. Landholding, professional, and mercantile families of great wealth and imperial standing tended to congregate in or near cultural and economic centers like Boston, New York, or Philadelphia, or they had convenient access to colonial capitals such as Williamsburg or Annapolis. Developing western regions, on the other hand, rarely produced individuals before 1774 with enough earned family status and personal wealth to gain the attention of royal governors living among leaders of the great families in eastern urban centers and capitals. Thus the better sort from coastal regions and cities were in a most favorable competitive position for high offices; they proved to be a major source of executive appointees.

But effective great family monopolization could not continue with election districts located all over the states, with the diffusion of the appointive power downward into the hands of voters and elected leaders in lower and upper houses, and with residency requirements placed on elective offices. As a third safeguard to the insurgents' interest, several of the state constitutions made it mandatory for senatorial candidates to live, not just own property, in election districts. Actual inhabitants were to represent constituents.[11] Thus families with extensive kinship connections, even if present in several communities, were unlikely to have relatives with residences in enough districts so that domination of executive offices could continue. Even in those areas where great families lived, they now had to compete for high offices at the polls with men of somewhat lesser stature, but nonetheless community leaders. The data suggest that the importance of family ties declined with the invocation of new governments. Diffusion of the appointive power and fixed election districts along with residency requirements broke the hold that many eastern families of distinction exercised over high offices while at the same time strengthening the competitive position of local community leaders everywhere.

The constitution-makers, fourth, attacked privileged control and political immobility by setting tenure restrictions upon executive offices. Unchecked tenure had been one major source of immobility before the Revolution. But after 1776 there were few cases where the incumbent might presume that there would be no challenge to his authority. The governors of New Jersey, Delaware, Virginia, North Carolina, and South Carolina had to face joint balloting and the threat of expulsion from office each year. The popularly elected upper houses of New Hampshire, New Jersey, and North Carolina were to be contested at the polls annually. Delaware chose a three-year term of office for state senators; New York and Virginia, wanting more stability, agreed upon four-year terms. Maryland again demonstrated its upper-class conservatism by placing senators under five-year terms of office. In those executive positions in which joint balloting determined the incumbent, terms of office varied but were normally longer than elective positions. Judges of the New Jersey supreme court had seven years; the attorney general and secretary five; the treasurer but one year. Delaware decided that the secretary and attorney general should hold office for five years yet permitted supreme court judges to serve during "good behavior," the norm for judicial tenure in some states.[12] New York supreme court judges, in a novel provision, were to have office during good behavior or until they reached a mandatory retirement age of sixty.

Such limitations had two definite effects upon leadership change and prospects for political mobility. First, tenure checks made it more difficult to hold offices indefinitely. Second, it became possible for prospective candidates from among local leadership ranks to challenge officeholders periodically and even to gain offices for themselves without having to wait an inordinantly long number of years. The first observation is borne out in the data about the number of years that late colonial (open-ended tenure) and revolutionary executives (closed-ended tenure) were in office. The first group averaged 10.7 years before the Revolution cut them short while the second group averaged 5.9 years before other challengers stepped into their positions. The very fact that revolutionary executives held office for briefer terms establishes the second point that more men had greater opportunity to experience political mobility after 1776.[13]

Not only did the constitution-makers place checks on tenure by assigning definite terms to offices, but in a few notable instances they also went so far as to adopt the principle of "rotation of office." Both the Virginia and Maryland governors, for example, were not to serve any more than three years in succession out of seven. The same provision applied to supreme executive councilors in Pennsylvania. According to constitution-makers there, rotation stopped "the danger of establishing an inconvenient aristocracy" while it also meant that "more men will be trained to public business." [14] As David Ramsay stated, "The favorers of this system of rotation contended for it, as likely to prevent a perpetuity of office and power in the same individual or family, and as a security against hereditary honors." [15]

The constitution-makers, finally, sanctioned a variety of provisions directed against plural officeholding. But there was no pattern to the procedures. Supreme court judges in New York were not permitted to hold any other office, except that of delegate to the Continental Congress. The treasurer and attorney general of Pennsylvania were not to sit consecutively in the Assembly or the supreme executive council. Senators and assemblymen in Maryland and South Carolina could not at the same time hold salaried offices, but the South Carolinians could accept officers' commissions in local or Continental military units. Treasurers in North Carolina were barred from the house and senate until they had settled all accounts with the state. Many such clauses arose from the desires of constitution-makers to avoid conflicting interests among men in office, but the provisions likewise made it illegal for one man to acquire more than his share of executive offices. More men could compete for more offices.

Thus several constitutional procedures worked to the advantage of those lesser officials desiring the opportunity to hold high offices before 1774. Yet at the same time a strange paradox grew out of constitution-making, directly affecting those insurgents who became executives in 1776 and 1777. We may discern the paradox by looking at two dimensions of state constitution-making rather than just one. On one dimension provisions made mobility possible for rising community leaders. Yet on an equally important dimension, the new constitutions put several checks upon the prerogatives that revolutionary higher officials were to exercise while in office. Governors were hardest hit. Many of them lost the right to veto legislation, to make political appointments, to adjourn, prorogue, and dissolve self-willed Assemblies. New Hampshire and Pennsylvania went so far as to eliminate the governor altogether from politics. Many upper houses lost the ability to influence the nature and the scope of money bills. The new constitutions located more prerogatives and powers in lower houses than ever had been the de facto case under British sovereignty. [16] These two dimensions in constitu-

tion-making thus converged at a point where insurgent lesser officials moved into executive offices when the authority of lower
houses was reaching a new zenith. Insurgents gained access to offices which had fewer powers attached to them than at any previous
time in the century.

What caused the confusion in the efforts of the constitution-makers? Why would they work to open the door to executive offices
while stripping many of these same positions of powers? Why would
lesser officials rush to fill these offices, apparently weaker in range
of authority, in 1776 and 1777? The answer to these questions lies
in the nature of the insurgent quest for power and political preferment before the outbreak of revolution. Community socioeconomic
leaders found through experience that British advancement procedures did not favor men with their qualifications. Leaders in lower
houses, then, congregated into factions and used their political energy to cut into the prerogatives of higher officeholders frustrating
their political ambitions. The incessant factional duel over prerogatives reflected the desires of lesser officials to consolidate as much
authority as possible on the level of officeholding (lower houses)
that was within their range of acquisition. Even though Assembly
leaders slashed deeply into Crown and proprietary territory, their
victory was never complete, and reverses were setting in with
Crown support after 1763. Even in the years of collapsing imperial
authority, governors and other court faction leaders had the ability
to stymie local legislative wants. Governors still had the veto power
and the right to adjourn, prorogue, and dissolve Assemblies. When
the factional contest finally undermined all respect for imperial authority, constitution-makers resolved the contest by putting the
brunt of decision-making prerogatives in the lower houses, the base
of prerevolutionary insurgent operations. It was the logical culmi-
nation of the whig "quest for power" in the absence of restraining
imperial authority.

Constitution-makers, nonetheless, were aware of the need to promote political mobility for community socioeconomic leaders. Political preferment remained the deferred aspect of the insurgent
quest; frustrations about political advancement had been a precondition to the solidification of factional lines on a vertical plane dic-
tating the drive against the prerogatives of upper-hierarchy appoin-

tive officials before 1774.[17] Hence the constitution-makers also responded to the needs of men for access to high office. Community leaders, most certainly aware of the circumscribed authority of high offices, did not hesitate but rushed into the void in executive leadership. These positions, moreover, still had some powers, and being the most visible offices, were prestigious, adding greatly to the status of known community leaders of talent and merit. Denied high offices before the Revolution, the first constitutional settlement denied lesser officials some authority once in high office. It would take time and further constitutional settlements before the imbalance would redress itself.

III

For common citizens, by comparison, state constitution-making and the implementation of popular sovereignty for the first time in the American experience represented something more than a pyrrhic victory. Whig insurgents, despite their concern with balance and fear of anarchy, expanded the political rights of the commonalty to insure, among other matters, political mobility and autonomy over all offices for men like themselves. If insurgent motives did not stem from principle alone, the end result of the first revolutionary constitutional settlement did redound to the advantage of enfranchised citizens in the American political community. To grasp the magnitude of gain in rights for voting citizens, we must compare the executive officeholders in a sample of provincial and revolutionary governments (Tables 7.1, 7.2, and 7.3). Comparisons allow for a better perception of why whig insurgents cautiously transferred new privileges to common citizens and yield hypotheses about the changing nature of political relationships in early American history.

New York, Virginia, and North Carolina represent in the sample the dominant type of royal province before 1776 in which governors along with councilors and ministers in England controlled executive appointments. Maryland as the fourth colony serves as the proprietary example, also having had the executive appointive power located in a few people. Calvert family proprietors substituted for governmental ministers in England. We note from the first table that few of the late colonial executives in these four colonies

Table 7.1

*Comparative Family Wealth of Late Colonial
and Revolutionary Executives by Colony Type*

Level of Family Wealth	Massachusetts				Rhode Island			
	Late Colonial		Revolutionary		Late Colonial		Revolutionary	
	(N)	%	(N)	%	(N)	%	(N)	%
Wealthy	(9)	26.5	(2)	6.3	(1)	6.3	(1)	5.6
Well-to-do	(9)	26.5	(13)	40.6	(7)	43.7	(7)	38.9
Average	(16)	47.0	(17)	53.1	(8)	50.0	(10)	55.5
Below Average	(0)	0.0	(0)	0.0	(0)	0.0	(0)	0.0
TOTAL	(34)	100.0	(32)	100.0	(16)	100.0	(18)	100.0

Level of Family Wealth	New York				Maryland			
	Late Colonial		Revolutionary		Late Colonial		Revolutionary	
	(N)	%	(N)	%	(N)	%	(N)	%
Wealthy	(11)	57.9	(9)	31.0	(11)	78.6	(19)	70.4
Well-to-do	(5)	26.3	(10)	34.5	(3)	21.4	(6)	22.2
Average	(3)	15.8	(10)	34.5	(0)	0.0	(2)	7.4
Below Average	(0)	0.0	(0)	0.0	(0)	0.0	(0)	0.0
TOTAL	(19)	100.0	(29)	100.0	(14)	100.0	(27)	100.0

Level of Family Wealth	Virginia				North Carolina			
	Late Colonial		Revolutionary		Late Colonial		Revolutionary	
	(N)	%	(N)	%	(N)	%	(N)	%
Wealthy	(12)	85.7	(14)	46.6	(3)	23.1	(4)	18.2
Well-to-do	(2)	14.3	(11)	36.7	(6)	46.2	(4)	18.2
Average	(0)	0.0	(5)	16.7	(4)	30.7	(14)	63.6
Below Average	(0)	0.0	(0)	0.0	(0)	0.0	(0)	0.0
TOTAL	(14)	100.0	(30)	100.0	(13)	100.0	(22)	100.0

were products of average family financial circumstances. North
Carolina was the least restrictive with 30.7 per cent of its late colonial higher officials in that category. Virginia was the most exclusive, drawing upon the great tobacco-planting families.[18] Maryland
was almost as restrictive as Virginia in terms of family credentials,
but then again the power of appointment resided in a few upper-
class proprietary hands. It should also be noted from the third table

that none of the late colonial executives was personally less than well-to-do, placing them in what we already have defined as the propertied upper class.

In Massachusetts and Rhode Island, by comparison, the data indicate a different pattern. Massachusetts may be described as a modified royal province in that some executive offices were indirectly elective. The 1691 charter provided that representatives in

Table 7.2

*Comparative Social Origins of Late Colonial
and Revolutionary Executives by Colony Type*

Social Origins	Massachusetts				Rhode Island			
	Late Colonial		Revolutionary		Late Colonial		Revolutionary	
	(N)	%	(N)	%	(N)	%	(N)	%
Class I	(12)	35.3	(7)	21.9	(2)	12.5	(1)	5.6
Class II	(14)	41.2	(18)	56.2	(8)	50.0	(9)	50.0
Class III	(8)	23.5	(7)	21.9	(6)	37.5	(8)	44.4
Class IV	(0)	0.0	(0)	0.0	(0)	0.0	(0)	0.0
TOTAL	(34)	100.0	(32)	100.0	(16)	100.0	(18)	100.0

Social Origins	New York				Maryland			
	Late Colonial		Revolutionary		Late Colonial		Revolutionary	
	(N)	%	(N)	%	(N)	%	(N)	%
Class I	(15)	78.9	(9)	31.0	(11)	78.6	(20)	74.1
Class II	(3)	15.8	(11)	38.0	(3)	21.4	(6)	22.2
Class III	(1)	5.3	(9)	31.0	(0)	0.0	(1)	3.7
Class IV	(0)	0.0	(0)	0.0	(0)	0.0	(0)	0.0
TOTAL	(19)	100.0	(29)	100.0	(14)	100.0	(27)	100.0

Social Origins	Virginia				North Carolina			
	Late Colonial		Revolutionary		Late Colonial		Revolutionary	
	(N)	%	(N)	%	(N)	%	(N)	%
Class I	(14)	100.0	(15)	50.0	(6)	46.2	(4)	18.2
Class II	(0)	0.0	(11)	36.7	(4)	30.7	(6)	27.3
Class III	(0)	0.0	(4)	13.3	(3)	23.1	(12)	54.5
Class IV	(0)	0.0	(0)	0.0	(0)	0.0	(0)	0.0
TOTAL	(14)	100.0	(30)	100.0	(13)	100.0	(22)	100.0

Table 7.3

Comparative Personal Wealth of Late Colonial
and Revolutionary Executives by Colony Type

Level of Personal Wealth	Massachusetts				Rhode Island			
	Late Colonial		*Revolutionary*		*Late Colonial*		*Revolutionary*	
	(N)	%	(N)	%	(N)	%	(N)	%
Wealthy	(12)	35.3	(3)	9.7	(1)	6.3	(2)	11.1
Well-to-do	(15)	44.1	(21)	67.7	(11)	68.7	(12)	66.7
Average	(7)	20.6	(7)	22.6	(4)	25.0	(4)	22.2
Below Average	(0)	0.0	(0)	0.0	(0)	0.0	(0)	0.0
TOTAL	(34)	100.0	(31)	100.0	(16)	100.0	(18)	100.0

	New York				Maryland			
	Late Colonial		*Revolutionary*		*Late Colonial*		*Revolutionary*	
	(N)	%	(N)	%	(N)	%	(N)	%
Wealthy	(18)	94.7	(11)	36.7	(13)	92.9	(21)	77.8
Well-to-do	(1)	5.3	(16)	53.3	(1)	7.1	(6)	22.2
Average	(0)	0.0	(3)	10.0	(0)	0.0	(0)	0.0
Below Average	(0)	0.0	(0)	0.0	(0)	0.0	(0)	0.0
TOTAL	(19)	100.0	(30)	100.0	(14)	100.0	(27)	100.0

	Virginia				North Carolina			
	Late Colonial		*Revolutionary*		*Late Colonial*		*Revolutionary*	
	(N)	%	(N)	%	(N)	%	(N)	%
Wealthy	(14)	100.0	(17)	50.0	(11)	68.7	(11)	28.9
Well-to-do	(0)	0.0	(15)	44.1	(5)	31.3	(24)	63.2
Average	(0)	0.0	(2)	5.9	(0)	0.0	(3)	7.9
Below Average	(0)	0.0	(0)	0.0	(0)	0.0	(0)	0.0
TOTAL	(14)	100.0	(34)	100.0	(16)	100.0	(38)	100.0

the General Court should annually elect qualified citizens to the upper house. The royal governor had the veto power over General Court selections, but it is doubtful that the veto ever was used to eliminate a man of modest family origins.[19] Indeed, fourteen of the sixteen Massachusetts late colonial higher officials who came from average family circumstances were councilors. Gubernatorial and

Crown-appointed executives, on the other hand, invariably were men of higher than average family wealth and status.

Of all the sampled colonies Rhode Island had the greatest amount of citizen control over executive appointments. The 1663 charter permitted the direct annual election of many upper-hierarchy leaders. The data demonstrate that voting Rhode Island freemen did not worry as much about a man's family background when they went to the polls. Fifty per cent of the late colonial executives were of average family means and 37.5 per cent were of Class III origins. The evidence does suggest, however, that voters considered the immediate, personal qualifications of the candidate as they viewed him at election time. With high frequency freemen favored men who personally had gained high economic standing—68.7 per cent were well-to-do. Here were community socioeconomic leaders who were upwardly mobile, given their personal economic success, men who had established themselves as talented local entrepreneurs.

The general pattern extrapolated from the data appears to be that late colonial voters put more emphasis upon a man's personal accomplishments, regardless of family background. Voters deferred in politics to recognizable community leaders. Crown and proprietary officials, on the other hand, preferred to appoint men with family as well as personal standing and wealth. Clearly the first kind of officeholder came closer to representing community entrepreneurs who had evidenced ability and talent on the local level. The latter kind of individual more nearly fitted the image of provincial America's untitled aristocracy. The former man, imbedded in community contacts and interests, would have more potential to think in terms of local needs—he was a community leader and had an immediate stake in local problems. The latter man, entrenched in imperial associations and dependent upon the Crown rather than enfranchised citizens for office, more likely would define his role in government as acting the part of counterweight to democratic excesses.

The measurable difference between elected and appointed officials in late colonial America was indicative of the trend which developed once state constitution-makers made executive positions directly or indirectly elective. The new advancement procedures resulted in the greater presence of men of community stature. Before the Revolution all but one of New York's executives had been personally wealthy, but now 53.3 per cent were well-to-do and another 10 per cent were men of average means. There was almost a perfect distribution in family backgrounds with a few more having average than wealthy origins. Freemen and freeholders turned to men of modest wealth (those community leaders with whom they were most familiar and had the most contact) more often than to men of great wealth. Men of humble backgrounds, but upwardly mobile, at the same time found the opportunity to gain high offices.

The same pattern is discernible in the examples of Virginia and North Carolina. In both states senatorial aspirants had to win favor from local voters; other prospective higher officials needed the approval of elected representatives in Assemblies. The effect again was that the Revolutionaries were men of less personal wealth from a greater diversity of family backgrounds. More executive offices were open to leaders who lacked the status to move into high offices before the Revolution.

Maryland constitution-makers, on the other hand, were more concerned that men with the highest personal credentials hold executive offices. Stiff property-holding qualifications and complex procedures for the election of senators worked to keep wealthy planters at the head of the revolutionary government. Over 70 per cent of the Maryland Revolutionaries came from wealthy families and had Class I social origins. A definite sense of hierarchical balance had been maintained, despite the passing of the old order. Yet Maryland was one exception to the new sense of constitution-making and leadership selection for higher-level offices.

Rhode Island showed little change, but there had been no new constitution there. High offices continued to be open to men from a variety of family backgrounds and modest levels of personal wealth. The Massachusetts insurgents temporarily eliminated the governorship in reinstituting the 1691 charter, and they filled other upper-hierarchy offices by joint balloting instead of gubernatorial nomination. The result was that a downward shift in wealth and status occurred with the demise of Crown-controlled appointments.

The appearance of so many community socioeconomic leaders

in executive offices during 1776 and 1777 leads to the conclusion that whig insurgents as constitution-makers and as lesser officials prior to revolution understood the voting habits of local citizens. They perceived that it was commonplace for the electorate, given the deferential norm in politics, to return men of proven ability from their communities to elective offices, whether to lower houses or to the few elective upper-hierarchy offices, as in the case of Rhode Island. Constitution-makers, therefore, transferred some of the rights of executive selection to enfranchised citizens. It was the "trickle down" approach in the expansion of popular authority. Constitution-makers at most were taking a calculated risk in an age of deferential voting practices when many men still feared the potential for democratic anarchy.

Thus common citizens found in 1776 and 1777 that they could vote for more offices. They also discovered that they could go to polling places with greater regularity to decide what local elite leader would serve in high office. The right to vote simply meant more because it was not so fettered as it had been before the Revolution. Citizens, moreover, now had community leaders representing them in lower and upper houses of Assemblies. More officials had to have some knowledge of community needs—perhaps even to respond to them. More officials had to think in terms of what constituents wanted from government and at least act like they were being responsive. The impact of constitution-making, then, was that more factors in the modern democratic paradigm became operative in the early years of revolutionary republicanism. Insurgent whigs drew citizens more directly into the political arena by broadening political rights. They did so in residual fashion to alleviate personal frustrations and to satisfy their own needs for the right to compete for all political offices. The nature of politics and political action could not be the same after 1776.

IV

One revolutionary Virginian visiting Williamsburg in November 1776 commented that he had taken "a view of our new Assembly, now sitting—under the happy auspices of the People only." He described the scene in vivid fashion:

I confess I am pleased—and though it is composed of men not quite so well dressed, nor so politely educated, nor so highly born as some Assemblies I have formerly seen—yet upon the whole I like their Proceedings—and upon the whole rather better than formerly. They are the People's men (and the People in general are right). They are plain and of consequence less disguised, but I believe to be full as honest, less intriguing, more sincere.[20]

The Virginian did not feel detachment but a new sense of involvement in government and the process of political decision-making. He did not write deferentially but almost scornfully about upper-class gentlemen. He betrayed a faith that the people knew their needs best, and he thought the people were in control of Virginia's government. His comments about the emerging political order were premature, if not overly optimistic.

A new political order was developing, no doubt, but not necessarily because of popular upheaval and the appearance of common men in high political office. The question of who should rule at home had been vital to the process making for revolution, as Carl Becker described it so ably many years ago, but the nature of the internal crisis was not so much a contest between the masses and the upper classes. It was not so much a direct, internal confrontation between those few with great wealth and the vast majority of citizens with little or no property. Neither did the Revolution solely gain momentum, as Robert E. Brown suggested, from the desires of middle-class men to preserve and sustain a democratic order. Indeed, leadership analysis leads to the conclusion that the confrontation after 1763 resulted not so much from a class struggle as from a struggle within the ruling class, if we may apply those terms to the lesser and higher officials making up the late colonial political elite. Were community socioeconomic leaders to control the destiny of American politics and to have open access to all, not just some, offices in government? Or were a few nonnative placemen and privileged native gentlemen of wealth, education, family standing, and imperial connections to dominate in high offices and frustrate community leaders by their presence and their willingness to carry through on imperial programs? Were lesser officials to have autonomy in political matters, or were higher officials (dependent upon Crown patronage) to corrupt American liberties because of their lust for power and preferment? More specifically, was it to be Patrick Henry or Lord Dunmore in the governorship of Virginia? Was William Henry Drayton to be denied a judgeship on the South Carolina circuit court? Were the Otises to be frustrated in their family political ambitions in Massachusetts by the better-placed Hutchinsons and Olivers? American community leaders, in the end, unwilling to accept imperial plans and all that such programs implied about subordination to royal authority and higher officials, resolved all such questions resoundingly in their favor.

This is not meant to imply that common citizens were wholly passive agents in the process of revolution. Citizens protested, imbibed phrases like "no taxation without representation," formed mobs, and struck out in selective fashion against imperial-oriented officials in government. But mobs are not always class conscious and solely made up of poor and desperate individuals. Mobs have organizers and leaders who determine targets and specify the goals in the coercion of people and destruction of property. Organizers of mobs after 1763 often were those lesser officials and whig faction leaders in government who were contesting with higher officials attempting to do the will of Parliament. The crowd was a means to an end; it was brute force with the power of intimidation and destruction to be used when men could not get what they wanted through the normal channels of politics. In the end common citizens, those who participated in mob activity and those who remained silent, benefited from the insurgent drive against higher officials. Their reward for supporting the insurgents was broader participation in the revolutionary political arena.

Thus common citizens became involved, but they rarely led. The weight of their numbers made whig threats and entreaties against imperial policies and higher officials all that more forceful. Citizens lent strength, but the preconditions and precipitants of revolution grew out of the frustrations of insurgent community leaders. The American Revolution from the outset was a contest for power involving men in power.

And the weight of popular support was the trump card of insurgent leaders. Royal and proprietary authorities lacked numbers in their collection of resources. They depended far too much upon lackadaisical ministries and popular consensus about the advantages of British sovereignty. Indeed, when Crown officials tried to balance off the void in numbers through the counterforce of redcoated British regular troops, they only further aggravated tensions and made the whig appeal about conspiracy and loss of liberties more vividly real. One need only think of the ineffectiveness of British regiments sent to Boston in the late summer of 1768 to quell popular disturbances directed against Crown officials. Confrontation of significant proportions eventually came in the Boston Massacre of March 1770, and a greater victory could not have been had for insurgent leaders. British troops, no matter who was at fault, now were killing *Americans* on *American* soil. British troops as a counterforce to the popular numbers backing whig insurgents abetted rather than deterred attitudes of American community solidarity and identity.

Royal and proprietary officials were losing control, moreover, because they failed to perceive that the unity of whig factions had some potential to be broken by the promotion of some lesser officials with fewer imperial credentials into higher offices. Would the sequence of events in Massachusetts have been different had James Otis, Sr., become the chief justice in 1760? Was the problem that court faction leaders were so hungry for their own political preferment that they could not perceive the need to keep political systems fluid and to provide opportunities for community leaders of merit who were lesser officials to move up the political hierarchy of offices? Would insurgent leaders have responded to such offers after the pull of the current of rebellion became so strong and have agreed to political elevation for themselves rather than destroying the political system sustaining so many Wentworths, Hutchinsons, Olivers, De Lanceys, Penns, Carters, and Bulls in higher offices? Such questions are speculative and based upon hindsight. Yet they point to a flaw, a blind spot in the counterstrategy of British officials, a failure to understand that systems lacking in mobility for qualified candidates have the potential to be disrupted through open rebellion. That failure of vision on the part of British officials abetted the destruction of the Anglo-American empire.

V

The coming of the American Revolution gained momentum from the factional contest for power, autonomy, and political preferment. But we should not leave the clash within the prerevolutionary political elite at that. We should consider the overall impact of the whig drive for complete authority in relation to the broader phenomenon of organizational change in the structure of eighteenth-century American politics. A useful concept is that of political modernization in the creation of a more democratic polity. We may set off three distinct but *overlapping* stages pertaining to the process as it affected American political development. One stage commenced within the colonial and two within the revolutionary political arenas. Each worked to reinforce what came before.

The abundance of land and the opportunity to acquire massive amounts of property made it difficult to recreate the stratified sociopolitical systems of England and Europe in America, hence setting the first stage in motion. Great numbers of white adult males turned the soil and gained title to land. By comparison with the Old World, the American environment offered limitless rather than fixed and even declining resources in land; property (even when held in modest amounts) meant the right to vote. Thus the first stage in American political modernization began when Englishmen came into contact with New World resources. There is no longer any doubt that white male colonists gained the right to vote and often did vote as a function of widespread property-holding opportunities.

Yet the provincial political order, nurtured during a hierarchical era when individuals accepted differences in people (whether artificial or real), contained important checks upon the efficacy of popular balloting in the process of decision-making. Most important, colonists could not vote for very many offices, in some areas only for a handful of local officials and for assemblymen, and in many districts (those on or near the frontier) not even for assemblymen. Voters, moreover, deferred to their socioeconomic betters as political leaders. They recognized wealth in property as the prime basis of distinction among men. There was no guarantee that men who believed they were the better sort would be sensitive to or quickly respond to constituency needs. They represented the people from a position of stewardship. The better sort were presumed to be the wisest men in society. Even if some were sensitive to constituency wants, there were upper-hierarchy checks in the form of appointed executives who believed that the democracy had to be closely watched in its political actions to preserve balance among the social orders in government. Higher officials felt that they must avoid popular extremes or face civil disorder and anarchy. The hierarchical conception of balanced government along with the deferential norm in leadership selection blocked the emergence of a democratic polity in provincial America, despite voting rights.

These obstacles came under serious scrutiny on the eve of the American Revolution. The second and third stages in the process blossomed with state constitution-making. The second stage grew out of the insurgent quest to open blocked avenues to high offices. Thus citizens were now to vote for more offices and with greater frequency in elections. Candidates needed to develop a greater awareness that retention of official authority depended upon pleasing a constituency, if for no other reason than that local citizens controlled for the first time the election of men to most if not all offices involved in state-wide legislative matters. Thus the power of the citizen ballot grew proportionately with the writing of state constitutions. The new constitutions *confirmed* the latently democratic tendencies of the colonial political environment by *expanding* citizen participation in the American political community.

Those with the right to vote were in a stronger position than they had been before 1774. They had more rights and even the potential to compete for some offices. Indeed, the third stage of political modernization, involving the decline of deferential assumptions about who should rule in state and society, had its origins in the tensions making for the American Revolution. The constitutional settlement cast doubt on the lines of distinction among the three traditional social orders to be represented in government. The transfer of so much legislative authority to the elected representatives of the people in lower houses tilted the balance ever more toward those elected officials in lower houses and the people they presumably represented. The constitution-makers, whether wittingly or inadvertently, threw hierarchical assumptions into confusion and made it increasingly difficult to conceptualize government in terms of mixing and balancing orders, especially when those orders did not exist in the traditional European sense. There was no longer the perception that higher officials (representing an untitled aristocracy and defunct monarchy) should inhibit the decisions of representatives of the democracy in lower houses. Indeed, there were only a few constitutions that included clauses suggesting that higher officials should be men of great wealth relative to the community of citizens.[21] The lines of distinction, therefore, blurred in 1776 and 1777. Hierarchical assumptions would become moribund in the next decade or two, leaving only the hollow shell of what formerly had been the monarchy, the aristocracy, and the democracy in government.[22]

The confusion in lines of distinction was symptomatic of the fate of the deferential norm. If higher branches in government were no longer to represent higher orders of citizens, then whom did the branches represent? Community leaders made it clear that it was within their right to hold such offices. The feeling in 1776 was no longer that a few privileged individuals of great wealth, family standing, and imperial connections should be dominant. Insurgents established the point that men who had proven themselves in local communities through personal exertion as much as through privilege of birth could compete for high offices. Thus the acquisition of executive positions by a number of men who began life in humble circumstances, but who had proven themselves, indicated that more flexible boundaries surrounded officeholding attitudes. The issue was not resolved in 1776, but decline had begun, and the rules of politics had moved one step closer to the era when citizens accepted as commonplace the assumption that all men, common or uncommon, should have the right to compete for all political offices.

It would be erroneous in closing to assume that all revolutionary leaders felt satisfied with the results of the first constitutional settlement. Dissident men of wealth, disgusted with what they saw as too great an influx of lowly men into state political offices, would gather their forces during the 1780s and attempt to redress the confusion surrounding the question of who should rule. They complained about popular excesses and too much participation by the democracy in governmental leadership. They found evidence to prove their fears that state republican governments were on the verge of anarchy. The wrong kind of men had gained power because of the destruction of balance, or so they claimed. All sense of deference was lost. Rational decision-making had become impossible. Some of these men would gather in Philadelphia during the long, hot summer months of 1787 to mold the constitutional framework for a new national government designed to redistribute the perquisites of office and authority in their favor, hoping thereby to restore stability for the republican experiment. They thought, like some of their prerevolutionary counterparts, that they were saving the American polity from corruption and destruction of liberties. The only difference was that the source of corruption was now coming from below rather than from above. Once again, it seems, the wrong men had moved into office.[23]

But the story of the countercharge against the first constitutional settlement lies beyond the scope of this study. Still the concerns of those who called themselves Federalists during the 1780s suggests that the deferential norm as it applied to leadership selection was losing its meaning, at least in their interpretation of events. Try as they might, men of the Federalist persuasion at best could delay the redefinition of democracy that was taking place in the American political arena during the late eighteenth century. Men were talking less about common citizens as a lower social order to be checked in political matters. A new, more modern definition of democracy was emerging as the three stages interacted with one another and as more people, regardless of background and personal property holdings, became directly involved in politics. Individuals were beginning to speak of a community of citizens making up the American democracy.[24] No doubt men of uncommon standing continued to dominate in political offices, but the new definition had revolutionary potential in the history of the modernization of American politics. Whether that potential ever has been realized, though, is yet another question.

Chapter Seven: Notes

[1] Jack P. Greene, *The Quest for Power*, pp. 3–18, 357–79.

[2] Bernard Bailyn, *The Ideological Origins of the American Revolution*, pp. 55–93.

[3] For differing interpretations about the nature, composition, and goals of revolutionary mobs, consult Jesse Lemisch, "Jack Tar in the Streets," *William and Mary Quarterly* (1968), pp. 371–407; Pauline Maier, "Popular Uprisings and Civil Authority in Eighteenth-Century America," *William and Mary Quarterly* (1970), pp. 3–35; James H. Hutson, "An Investigation of the Inarticulate: Philadelphia's White Oaks," *William and Mary Quarterly*, 3rd Sers. 28 (1971), pp. 3–25.

[4] Gordon S. Wood elaborates on the theme of popular virtue as a key to republicanism in *The Creation of the American Republic*, pp. 46–90, 127–255.

[5] A variety of studies have dealt with constitution-making from the traditional perspective. See in particular William C. Brewster, "Comparative Study of the State Constitutions in the American Revolution," American Academy of Political and Social Science, *Annals* 9 (1897), pp. 380–420; Elisha P. Douglass, *Rebels and Democrats;* Fletcher M. Green, *Constitutional Development in the South Atlantic States, 1776–1860: A Study in the Evolution of Democracy* (Chapel Hill, 1930), pp. 47–98; William C. Morey, "The First State Constitutions," American Academy of Political and Social Science, *Annals* 4 (1893), pp. 201–32; J. R. Pole, *Political Representation in England and the Origins of the American Republic* (London, 1966), pp. 169–338; Wood, *Creation of the American Republic,* pp. 127–255.

In Maryland prospective state senators had to be worth at least £1,000 current money; the governor had to establish personal wealth of £5,000, £1,000 of which at least was to be in a freehold estate. The short-lived South Carolina constitution of 1776 did not make distinctions among officers on various levels of government, but the 1778 constitution did. The governor and lieutenant governor needed wealth of £10,000 local currency free of debt. Candidates for the senate who were residents in the election district had to have property worth £2,000 local currency value, and if they were nonresidents who owned property in the district, they had to have £7,000 in property in that district in order to run as a nonresident candidate. All the constitutions are in Francis N. Thorpe, ed., *The Federal and State Constitutions, Colonial Charters, and Other Organic Laws of the States, Territories, and Colonies . . . Forming the United States of America* (7 vols., Washington, 1909), as follows: New Hampshire (1776), IV, 2451–53; Massachusetts (1691 charter), III, 1870–86; Rhode Island (1663 charter), VI, 3211–22; Connecticut (1662 charter), I, 529–36; New York (1777), V, 2623–38; New Jersey (1776), V, 2594–98; Pennsylvania (1776),

V, 3081–92; Delaware (1776), I, 562–68; Maryland (1776), III, 1686–1701; Virginia (1776), VII, 3812–19; North Carolina (1776), V, 2787–94, South Carolina (1776), VI, 3241–48; Georgia (1777), II, 776–85. All references in this chapter to specific clauses are drawn from these pages.

⁶ There was little agreement among revolutionary leaders about the ability of common people to hold office and to rule themselves in state and society. Thomas Paine represented the radical extreme; he wrote about unchecked popular rule in *Common Sense*. See Philip S. Foner, ed., *The Complete Writings of Thomas Paine* (2 vols., New York, 1945), I, pp. 3–46. Another advocate of popularly based leadership was the anonymous pamphleteer who published in 1776 *The People the Best Governors, or, a Plan of Government Founded on the Just Principles of Natural Freedom,* reprinted in Frederick Chase, *A History of Dartmouth College and the Town of Hanover New Hampshire (to 1815),* 2nd ed. (Brattleboro, 1928), pp. 654–63. John Adams penned his *Thoughts on Government* in reacting to Paine's *Common Sense* in the spring of 1776. Adams represented a middle position in that he desired men of proven ability and merit in political offices. His position perhaps was most representative of what other constitution-makers thought. Property qualifications for office were not that high for officials in most states, except for Maryland and South Carolina. Adams clearly wanted community leaders of proven standing in political office. He did not trust rampant popular rule. The *Thoughts* are reprinted in Charles F. Adams, ed., *The Works of John Adams,* IV, pp. 193–200. But there were a few who were more conservative than Adams, such as Carter Braxton, a Virginia planter who prepared a plan of government for the Virginia state constitutional convention. Braxton insisted that the senate should be appointed for life. He felt that men completely secure in their offices would stand more willingly against the unreasonableness of the public will. But Braxton's arguments, implying a native officeholding aristocracy of wealth and presumed talent, were rejected. They implied political immobility among other matters. Braxton wrote as "A Native" to the Virginia convention, and his comments are in Peter Force, ed., *American Archives,* 4th Sers. (6 vols., Washington, 1837–1846), VI, pp. 748–54. For secondary accounts, consult Bailyn, *Ideological Origins,* pp. 272–301, and Douglass, *Rebels and Democrats,* pp. 10–32.

⁷ The South Carolina 1776 constitution, likewise, called for the indirect election of a legislative council to function as an upper house. Legislative councilors were to be elected from among members of the lower house. But the 1778 South Carolina constitution provided for the direct election of state senators, yet like Maryland with higher than usual property-holding qualifications for candidates.

⁸ The anonymous author of *The People the Best Governors* was reacting to the first New Hampshire constitutional settlement when he wrote his pamphlet denouncing among other things property-holding clauses for both electors and the elected. For a succinct summary of the western secessionist

attempt as it involved Vermont, consult Matt B. Jones, *Vermont in the Making, 1750–1777* (Cambridge, 1939).

[9] In New York, though, prominent leaders in each of the four districts had the advantage in competing for senatorial positions. The larger the district, the easier it was for men of birth, wealth, and family name to predominate over all others. Such men would be more visible and better known by reputation.

[10] The septennial census clauses contained in the New York and Pennsylvania constitutions were exceptions to the rule. Eastern interests usually had the initial advantage in legislative matters, given the location of population in 1776.

[11] Residency requirements for legislators and senators were adopted in many states, including New Jersey, Delaware, Virginia, and North Carolina. The constitutions usually required that the candidate reside within his district for at least one year before the election took place. The requirements were designed to cut out those men who owned large tracts of land in districts but were nonresidents. The South Carolina constitutional provision of 1778 was unique in that it endorsed much higher property-holding qualifications for nonresidents than for residents seeking senatorial positions.

[12] Before the Revolution imperial instructions had dropped the phrase "good behavior" in favor of that of "during pleasure" only. Many insurgents felt that judges in office who served during the pleasure of the Crown were not truly independent. For one manifestation of the controversy, consult Jerome J. Nadelhaft, "Politics and the Judicial Tenure Fight in Colonial New Jersey," *William and Mary Quarterly*, 3rd Sers. 28 (1971), pp. 46–63.

[13] In North Carolina, for example, only eighteen men gained council appointments in the decade before 1774. But after 1776 each county had a state senator who was to be elected to office each year. The first state senate had thirty-four members, and in the twelve years following 1776 some 250 individuals had the opportunity to sit in the North Carolina senate. The figures indicate the dramatic increase in political mobility resulting from changes in the constitutional environment. The data about North Carolina are contained in Jackson T. Main, *The Upper House in Revolutionary America*, p. 154.

[14] Thorpe, *Federal and State Constitutions*, V, p. 3087.

[15] *The History of the American Revolution*, I, p. 353.

[16] For the impact of the pattern reducing the authority of senators in the legislative arena, consult Main, *Upper House in Revolutionary America*, pp. 99–191. See also Merrill Jensen, "Democracy and the American Revolution," *Huntington Library Quarterly* 20 (1957), pp. 321–41.

[17] Factionalism before 1776 generally followed a vertical plane. Members of lower houses fought with higher officials. But after 1776 factional disputes took more of a horizontal plane. Indeed, state constitution-making was largely responsible for the shift in that so much power came to rest in lower houses. Thus after 1776 factions in politics became more readily identifiable

in lower houses. It was a shift portending the emergence of formalized party politics.

[18] There is much evidence to show that prominent late colonial Virginia planters were heavily in debt to British creditors. Surely the John Robinson scandal points to such financial problems. But the planters still had assets. For a summary statement about the problem of debts, see Emory G. Evans, "Planter Indebtedness and the Coming of the Revolution in Virginia," *William and Mary Quarterly,* 3rd Sers. 19 (1962), pp. 511–33. I rated planter wealth on the basis of known assets.

[19] See Chapter Two and Francis G. Walett, "The Massachusetts Council, 1766–1774," *William and Mary Quarterly* (1949), pp. 605–27.

[20] Roger Atkinson to Samuel Pleasants, Williamsburg, November 23, 1776, *Virginia Magazine of History and Biography* 15 (1908), pp. 357–58.

[21] Those of Maryland and South Carolina stand out in particular, as mentioned in footnote 5. New Jersey, likewise, had fairly high property-holding qualifications for officeholders. Whereas voters needed to be worth only £50 proclamation money, legislators had to be worth £500 and councilors £1,000 in proclamation money. Elsewhere, though property-holding requirements existed (either in money or land) and were usually higher for state senators and governors than for voters or legislators, they were not so high as to prohibit a great number of citizens from competing for office. Thus the lines of hierarchical distinction were there after state constitution-making, but the lines were not necessarily prohibitive for men of less than wealthy means seeking high office.

[22] Wood, *Creation of the American Republic,* pp. 471–615, confirms the collapse of hierarchical assumptions about balancing social orders in government in his discussion of the new science of politics emerging from the work of the Founding Fathers in Philadelphia during 1787 and after. For those men, the traditional divisions of government (house, senate, and executive branch) no longer served to balance social orders but to check rampant factional conflict among interest groups in society.

[23] *Ibid.,* pp. 471–518. Wood implies that a social analysis of the constitutional convention would be in order, given the fears about impending social chaos among the delegates who largely blamed instability in state governments upon the presence of common citizens turned demagogues in state offices.

[24] Historians often have asked the question: How revolutionary was the American Revolution? In its political aspects there can be no doubt that the Revolution sped up the transformation of American political thought and action. The people had become the "constituent power," as R. R. Palmer observed in his *The Age of the Democratic Revolution: A Political History of Europe and America, 1760–1800* (2 vols., Princeton, 1959–1964), I, pp. 213–35. But whether the people had become the actual power in political decision-making is another question. Until further research to the contrary,

we may presume that the Revolution confirmed the right of local community leaders to rule, and that political elites made up of men of ability, wealth, education, and family standing continued to control decision-making. The Revolution was not very revolutionary in that sense.

The Combined Executive Elite Serving in Upper-Hierarchy Offices at the Time of the Outbreak of the American Revolution

LATE COLONIAL:	REVOLUTIONARY:

New Hampshire

LATE COLONIAL:	REVOLUTIONARY:
Governor: John Wentworth (1767-1775)	*Governor:* None
Lt. Governor: None	*Lt. Governor:* None
Secretary: Theodore Atkinson (1741-1762, 1769-1775)	*Secretary:* Ebenezer Thompson (1776-1786)
Treasurer: George Jaffrey (1749-1775)	*Treasurer:* Nicholas Gilman (1776-1783)
Attorney General: Samuel Livermore (1769-1776, 1778-1781)	*Attorney General:* Wyseman Claggett (1765-1769, 1776-1778)
Chief Justice: Theodore Atkinson (1754-1775)	*Chief Justice:* Meshech Weare (1776-1782)
Associate Justices: Leverett Hubbard (1763-1784) William Parker (1771-1775) Meshech Weare (1747-1775)	*Associate Justices:* Leverett Hubbard (1763-1784) Matthew Thornton (1776-1782) John Wentworth (1776-1781)
Councilors: Theodore Atkinson (1734-1775) Peter Gilman (1771-1775) George Jaffrey (1766-1775) Peter Livius (1765-1772) [1] Daniel Rindge (1766-1775) Daniel Rogers (1766-1775)	*Councilors:* Samuel Ashley (1776-1779) Josiah Bartlett (1776-1784) Jonathan Blanchard (1776-1778) Wyseman Claggett (1776-1777, 1780-1781)

LATE COLONIAL:

John Sherburne (1774-1775)
Thomas Westbrook Waldron
    (1772-1776)
Daniel Warner (1753-1775)
Jonathan Warner (1766-1775)
Mark Hunking Wentworth
    (1759-1775)
Paul Wentworth (1770-1775)

REVOLUTIONARY:

Nathaniel Folsom (1776-1777,
    1783-1784)
Benjamin Giles (1776-1777)
John Hurd (1776-1777)
Ebenezer Thompson (1776-1780)
Matthew Thornton (1776-1777,
    1779-1780)
Thomas Westbrook Waldron
    (1772-1776) [2]
Meshech Weare (1776-1784)
John Wentworth (1776-1781) [3]
William Whipple (1776-1777)

Massachusetts

Governor:
Thomas Hutchinson
    (1771-1774)

Governor:
None

Lt. Governor:
Andrew Oliver (1771-1774)

Lt. Governor:
None

Secretary:
Thomas Flucker (1770-1774)

Secretary:
Samuel Adams (1775-1780) [4]
John Avery, Jr. (1776-1806) [5]

Treasurer:
Harrison Gray (1753-1774)

Treasurer:
Henry Gardner (1775-1782)

Attorney General:
Jonathan Sewall (1767-1774)

Attorney General:
None

Chief Justice:
Peter Oliver (1771-1774)

Chief Justice:
John Adams (1775-1777)

Associate Justices:
William Cushing (1772-1777)
Foster Hutchinson (1771-1774)
Nathaniel Ropes (1772-1774)
Edmund Trowbridge
    (1767-1774)

Associate Justices:
William Cushing (1772-1777)
Jedidiah Foster (1776-1779) [6]
Robert Treat Paine (1775-1776,
    1790-1804) [6]
William Reed (1775-1776) [6]
Nathaniel Peaslee Sargent
    (1775-1790)
James Sullivan (1776-1782) [6]

LATE COLONIAL:

Councilors:
James Bowdoin (1757-1769,
1770-1774, 1775-1777)
William Brattle (1755-1769,
1770-1774)
Caleb Cushing (1771-1774,
1775-1780)
Samuel Danforth (1739-1774)
Samuel Dexter (1768-1774)
John Erving (1754-1774)
James Gowen (1770-1774)
Benjamin Greenleaf (1770-1774,
1775-1776, 1777-1780)
John Hancock (1772-1774,
1775-1776)
Humphrey Hobson (1773-1774)
James Humphrey (1770-1774)
George Leonard, Jr. (1770-1774,
1792-1794)
James Otis, Sr. (1762-1766,
1770-1774, 1775-1776)
Samuel Phillips (1772-1774)
James Pitts (1766-1774,
1775-1776)
Jedidiah Preble (1773-1774,
1778-1779, 1780-1781)
Isaac Royall (1752-1774)
James Russell (1761-1774)
William Sever (1769-1774,
1775-1783)
Walter Spooner (1770-1774,
1775-1787)
Artemas Ward (1770-1774,
1778-1780, 1788-1789)
John Whitcomb (1773-1774,
1776-1780)
John Winthrop IV (1773-1774,
1775-1777)
TimothyWoodbridge(1771-1774)

REVOLUTIONARY:

Councilors:
John Adams (1775-1776)
Samuel Adams (1775-1776,
1779-1780, 1781-1787)
James Bowdoin (1757-1769,
1770-1774, 1775-1777)
Benjamin Chadbourne
(1775-1777, 1781-1785)
Charles Chauncy (1775-1776)
Caleb Cushing (1771-1774,
1775-1780)
Thomas Cushing (1775-1780)
Michael Farley (1775-1776)
Jabez Fisher (1775-1784)
Jedidiah Foster (1775-1776)
Enoch Freeman (1775-1776)
Joseph Gerrish (1770-1771,
1775-1776)
Moses Gill (1775-1795)
Benjamin Greenleaf (1770-1774,
1775-1776, 1777-1780)
John Hancock (1772-1774,
1775-1776)
Samuel Holten (1775-1778,
1780-1782, 1784-1785,
1786-1787, 1789-1791)
Benjamin Lincoln (1775-1776)
Azor Orne (1775-1777,
1780-1782, 1788-1796)
James Otis, Sr. (1762-1766,
1770-1774, 1775-1776)
Robert Treat Paine (1775-1776,
1779-1781)
Joseph Palmer (1775-1776,
1777-1778)
James Pitts (1766-1774,
1775-1776)
James Prescott (1775-1776,
1780-1784, 1786-1787)

LATE COLONIAL:

REVOLUTIONARY:

William Sever (1769-1774,
  1775-1783)
Walter Spooner (1770-1774,
  1775-1787)
Eldad Taylor (1775-1776)
John Taylor (1775-1778)
John Winthrop IV (1773-1774,
  1775-1777)

Rhode Island

Governor:
Joseph Wanton (1769-1775)

Lt. Governor:
Darius Sessions (1769-1775)

Secretary:
Henry Ward (1760-1797)

Treasurer:
Joseph Clarke (1761-1792)

Attorney General:
Henry Marchant (1771-1777)

Chief Justice:
Stephen Hopkins (1751-1756,
  1770-1776)

Associate Justices:
Job Bennet, Jr. (1763-1768,
  1773-1776)
Metcalf Bowler (1768-1768,
  1770-1776)
William Greene (1768-1769,
  1774-1777)
Joseph Russell (1751-1759,
  1761-1762, 1774-1776)

Assistants:
John Almy (1772-1775)
Peleg Barker (1774-1775)
John Collins (1774-1778)
John Congdon (1771-1775)

Governor:
Nicholas Cooke (1775-1778)

Lt. Governor:
William Bradford (1775-1778)

Secretary:
Henry Ward (1760-1797)

Treasurer:
Joseph Clarke (1761-1792)

Attorney General:
Henry Marchant (1771-1777)

Chief Justice:
Metcalf Bowler (1776-1777)

Associate Justices:
Shearjashub Bourne (1776-1778)
Jabez Bowen (1776-1778)
William Greene (1768-1769,
  1774-1777)
Thomas Wells, Jr. (1776-1780)

Assistants:
James Arnold, Jr. (1775-1781,
  1786-1787, 1788-1790,
  1792-1793)
Thomas Church (1775-1777)

LATE COLONIAL:

David Harris (1769-1775)
William Potter (1774-1775,
 1776-1778)
Jonathan Randall (1745-1746,
 1747-1748, 1758-1761,
 1763-1765, 1767-1768,
 1770-1777)
William Richmond (1769-1770,
 1771-1772, 1773-1775)
John Sayles, Jr. (1774-1782)
Thomas Wickes (1767-1768,
 1769-1771, 1772-1775)

REVOLUTIONARY:

John Collins (1775-1777)
John Jepson (1765-1767,
 1776-1777)
Ambrose Page (1775-1778)
Peter Phillips (1775-1777,
 1779-1781)
Simeon Potter (1776-1777)
William Potter (1774-1775,
 1776-1778)
Jonathan Randall (1745-1746,
 1747-1748, 1758-1761,
 1763-1765, 1767-1768,
 1770-1777)
John Sayles, Jr. (1774-1782)

Connecticut

Governor:
Jonathan Trumbull (1769-1784)

Lt. Governor:
Matthew Griswold (1769-1784)

Secretary:
George Wyllys (1735-1796)

Treasurer:
John Lawrence (1769-1789)

Attorney General:
None

Chief Justice:
Matthew Griswold (1769-1784)

Associate Justices:
Eliphalet Dyer (1766-1789)
Samuel Huntington (1773-1784)
William Pitkin (1769-1789)
Roger Sherman (1766-1789)

Assistants:
Shubael Conant (1760-1775) dead
Abraham Davenport (1766-1784)
Eliphalet Dyer (1762-1784)

Governor:
Jonathan Trumbull (1769-1784)

Lt. Governor:
Matthew Griswold (1769-1784)

Secretary:
George Wyllys (1735-1796)

Treasurer:
John Lawrence (1769-1789)

Attorney General:
None

Chief Justice:
Matthew Griswold (1769-1784)

Associate Justices:
Eliphalet Dyer (1766-1789)
Samuel Huntington (1773-1784)
William Pitkin (1769-1789)
Roger Sherman (1766-1789)

Assistants:
Abraham Davenport (1766-1784)
Eliphalet Dyer (1762-1784)
Jabez Hamlin (1758-1766,
 1773-1785)

LATE COLONIAL:

Jabez Hamlin (1758-1766,
1773-1785)
James A. Hillhouse (1773-1775)
Jabez Huntington (1764-1781)
William Samuel Johnson
(1766-1776, 1786-1789)
William Pitkin (1766-1786)
Elisha Sheldon (1762-1779)
Roger Sherman (1766-1786)
Joseph Spencer (1766-1778,
1779-1789)
Oliver Wolcott (1771-1786)

REVOLUTIONARY:

Jabez Huntington (1764-1781)
Samuel Huntington (1775-1784)
Richard Law (1776-1786)
William Pitkin (1766-1786)
Elisha Sheldon (1762-1779)
Roger Sherman (1766-1786)
Joseph Spencer (1766-1778,
1779-1789)
William Williams (1776-1780,
1784-1803)
Oliver Wolcott (1771-1786)

New York

Governor:
William Tryon (1771-1775)

Lt. Governor:
Cadwallader Colden (1761-1776)

Secretary:
George Clarke, Jr. (1738-1745,
1746-1775)

Treasurer:
Abraham Lott (1767-1776)

Attorney General:
John Tabor Kempe (1759-1775)

Chief Justice:
Daniel Horsmanden (1763-1776)

Associate Justices:
Thomas Jones (1773-1776)
Robert R. Livingston
(1763-1775)
George Duncan Ludlow
(1769-1776)

Governor:
George Clinton (1777-1795,
1801-1804)

Lt. Governor:
Pierre Van Cortlandt
(1777-1795)

Secretary:
John Morin Scott (1778-1784)

Treasurer:
Peter V. B. Livingston
(1776-1778)

Attorney General:
Egbert Benson (1777-1787)

Chief Justice:
John Jay (1777-1779)

Associate Justices:
John Sloss Hobart (1777-1798)
Robert Yates (1777-1790)

LATE COLONIAL:

Councilors:
Charles Warde Apthorpe
  (1764-1776)
William Axtell (1771-1776)
Cadwallader Colden (1721-1776)
John Harris Cruger (1773-1776)
Oliver De Lancey (1760-1776)
Daniel Horsmanden
  (1733-1747, 1755-1776)
James Jauncey, Jr. (1775-1776)
Roger Morris (1764-1776)
William Smith, Jr. (1767-1776)
Hugh Wallace, (1769-1776)
John Watts (1758-1776)
Henry White (1769-1776)

REVOLUTIONARY:

Senators:
William Duer (1777-1778)
William Floyd (1777-1788,
  1807-1808)
Jellis Fonda (1777-1778,
  1779-1781, 1788-1791)
John Jones (1777-1778) [7]
Jonathan Landon (1777-1779)
Jonathan Lawrence (1777-1783)
Philip Livingston, Jr.
  (1777-1783)
Lewis Morris (1777-1781,
  1784-1790)
Richard Morris (1778-1790) [7]
Rinier Mynderse (1777-1781)
Isaac Paris (1777-1777)
Arthur Parks (1777-1788)
Levi Pawling (1777-1782)
Zephaniah Platt (1777-1783)
Isaac Roosevelt (1777-1786,
  1788-1792)
John Morin Scott (1777-1782)
William Smith (1777-1783)
Dirck W. Ten Broeck
  (1777-1779)
Pierre Van Cortlandt
  (1777-1778)
Anthony Van Schaick
  (1777-1780)
Alexander Webster (1777-1778,
  1779-1785, 1789-1793)
John Williams (1777-1778,
  1782-1783, 1795-1796)
Henry Wisner (1777-1782)
Jesse Woodhull (1777-1781)
Abraham Yates, Jr. (1777-1790)

LATE COLONIAL: REVOLUTIONARY:

New Jersey

Governor:
William Franklin (1763-1775)

Governor:
William Livingston (1776-1790)

Lt. Governor:
None

Lt. Governor:
None

Secretary:
Maurice Morgann (1767-1775) [8]
Charles Pettit (1769-1775,
   1776-1778) [8]

Secretary:
Charles Pettit (1769-1775,
   1776-1778)

Treasurer:
John Smyth (1774-1775) [9]
Samuel Smith (1750-1775) [10]

Treasurer:
Richard Smith (1776-1777)

Attorney General:
Cortlandt Skinner (1754-1775)

Attorney General:
William Paterson (1776-1783)

Chief Justice:
Frederick Smyth (1764-1775)

Chief Justice:
Richard Stockton (1776-1776) [11]
John DeHart (1776-1777) [11]
Robert Morris (1777-1779) [11]

Associate Justices:
David Ogden (1772-1775)
Richard Stockton (1774-1775)

Associate Justices:
Francis Hopkinson
   (1776-1776) [12]
Isaac Smith (1777-1805) [12]
John Cleves Symmes
   (1777-1788) [12]
Samuel Tucker (1776-1777) [12]

Councilors:
William Alexander (1758-1775)
Daniel Coxe IV (1771-1775)
Francis Hopkinson (1774-1775)
Peter Kemble (1745-1775)
John Lawrence (1771-1775)
David Ogden (1751-1775)
James Parker (1764-1775)
Stephen Skinner (1769-1775)
Samuel Smith (1763-1775)
Frederick Smyth (1764-1775)

Councilors:
Silas Condict (1776-1781)
John Cooper (1776-1781,
   1784-1785)
Stephen Crane (1776-1778,
   1779-1780)
Theophilus Elmer (1776-1778,
   1782-1783)
John Fell (1776-1777,
   1782-1784)
Jonathan Hand (1776-1777)

LATE COLONIAL:

John Stevens (1762-1775,
 1776-1782)
Richard Stockton (1768-1775)

REVOLUTIONARY:

William Paterson (1776-1777)
Nathaniel Scudder (1776-1777)
Andrew Sinnickson (1776-1777,
 1778-1780)
Richard Smith (1776-1777)
John Stevens (1762-1775,
 1776-1782)
John Cleves Symmes
 (1776-1777, 1785-1786)
John Wetherill (1776-1777)

Pennsylvania

Governor:
John Penn (1773-1776)

Lt. Governor:
None

Secretary:
Joseph Shippen, Jr. (1762-1776)

Treasurer:
Owen Jones (1768-1775)

Attorney General:
Andrew Allen (1769-1776)

Chief Justice:
Benjamin Chew (1774-1776)

Associate Justices:
John Lawrence (1767-1776)
John Morton (1774-1776)
Thomas Willing (1767-1776)

Councilors:
Andrew Allen (1770-1775)
Thomas Cadwalader
 (1755-1776)
Benjamin Chew (1755-1776)
James Hamilton (1746-1776)

Governor:
None

Lt. Governor:
None

Secretary:
Timothy Matlack (1777-1782)

Treasurer:
David Rittenhouse (1777-1789)

Attorney General:
Jonathan D. Sergeant
 (1777-1780)

Chief Justice:
Joseph Reed (1777-1777) [13]
Thomas McKean (1777-1799) [13]

Associate Justices:
William Augustus Atlee
 (1777-1791)
John Evans (1777-1783)

Supreme Executive Councilors:
John Bailey (1777-1778) [14]
George Bryan (1777-1779)
John Evans (1777-1777) [15]
Joseph Hart (1777-1780)
Jonathan Hoge (1777-1778,
 1784-1787)

LATE COLONIAL:

Lynford Lardner (1755-1776)
William Logan (1747-1776)
John Penn (1752-1776)
Richard Penn (1764-1776)
Richard Peters (1749-1776)
Edward Shippen, Jr.
 (1770-1776)
James Tilghman (1767-1776)
Joseph Turner (1747-1776)

REVOLUTIONARY:

John Hubley (1777-1777) [14]
John Lowdon (1777-1777)
Jacob Morgan (1777-1778) [16]
John Proctor (1777-1777)
George Taylor (1777-1777)
Richard Tea (1777-1777) [16]
Thomas Wharton, Jr.
 (1777-1778)

Delaware

Governor:
See Pennsylvania

Lt. Governor:
None

Secretary:
See Pennsylvania

Treasurer:
See Pennsylvania

Attorney General:
Jacob Moore (1774-c.1777) [17]
George Read (1763-1774)

Chief Justice:
Richard McWilliams
 (1773-1776, 1777-1777)

Associate Justices:
Samuel Chew (1773-1776)
David Hall (1769-1776)
Caesar Rodney (1769-1776)

Councilors:
See Pennsylvania

Governor:
John McKinly (1777-1777)

Lt. Governor:
None

Secretary:
James Booth (1778-1799)

Treasurer:
Samuel Patterson (1778-1781)

Attorney General:
Jacob Moore (1774-c.1777) [17]
Gunning Bedford, Jr.
 (c.1779-1789) [17]

Chief Justice:
Richard McWilliams
 (1773-1776, 1777-1777) [18]
William Killen (1777-1793) [18]

Associate Justices:
John Cook (1777-1778) [19]
John Evans (1777-1778) [19]
Caesar Rodney (1777-1777) [19]
James Sykes (1777-1777) [19]

Councilors:
Richard Bassett (1776-1780,
 1782-1785)
Richard Cantwell (1776-1777,
 1779-1782)

LATE COLONIAL:

REVOLUTIONARY:

Thomas Collins (1776-1782)
Daniel Dingee (1776-1778)
William Polk (1776-1777,
    1778-1782)
George Read (1776-1779,
    1782-1788)
James Sykes (1776-1777)
Nicholas Van Dyke (1776-1778,
    1786-1789)
John Wiltbank (1776-1777)

Maryland

Governor:
Robert Eden (1769-1776)

Governor:
Thomas Johnson, Jr. (1777-1779)

Lt. Governor:
None

Lt. Governor:
None

Secretary:
Daniel Dulany the Younger
    (1761-1774)

Secretary:
Extant records make it unclear
    as to who was appointed, if
    someone was appointed dur-
    ing the Revolution.

Treasurer:
William Fitzhugh
    (1772-1775) [20]
William Hemsley, Jr.
    (1769-1775) [21]

Treasurer:
Thomas Harwood, Jr.
    (1775-1804) [20]
James Hindman (1777-1779) [21]
William Hindman
    (1775-1777) [21]

Attorney General:
Thomas Jenings (1768-1776)

Attorney General:
Benjamin Galloway
    (1777-1777) [22]
Thomas Jenings (1777-1777) [22]
Luther Martin (1778-1805,
    1818-1822) [22]
James Tilghman (1777-1777) [22]

Chief Judge:
William Hayward (c.1771-1776)

Chief Judge:
Benjamin Rumsey (1778-1805)

LATE COLONIAL:

Associate Judges:
John Beale Bordley (1766-1776)
John Cooke (c.1773-1776)
John Hepburn (c.1766-1776)
Daniel of St. Thomas Jenifer
(1766-1776)
Philip Thomas Lee
(c.1773-1776)
John Leeds (c.1766-1776)
Joseph Sim (c.1773-1776)

Councilors:
John Beale Bordley (1767-1776)
Benedict Calvert (1748-1776)
Daniel Dulany the Younger
(1757-1776)
William Fitzhugh (1769-1776)
William Hayward (1770-1776)
Daniel of St. Thomas Jenifer
(1771-1776, 1777-1781)
Philip Thomas Lee (1773-1776)
Richard Lee (1745-1776)
Benjamin Ogle (1773-1776)
George Plater (1771-1776,
1777-1791)
John Ridout (1760-1776)
George Steuart (1769-1776)

REVOLUTIONARY:

Associate Judges:
Thomas Jones (1778-1805)
Benjamin Mackall (1778-1806)
James Murray (1778-1804)
Solomon Wright (1778-1792)

Senators:
Charles Carroll, Barrister
(1777-1780)
Charles Carroll, Carrollton
(1777-1801)
Thomas Contee (1777-1778)
Robert Goldsborough
(1777-1783)
Charles Grahame (1777-1779) [23]
Thomas B. Hands
(1777-1777) [24]
William Hindman (1777-1784,
1791-1792, 1799-1800) [24]
Daniel of St. Thomas Jenifer
(1771-1776, 1777-1781)
Thomas Johnson, Jr.
(1777-1777) [23]
Joseph Nicholson, Jr.
(1777-1780)
William Paca (1777-1779)
George Plater (1771-1776,
1777-1791)
Thomas Stone (1777-1787)
Edward Tilghman
(1777-1777) [24]
James Tilghman (1777-1777) [24]
Matthew Tilghman
(1777-1783)
Samuel Wilson (1777-1780)

LATE COLONIAL:

REVOLUTIONARY:

Brice Thomas Beale Worthington
(1777-1781, 1791-1793)
Turbutt Wright (1777-1779)

Virginia

Governor:
John Murray, Earl of Dunmore
(1771-1775)

Governor:
Patrick Henry (1776-1779,
1784-1786)

Lt. Governor:
None

Lt. Governor:
None

Secretary:
Thomas Nelson (1743-1782)

Secretary:
Thomas Nelson (1743-1782)

Treasurer:
Robert Carter Nicholas
(1766-1776, 1776-1776)

Treasurer:
Robert Carter Nicholas
(1766-1776, 1776-1776) [25]
George Webb (1776-1778) [25]

Attorney General:
John Randolph (1766-1776)

Attorney General:
Edmund Randolph (1776-1786)

Chief Justice:
See General Court

Chief Justice:
See Supreme Court

General Court:
The council served as the supreme court in Virginia.

Supreme Court: [26]
John Blair, Jr. (G)
(1778-c.1789)
Paul Carrington (G)
(1778-1807)
Richard Cary (A) (1776-1788)
William Holt (A) (1776-1778)
Joseph Jones (G) (1778-1779,
1789-1805)
Bernard Moore (A) (1776-1778)
Robert Carter Nicholas (C)
(1778-1780)
Edmund Pendelton (C)
(1778-1803)
George Wythe (C) (1778-1806)

Councilors:
Robert Carter Burwell
(1764-1776)

Senators:
John Armistead (1776–1777)

LATE COLONIAL:

William Byrd III (1754-1776)
Robert Carter (1758-1776)
Richard Corbin (1750-1776)
George William Fairfax
  (1768-1776)
Philip Ludwell Lee (1757-1775)
Thomas Nelson (1749-1776)
John Page (1768-1774)
John Page II (1773-1776)
John Tayloe II (1757-1776)
Ralph Wormeley III
  (1771-1776)

REVOLUTIONARY:

Theodorick Bland, Jr.
  (1776-1779)
George Brooke (1776-1779)
William Cabell (1776-1781)
Paul Carrington (1776-1778)
Archibald Cary (1776-1787)
William Christian (1776-1777,
  1780-1784)
William Ellzey (1776-1787)
James Holt (1776-1780)
David Jameson (1776-1777,
  1781-1784)
John Jones (1776-1791)
Henry Lee (1776-1787)
Thomas Ludwell Lee
  (1776-1778)
Warner Lewis, Jr. (1776-1779)
Thomas Lomax (1776-1778)
David Mason (1776-1777,
  1779-1781)
Sampson Mathews (1776-1782,
  1790-1792)
Richard Mitchell (1776–1778)
Thomas Mann Randolph
  (1776-1778)
David Rogers (1776-1779)
Robert Rutherford (1776-1791)
Isaac Smith (1776-1777)
Edward Stevens (1776-1777,
  1779-1791)
Edmund Winston (1776-1784)

North Carolina

Governor:
Josiah Martin (1771-1775)

Governor:
Richard Caswell (1776-1780,
  1785-1787)

Lt. Governor:
None

Lt. Governor:
None

LATE COLONIAL:

Secretary:
Samuel Strudwick (1767-1775)

Treasurer:
Richard Caswell (1773-1776) [27]
Joseph Montfort (1764-1775) [28]

Attorney General:
Thomas McGuire (1767-1775)

Chief Justice:
Martin Howard (1767-1775)

Associate Judges:
Richard Henderson (1768-1773)
Maurice Moore (c.1765-1766,
   1768-1773)

Councilors:
Samuel Cornell (1770-1775)
Lewis Henry DeRosset
   (1752-1775)
William Dry (1764-1775)
Nathaniel Duckinfield
   (1771-1775)
James Hasell (1750-1775)
Martin Howard (1767-1775)
Alexander McCulloh
   (1762-1775)
Thomas McGuire (1774-1775)
John Rutherford (1751-1757,
   1761-1775)
John Sampson (1761-1775)
Samuel Strudwick (1772-1775)

REVOLUTIONARY:

Secretary:
James Glasgow (1777-1798)

Treasurer:
John Ashe (1777-1779) [27]
Samuel Johnston (1777-1777) [28]
William Skinner (1777-1784) [28]

Attorney General:
Waightstill Avery (1777-1779)

Chief Justice:
None so designated

Supreme Court Judges:
Samuel Ashe (1777-1795)
James Iredell (1777-1778)
Samuel Spencer (1777-1794)

Senators:
John McKnitt Alexander
   (1777-1778)
Samuel Ashe (1777-1779)
Elisha Battle (1777-1782,
   1783-1784, 1785-1788)
John Bradford (1777-1778)
Needham Bryan (1777-1778)
John Campbell (1777-1778)
John Carter (1777-1778)
James Coor (1777-1778)
Archibald Corrie (1777-1778)
William Cray (1777-1778)
Benjamin Exum (1777-1780)
Ralph Gorrell (1777-1779)
Thomas Hart (1777-1778)
Memucan Hunt (1777-1779,
   1781-1782, 1788-1789)
Samuel Jarvis (1777-1778,
   1780-1782)
Allen Jones (1777-1779,
   1783-1785, 1787-1788)
Joseph Jones (1777-1778)

LATE COLONIAL:	REVOLUTIONARY:
	James Kenan (1777-1784, 1787-1792, 1793-1794)
	Robert Lanier (1777-1778)
	David Love (1777-1778)
	Archibald Maclaine (1777-1779, 1782-1783)
	Charles McLean (1777-1778)
	James Parratt (1777-1778)
	Ambrose Ramsey (1777-1788)
	Thomas Respass (1777-1781)
	Thomas Robeson (1777-1778)
	Griffith Rutherford (1777-1781, 1783-1787)
	William Russell (1777-1784)
	Robert Salter (1777-1779)
	Benjamin Seawell (1777-1779)
	William Skinner (1777-1778, 1786-1787)
	Luke Sumner (1777-1781)
	Robert Sumner (1777-1780, 1785-1788)
	William Williams (1777-1778)

South Carolina

Governor: (Acting)
William Bull II (1760-1761, 1764-1766, 1768, 1769-1771, 1773-1775)

President:
John Rutledge (1776-1778, 1779-1782)

Lt. Governor:
None

Vice President:
Henry Laurens (1776-1777)

Secretary:
Thomas Skottowe (1763-1775)

Secretary:
John Huger (1776-1778)

Treasurer:
Benjamin Dart (1771-1775)
Henry Peronneau (1770-1775)

Treasurer:
Peter Bacot (1775-1778)
William Gibbes (1775-1778)
John Neufville (1775-1778)

Attorney General:
Sir Edgerton Leigh
(1765-1774) [29]

Attorney General:
Alexander Moultrie (1776-1778)

LATE COLONIAL:

James Simpson (1765,
1774-1775) [29]

Chief Justice:
Thomas Knox Gordon
(1771-1775)

Circuit Court Judges:
William Henry Drayton
(1774-1774) [30]
Matthews Gosslett (1772-1775)
John Fewtrell (1771-1775)
William Gregory (1774-1775) [30]
John Murray (1771-1774) [30]
Edward Savage (1771-1775)

Councilors:
Daniel Blake (1761-1775)
William Bull II (1748-1775)
John Burn (1763-1775)
Sir John Colleton (1764-1775)
John Drayton (1761-1775)
William Henry Drayton
(1772-1775)
Barnard Elliott (1771-1775)
Thomas Knox Gordon
(1771-1775)
Sir Edgerton Leigh
(1759-1775)
Henry Middleton (1755-1775,
1776-1777)
Thomas Skottowe (1763-1775)
John Stuart (1771-1775)

REVOLUTIONARY:

Chief Justice:
William Henry Drayton
(1776-1779)

Assistant Judges:
Thomas Bee (1776-1778,
1788-1790)
John Mathews (1776-c.1778)
Henry Pendleton (1776-1789)
Joshua Ward (1776-1776)

Legislative Councilors:
Thomas Bee (1776-1778) [31]
Stephen Bull (1776-1777,
1778-1780)
Thomas Ferguson (1776-1777)
Thomas Fuller (1776-1780) [31]
Le Roy Hammond (1776-1778)
Daniel Horry (1776-1777,
1778-1780) [31]
Joseph Kershaw (1776-1777)
Henry Laurens (1776-1776) [32]
Rawlins Lowndes
(1776-1778) [33]
Henry Middleton (1755-1775,
1776-1777)
William Moultrie (1776-1780,
1787-1791) [32]
David Oliphant (1776-1776,
1778-1788) [31]
John Parker (1776-1780,
1788-1790) [33]
Charles Pinckney (1776-1780)
George Gabriel Powell
(1738-1742, 1776-1777,
1778-1779)
Richard Richardson (1776-1777,
1778-1780)
Thomas Shubrick (1776-1778)

LATE COLONIAL: REVOLUTIONARY:

Georgia

Governor:
Sir James Wright (1762-1775)

Lt. Governor:
None

Secretary:
James Habersham (1754-1775)

Treasurer:
Noble Jones (1760-1775)

Attorney General:
James Hume (1770-1775)

Chief Justice:
Anthony Stokes (1769-1775)

Assistant Judges:
Elisha Butler (1755-1775)
James Deveaux (1755-1775)
Noble Jones (1754-1756,
   1759-1775)

Councilors:
Grey Elliott (1761-1775)
John Graham (1763-1775)
James Habersham (1754-1775)
James Hume (1772-1775,
   1780-1785) [34]
Lewis Johnston (1764-1775,
   1783-1784) [34]
Noble Jones (1754-1756,
   1759-1775)
James Mackay (1755-1775)
Clement Martin (1755-1775)
James Edward Powell
   (1755-1775)
James Read (1765-1775)
Anthony Stokes (1772-1775)
Henry Yonge (1771-1775)

Note: No Georgia revolutionary executive officers were included in this study. There was no stable revolutionary government in Georgia until after the fighting ended in the 1780s. Actually, more than one government competed for legitimacy during the late 1770s, including a royal government supported by British military units.

Appendix I: Notes

[1] Livius returned to England in 1772, but he was still on the official roles in 1774.

[2] Waldron considered his appointment, and then he finally refused to serve.

[3] John Wentworth (a distant relation of Governor John Wentworth), a man who had already assumed an associate justiceship of the superior court, replaced Waldron.

[4] Adams held the secretary's post as a sinecure.

[5] Since the secretary's position really paid Adams for service to the Continental Congress, John Avery did the actual secretarial work.

[6] Neither Paine nor Reed actually served, even though appointed. Foster and Sullivan replaced them in 1776.

[7] Jones vacated his seat early in 1778 because of ill health. His immediate replacement was Richard Morris.

[8] Morgann was a placeman who never actually filled the office in New Jersey. Charles Pettit carried out the duties as Morgann's resident assistant.

[9] East Jersey treasurer.

[10] West Jersey treasurer.

[11] Both Richard Stockton and John DeHart resigned their appointments to the office before Robert Morris finally accepted it.

[12] Both Hopkinson and Tucker accepted, but they later resigned. Smith and Symmes took their places.

[13] Joseph Reed declined to accept. He preferred to fill a military commission he had at the time.

[14] John Bailey took the place of John Hubley when the latter resigned.

[15] John Evans resigned to accept an appointment to the state supreme court.

[16] Richard Tea did not serve. He was replaced by Jacob Morgan.

[17] There is some confusion as to who actually filled the Delaware attorney generalship. Moore appeared to serve briefly under the new government, but only briefly. Bedford, offered the post in 1779, was technically the first state attorney general.

[18] McWilliams refused the post, and Killen was named in his place.

[19] Caesar Rodney and James Sykes refused to serve because of other offices. Cook and Evans were appointed in their places.

[20] Western shore treasurers.

[21] Eastern shore treasurers. James Hindman replaced his brother William when the latter was elected to the new senate in 1777.

[22] Luther Martin finally accepted the attorney generalship after Thomas Jenings, James Tilghman, and Benjamin Galloway turned down offers to fill the post.

[23] When Thomas Johnson became the first state governor, Charles Grahame was elected to fill his place.

[24] William Hindman finally took a senate seat and left his treasurership when James Tilghman, Edward Tilghman, and Thomas B. Hands refused to accept that particular seat.

[25] Nicholas served until the new government was established. He then relinquished the office to George Webb.

[26] The Virginia revolutionary supreme court consisted of three judges from the general court (G), three from the admiralty court (A), and three from the chancery court (C).

[27] Southern district treasurers.

[28] Northern district treasurers. Samuel Johnston resigned shortly after assuming the office, and William Skinner took his place.

[29] When Leigh returned to England permanently in 1774, Simpson replaced him.

[30] John Murray died early in 1774. William Henry Drayton temporarily filled his position until William Gregory arrived later in 1774.

[31] Fuller and Horry replaced Bee and Oliphant. Thomas Bee took a court appointment, then was later reelected to the legislative council.

[32] When Laurens assumed the vice-presidency, William Moultrie replaced him.

[33] Rawlins Lowndes at first refused to serve. John Parker took his seat.

[34] The last dates for Hume and Johnston refer to their tenure on the East Florida council.

Further Information about Officeholding

The late colonial, loyalist, and revolutionary executives held a variety of offices before moving up the political hierarchy into executive positions, whether before or with the coming of the Revolution. As noted in the second chapter, the prerevolutionary group had greater appointive favor in such offices whereas the revolutionary group had more elective pull. Overall, each of the 487 leaders gained an average of three offices per man before the Revolution turned out so many of the late colonial upper-hierarchy leaders.

Another measure of officeholding has to do with the actual number of offices held *before* the individual took one or more executive positions. For the individual who became a councilor in 1758, we are considering those offices which he filled before that time. For the revolutionary official, we are looking at those positions which he held before becoming an executive in 1776 or 1777. In all cases, including the fifty-two late colonial executives who joined the Revolutionaries, we are investigating the number of other offices before movement into an upper-hierarchy office occurred.

At least two important patterns emerge from the data listed below:

Number of Offices:	Late Colonial:	Loyalist:	Revolutionary:
At least 1	82.5%	79.1%	93.1%
At least 2	52.6	49.3	70.8
At least 3	35.9	31.3	47.1
At least 4	17.1	14.2	25.0
At least 5	8.9	6.7	9.7

First, a greater number of the Revolutionaries had earned political experience in at least one position before becoming an executive. Only 6.9 per cent had not served in at least one other office, as compared to 17.5 per cent of the late colonial and 20.9 per cent of the loyalist leaders. The revolutionary insurgents, second, consistently held more offices per man in terms of raw numbers before personal political mobility occurred. Whereas 25 per cent of the Revolutionaries were in at least four offices, only 17.1 per cent and 14.2 per cent of the late colonial and loyalist executives respectively had a similar numerical range of political experiences. For those revolutionary leaders with such extensive political backgrounds, it may have been a real source of frustration to see men with fewer offices promoted over them into upper-hierarchy positions. Thus such men had to be satisfied with what were mostly lesser positions (see Table 2.1) until the Revolution gave them the opportunity to advance.

Despite the relatively high average age (47.6 years) of those who became revolutionary executives, many moved beyond the particular statewide offices that they acquired in 1776 or 1777. Such a man was John Mathews of South Carolina, who became an assistant circuit court judge (1776–c. 1778). Even though from a respected family, even though a student at the Middle Temple, and even though married into the Charleston elite, Mathews' political career really began when he represented St. George's parish in the first and second provincial congresses. Mathews soon found himself speaker of the first state Assembly under the 1776 constitution, besides holding the assistant judgeship. In 1778 he began four years of service in the Continental Congress; in 1782 he became South Carolina's governor and negotiated the final settlement with the British leading to the evacuation of Charleston. When South Carolina established a chancery court in 1784, Mathews became chancellor, and when the government organized the courts of law and equity in 1791, he remained on as an equity court judge. For a man with restricted political experiences before 1774, Mathews had an extensive career.[1]

The Revolution also burgeoned the careers of Moses Gill of Massachusetts and Silas Condict of New Jersey. Both came from farming families locating in the colonies during the seventeenth century. Moses Gill married well, prospered as a Boston merchant, retreated to Princeton in Worcester County, and built a good-sized mansion. Condict was a commercial farmer and land speculator. Until 1774 Gill confined his political offices to town moderator and selectman. Condict had no identifiable offices. Both were elected to provincial congresses. For Gill his revolutionary stand meant a common pleas court judgeship in 1775, election to the council (1775–1795), the lieutenant governorship from 1795 until he took over as acting governor in 1799, a position he held until he died in 1800. For Condict his association with New Jersey Revolutionaries resulted in a five-year term on the state council (1776–1781), election to the Continental Congress, a common pleas court judgeship, and later in life the Assembly speakership. Neither Gill nor Condict had any reason to regret their decision for revolution. A broad range of new political opportunities characterized their lives after 1776.[2]

Some of the revolutionary insurgents of 1776 lived long enough, or were young enough, to obtain important offices in the national government approved under the Constitution of 1787. Egbert Benson of New York personified this career pattern. Only twenty-eight in 1774, Benson had graduated from King's College in the mid-1760s and studied law in John Morin Scott's law office. In 1772 he opened his own law office in Dutchess County. Almost at once he went with the current of revolution. Benson was active on local and state revolutionary committees. In 1777 he was elected to the first state Assembly and later appointed the state's attorney general (1777–1787). During the 1780s he attended several sessions of the Continental Congress. (So had 26.2 per cent of the other revolutionary insurgents.) Benson agreed with those who wanted a stronger national government than that provided under the Articles of Confederation. He went to the Annapolis Convention in 1786 with Alexander Hamilton and later supported efforts in New York to ratify the 1787 Constitution. His constituents elected him to the first two United States congresses. Later, in February 1801, President John Adams appointed Benson as one of the so-called "midnight" judges. He was to fill the second United States circuit court judgeship, but Jeffersonian-Republicans retracted Adams's work. Benson lived on into the nineteenth century, assuming a state associate justiceship, receiving three doctors of law degrees—Union

College (1779), Harvard (1808), and Dartmouth (1811)—and filling an unexpired congressional term for a few months in 1813. The coming of the Revolution and the formation of a national government had worked well for Benson's political aspirations.[3]

Richard Bassett of Delaware had many points in common with Egbert Benson. He too attended the Annapolis Convention, worked for Delaware's ratification of the Constitution of 1787, and became one of John Adams's "midnight" judges. Just one year older than Benson, Bassett was the son of Michael, a tavern keeper at Bohemia Ferry, Maryland. Michael deserted Richard's mother, and Richard was taken in by a wealthy relative, Peter Lawson, who owned and eventually willed his plantation, Bohemia Manor, to Richard. Bassett's political career commenced with the Revolution. He attended the Delaware state constitutional convention in 1776 and won elections as a state councilor (1776–1780, 1782–1785) besides serving in the military. Delaware voters elected him a United States senator (1789–1799) before he returned to Delaware to fill a two-year term as governor. As a Delaware presidential elector in 1796, Bassett had voted for John Adams, a favor that Adams tried to return four years later. A lawyer and wealthy landholder—Bohemia Manor consisted of six thousand acres—Bassett retired from public life in 1801. A close friend of Bishop Francis Asbury, he had become an enthusiastic Methodist. Until his death in 1815 camp meetings replaced national politics as the prime focus for this revolutionary leader.[4]

Men like Mathews, Gill, Condict, Benson, and Bassett held very few offices before 1776. Generally they were younger than the average revolutionary state executive of 1776 and 1777. The Revolution meant unfettered political opportunity for them as it had for so many other community socioeconomic leaders who had a much wider range of political experiences, generally, though as lesser officials before 1776.

Appendix II: Notes

[1] *South Carolina Historical and Genealogical Magazine* 8 (1907), pp. 36–39; E. Alfred Jones, *American Members of the Inns of Court,* pp. 157–58; *D.A.B.,* XII, pp. 404–5.

[2] For Moses Gill, consult Francis E. Blake, *History of the Town of Princeton* (2 vols., Princeton, 1915), I, pp. 270–77, II, pp. 113–14. For Condict, Jotham H. Condit and Eben Condit, *Genealogical Record of the Condit Family* (Newark, 1885), pp. 172–76; Edmund Drake Halsey, ed., *History of Morris County, New Jersey* (New York, 1882), pp. 26, 32, 75–78, 113, 117, 148.

[3] Benjamin F. Thompson, *History of Long Island* (3 vols., New York, 1918), III, pp. 442–47; *D. A. B.,* II, p. 204.

[4] Robert E. Pattison, "The Life and Character of Richard Bassett," *Papers of the Historical Society of Delaware* 29 (1900), pp. 3–19; *D. A. B.,* II, pp. 39–40.

The Political Fortunes of Loyalist Executives
After the Outbreak of Revolution

Some 92 per cent of the late colonial governors, 75 per cent of the lieutenant governors, 61 per cent of the secretaries, 44 per cent of the treasurers, 93 per cent of the attorneys general, 75 per cent of the chief justices, 45 per cent of the associate justices, and 60 per cent of the councilors who were in office during 1773 and/or 1774 took some sort of a loyalist stand on the Revolution.[1] For most of those who were accused of loyalism or who sought sanctuary behind British lines, the Revolution ended their political careers. Many would live in obscurity for the remainder of their lives, but a few were able to begin anew by soliciting and gaining other appointive posts in the empire. They tended to be the exception, though, rather than the rule.

An excellent example of a prominent prerevolutionary leader who fell from power and never regained political standing was Peter Oliver of Massachusetts. Like Thomas Hutchinson, his crony, friend, and relative, Peter Oliver had a knack for acquiring offices. After a short but successful mercantile partnership with his brother Andrew during the 1730s, Peter retired to Middleborough, Plymouth County. He bought heavily in local real estate, constructed a slitting mill, and became involved in iron manufacturing. He also took political offices. In 1744 he was appointed a justice of the peace. Three years later he joined the county common pleas court, and two years after that he won his first election to the General Court. In 1756 Oliver was elevated to an associate justiceship of the superior court, a position he held until he took the chief justiceship in 1771. Meantime, the General Court began electing Oliver to the council. His political experience was extensive, but open and avowed attachment to the mother country cost him all. Oliver fled to England in 1776 and joined other Massachusetts exiles, including Thomas Hutchinson. The Massachusetts government confiscated his property in 1779 and attainted him. Even though he received some monetary compensation for his property losses from the Loyalists' Claims Commission, he died an unhappy exile in 1791. Oliver's political career ended with the Revolution. Indeed, his natural loyalist stance was a shattering blow economically and socially as well as politically.[2]

Perhaps had Oliver desired, he might have been able to obtain an office in Canada, the Bahamas, or other loyalist strongholds. The last colonial attorney general of Massachusetts, Jonathan Sewall (1767–1774) did. Like Hutchinson and Oliver, he came from old New England stock, but unlike them, he actively sought and received an appointment in 1788 as an admiralty court judge for Nova Scotia and New Brunswick. The admiralty position was at least some compensation for his losses after 1774.[3]

A few of the other late colonial loyalist executives followed Sewall's career pattern. The wealthy lawyer and historian of New York, William Smith, Jr., councilor (1767–1776), became the chief justice of the Nova Scotia supreme court in 1785. Another New Yorker, George D. Ludlow, associate justice (1769–1776), stayed behind British lines around New York City until 1783, then sailed for England. The ministry considered his case and appointed him chief justice of New Brunswick in 1784, besides awarding him a council position. Ludlow was able to recoup his lost fortunes in Canada and died a prosperous landholder in 1808. James Hume, Georgia's last colonial attorney general (1770–1775), likewise was fortunate in continuing his career. He retreated to nearby British strongholds in Florida and involved himself in civil government there. Hume became a member of the council before finally returning to England and receiving £1,525 sterling compensation from the Loyalists' Claims Commission for losses in land and slaves to confiscating insurgents in Georgia.[4]

There were those who were tainted by accusations of unwillingness to defend American liberties, such as Judge William Potter of Rhode Island and William Samuel Johnson of Connecticut. Although they suffered immediate loss of offices, such men were able to begin anew once time removed some of the stigma. Benjamin

Chew, the last proprietary chief justice of Pennsylvania (1774–1776), experienced much the same treatment as Potter and Johnson. The Chews were an old Virginia and Maryland family. Banjamin's father, Dr. Samuel Chew, had a large estate in Maryland; he acted as Delaware's chief justice during the early 1740s. Benjamin was approaching adulthood when his father took the justiceship. Dr. Samuel sent his son first to Philadelphia and then to the Middle Temple in London to study law. Benjamin returned, settled in Dover, Delaware, and practiced law. In 1754 he moved his office to Philadelphia. Through family connections he obtained the attorney generalship (1755–1769) and gained an appointment to the proprietary council (1755–1776) while holding other minor offices. When old Chief Justice William Allen resigned in 1774, Chew took his place. But the Revolution cut his career off. He was not considered trustworthy, and the Continental Congress paroled him to the area of the Union Iron Works in New Jersey. Suffering as a loyalist, Chew made a complete turnabout in 1778 and took an oath of allegiance to the revolutionary Pennsylvania government. He managed to save the remnants of his legal practice. After several more years, the revolutionary air had cleared enough so that in 1791 the former chief justice could become president of the new high court of errors and appeals. He continued in that post until the Assembly abolished the court in 1808, just before his death. Chew's submission, like that of Judge Potter, made it possible for him to hold at least one important office before his death.[5]

The charge of loyalism, however, signaled the end of political careers for most of the late colonial upper-hierarchy leaders. Whether from old families or whether placemen, the outbreak of the Revolution shoved most of them out of the political arena for good. Indeed, if we compare the number of *new offices* which the various groups held after 1776, we find the following pattern:

Number of New Offices:	Late Colonial:	Loyalist:	Revolutionary:
At least 1	31.2%	15.7%	56.2%
At least 2	17.3	5.9	32.8
At least 3	8.2	2.2	16.2

The percentages refer only to positions which had not been held previously by the particular executive, unless relating to an office that a loyalist gained outside the thirteen rebellious provinces after 1776. Thus if a man had been a justice of the peace before 1776 and held the same office under a revolutionary government, the office would not be counted here. As such we are better able to perceive the growing or declining range of offices held by men in each group. Those loyalists who took new offices after 1776 were like William Smith, Jr., of New York who left his colony for England, or like Benjamin Chew of Delaware and Pennsylvania, who recovered from charges of loyalism. The percentages dramatically demonstrate how the Revolution worked to cut off the political ascendancy of upper-hierarchy loyalists while expanding officeholding opportunities for insurgents, even beyond their new-found executive offices of 1776 and 1777. While the latter group now enjoyed untrammeled political mobility, the loyalists had few chances to gain new positions after the overthrow of provincial governments.

Appendix III: Notes

[1] In these percentages loyalism has been tabulated by office rather than by individual. The number of plural officeholders among the loyalists, representing men like Theodore Atkinson of New Hampshire and Thomas Knox Gordon of South Carolina, stand out more strikingly in such percentage figures.

[2] Clifford K. Shipton, *Sibley's Harvard Graduates*, VIII, pp. 737–63; *D. A. B.*, XIV, pp. 22–23. See also the excellent introduction to *Peter Oliver's Origin and Progress of the American Rebellion* by Douglass Adair and John A. Schutz.

[3] Shipton, *Sibley's Harvard Graduates*, XII, pp. 306–25; *D. A. B.*, XVI, pp. 607–8.

[4] For William Smith, Jr., see L. S. F. Upton, *The Loyal Whig;* William A. Benton, *Whig-Loyalism*, pp. 22–28, 182–89, 197–202; *D. A. B.*, XVII, pp. 357–58. For Ludlow, *D. A. B.*, XI, pp. 492–93. For Hume, Wilbur H. Siebert, *Loyalists in East Florida, 1774 to 1785*, Publications of the Florida Historical Society no. 9 (2 vols., Delano, 1929), I, pp. 80–81, II, pp. 37–41, 307; Lorenzo Sabine, *Biographical Sketches of Loyalists*, II, p. 534.

[5] Charles P. Keith, *The Provincial Councilors of Pennsylvania*, pp. 324–31; E. Alfred Jones, *American Members of the Inns of Court*, pp. 44–45; *D. A. B.*, IV, pp. 64–65.

Bibliographical Note

The greatest research obstacle for historians of early America who are interested in the analysis of socioeconomic and political elites is that of incomplete, often fragmentary data. Even for political leaders as visible in the eighteenth-century political arena as the late colonial and revolutionary executives, there are serious record shortages. At times, for instance, I found it quite difficult to find out exactly who was holding what high political office at what time, let alone trying to establish incumbency in lesser offices. Generally, the lives and public careers of a small number of men (those who left letters, diaries, and other materials for posterity and consumption by historians) have been treated with varying quality in numerous essays and biographies. Perhaps some seventy-five to one hundred of the leaders studied in the previous pages fall into that category. Since they preserved records about themselves, they too often are the men upon whom we have constructed our perceptions of the reality of the American Revolution. They include among other individuals Thomas Hutchinson, Peter Oliver, John Adams, Jonathan Trumbull, Cadwallader Colden, Thomas Willing, David Rittenhouse, Caesar Rodney, Daniel Dulany the Younger, Charles Carroll of Carrollton, Patrick Henry, and William Henry Drayton. Thus the primary problem turned out to be that of collecting adequate data about the other 350 to 425 executives, individuals not so well-known. As historical figures they are shrouded in obscurity, despite at least modest levels of prominence and importance in the revolutionary era, because among other reasons they lacked a keen sense of historical preservation.

One major research obstruction was that of determining who the executive officeholders were. Some states have maintained relatively complete listings of colonial and revolutionary governmental leaders. Other extant colony and state records are far from adequate. As offices became less visible, moreover, records were increasingly fragmentary. When all else fails, the researcher should read through the various legislative journals now preserved on microfilm as part of the Early State Records microfilm project. Sometimes, too, commissions issued to those holding particular offices have been microfilmed, depending of course on whether copies survived. For a summary of what is available, consult William S. Jenkins and Lillian A. Hamrick, eds., *Guide to the Microfilm Collection of Early State Records* (Washington, 1950).

But before one turns to this source, the following published materials should be consulted:

Armor, William C. *Lives of the Governors of Pennsylvania, with the Incidental History of the State from 1609 to 1872*. Trenton, 1872.

Bartlett, John R., ed. *Records of the Colony [and State] of Rhode Island and the Providence Plantations, in New England, 1636–1792*. 10 vols. Providence, 1856–1865.

Bouton, Nathaniel, *et al.*, eds. *Documents and Records Relating to the Province, Towns, and State of New Hampshire*. 40 vols. Manchester and Concord, 1867–1943.

Browne, William H., *et al.*, eds. *Archives of Maryland*. 70 vols. Baltimore, 1883 to date.

Candler, Allen D., *et al.*, eds. *The Colonial Records of the State of Georgia*. 26 vols. Atlanta, 1904–1916.

Conner, R. D. W., ed. *A Manual of North Carolina*. Raleigh, 1913.

Conrad, Henry C. *History of the State of Delaware*. 3 vols. Wilmington, 1908.

Cote, Armand H., and Brady, W. Stratton, eds. *Manual with Rules and Orders for the Use of the General Assembly of State of Rhode Island, 1949–1950*. Providence, 1950.

Governor's Register State of Delaware, Volume One: Appointments and Other Transactions by Executives of the State from 1674 to 1851. Wilmington, 1926.

Hoadley, Charles J., *et al.*, eds. *The Public Records of the State of Connecticut*. 9 vols. Hartford, 1894–1953.

Hollister, G. H. *The History of Connecticut*. 2 vols. New Haven, 1835.

Keasbey, Edward Q. *The Courts and Lawyers of New Jersey, 1661–1912*. 3 vols. New York, 1912.

Keith, Charles P. *The Provincial Councilors of Pennsylvania Who Held Office between 1733 and 1776*. Philadelphia, 1883.

Kemmerer, Donald L. *Path to Freedom: The Struggle for Self-Government in Colonial New Jersey, 1703–1776*. Princeton, 1940.

McClintock, John N. *History of New Hampshire.* Boston, 1889.

Reynolds, Emily B., and Raunt, Joan R., eds. *Biographical Directory of the Senate of the State of South Carolina, 1776–1964.* Columbia, 1964.

Roll of Officers and Members of the General Assembly of Connecticut, from 1776 to 1881. Hartford, 1881.

Saunders, William L., *et al.,* eds. *The Colonial [and State] Records of North Carolina.* 40 vols. Raleigh, 1886–1914.

Scharf, J. Thomas. *History of Delaware, 1609–1888.* 2 vols. Philadelphia, 1888.

Smith, Joseph J. *Civil and Military List of Rhode Island, 1647–1800.* Providence, 1900.

Smith, W. Roy. *South Carolina as a Royal Province, 1719–1776.* New York, 1903.

Stanard, William G., and Newton, Mary. *The Colonial Virginia Register.* Albany, 1902.

State of Connecticut: Register and Manual, 1945–1946. Hartford, 1946.

Swem, Earl G., and Williams, John W. *A Register of the General Assembly of Virginia, 1776–1918, and of the Constitutional Conventions.* Richmond, 1918.

Trumbull, J. Hammond, *et al.,* eds. *The Public Records of the Colony of Connecticut.* 15 vols. Hartford, 1850–1890.

Werner, Edgar A. *Civil List and Constitutional History of the Colony and State of New York.* Albany, 1889.

Whitmore, William H. *The Massachusetts Civil List for the Colonial and Provincial Periods, 1630–1774.* Nashua, 1873.

Once I had identified the men in upper-hierarchy offices, the next research problem was to obtain reliable biographical information, especially for those men whose lives have been obscured by the passage of time. Records are scattered, and in some individual cases seemingly nonexistent. The search, then, had to be conducted through countless state, county, and local histories, through various genealogical studies, through scholarly journals, and through published tax lists, and church, court, and probate records. Literally hundreds of local and county histories appeared during the late nineteenth century. Despite filiopietistic overtones, many such studies are immense compilations of otherwise scattered (and perhaps now even lost) data. Genealogies, too, proved to be a rewarding source, although one must guard against the tendency of compilers to overstate family credentials. For an introduction to the most revealing family studies (including genealogical journals), see Fremont Rider, ed., *The American Genealogical Index* (48 vols., Middletown, 1942–1952), and a newer, expanded version by Fremont Rider, *et al.*, eds., *The American Genealogical-Biographical Index to American Genealogical, Biographical, and Local History Materials* (64 vols. to date, Middletown, 1952–   ). Another solid starting point for the provincial years is George N. Mackenzie, *et al.*, eds., *Colonial Families of the United States of America* (7 vols., New York and Baltimore, 1907–1920).

Still other collections of biographical materials are contained in many early issues of state historical journals. Before such publications fell into the pattern of printing scholarly articles and book reviews to the general exclusion of other items, many journals filled their pages with miscellaneous data, including glimpses of the lives of long forgotten local leaders. The most helpful journals, that is in terms of their early issues, include *The Pennsylvania Magazine of History and Biography,* 1877 to date; the *Maryland Historical Magazine,* 1906 to date; *The Virginia Magazine of History and Biography,* 1893 to date; *The North Carolina Historical Review,* 1924 to date; and *The South Carolina Historical Magazine* [formerly titled *The South Carolina Historical and Genealogical Magazine*], 1900 to date. The first series of *The William and Mary Quarterly,* begun in 1891, falls into the same category.

A number of scholarly biographical aids have appeared over the years facilitating the labors of historians probing into socioeconomic and political elites. Although one must be careful because of the factual errors in many selections, the most important general work remains Allen Johnson and Dumas Malone, eds., *Dictionary of American Biography* (22 vols., New York, 1928–1944). Of greater value for the provincial and revolutionary periods is the massive undertaking begun by John Langdon Sibley in the nineteenth century and carried forward in the past several years by Clifford K. Shipton, now titled *Sibley's Harvard Graduates: Biographical Sketches of Those Who Attended Harvard College* (15 vols. to date, Cambridge and Boston, 1873–   ). Of somewhat less merit because of the lack of detail about individual lives is Franklin B.

Dexter, *Biographical Sketches of the Graduates of Yale College with Annals of the College History, 1701–1815* (6 vols., New York and New Haven, 1885–1912). Two other noteworthy collections include E. Alfred Jones, *American Members of the Inns of Court* (London, 1924), and the ongoing *Biographical Directory of the American Congress,* which is periodically brought up to date.

Loyalists in the American Revolution have had their share of superficial biographical treatment. Lorenzo Sabine's *Biographical Sketches of Loyalists of the American Revolution, with an Historical Essay* (2 vols., Boston, 1864) represents the first attempt to preserve information about those on the losing side of the Revolution. Even though the materials often are thin and disorganized, if not misleading, Sabine's was a bold undertaking in the mid-nineteenth century. There are also more modern state studies which too have ample summaries of prominent loyalists. Among the best are Alexander C. Flick, *Loyalism in New York during the American Revolution* (New York, 1902); Robert O. DeMond, *The Loyalists in North Carolina during the Revolution* (Durham, 1940); Harold B. Hancock, *The Delaware Loyalists* (Wilmington, 1940); Isaac S. Harrell, *Loyalism in Virginia* (Philadelphia, 1926); E. Alfred Jones, *The Loyalists in New Jersey* (Newark, 1927); Wilbur H. Siebert, *Loyalists in East Florida, 1774 to 1785* (2 vols., Delano, 1929); and James H. Stark, *The Loyalists of Massachusetts and the Other Side of the Revolution* (New York, 1910).

In the same vein, there is a mixture of biographical collections emphasizing notable state personalities. Some proved to be of assistance in tracking down less well-known provincial and revolutionary leaders. Representative of the better volumes are Samuel A. Ashe, *et al.,* eds., *Biographical History of North Carolina from Colonial Times to the Present* (8 vols., Greensboro, 1908–1925); Charles W. Brewster, *Rambles About Portsmouth: Sketches of Persons, Localities, and Incidents of Two Centuries* (2 vols., Portsmouth, 1859–1869); Thomas A. Glenn, *Some Colonial Mansions and Those Who Lived in Them* (Philadelphia, 1899); Horace Montgomery, ed., *Georgians in Profile: Historical Essays in Honor of Ellis Merton Coulter* (Athens, 1958); William J. Northen, *Men of Mark in Georgia* (6 vols., Atlanta, 1907–1912); Lyon G. Tyler, *Encyclopedia of Virginia Biography* (5 vols., New York, 1915);

and John H. Wheeler, *Historical Sketches of North Carolina from 1584 to 1851* (2 vols., Philadelphia, 1851). It is through such works, much too numerous to list in full here, that the lives and public careers of local men of prominence survive.

Turning to a related subject, there have been innumerable scholarly studies detailing the nature of the eighteenth-century provincial and revolutionary American political culture. Only a few such inquiries stress or see much importance in the organizing concept of political elites, but several were crucial to the formulation of my thoughts about the vital position that the late colonial political elite held in fomenting the coming of the American Revolution. The list that follows is admittedly selective. All of these studies aid in conceptualizing the political culture that characterized eighteenth-century America, and they are offered in this context below:

Abbot, W. W. *The Royal Governors of Georgia.* Chapel Hill, 1959.

Anderson, James L. "The Impact of the American Revolution on the Governor's Councilors," *Pennsylvania History* 34 (1967), pp. 131–46.

Aronson, Sidney H. *Status and Kinship in the Higher Civil Service: Standards of Selection in the Administrations of John Adams, Thomas Jefferson, and Andrew Jackson.* Cambridge, 1964.

Bailyn, Bernard. *The Ideological Origins of the American Revolution.* Cambridge, 1967.

———. *The Origins of American Politics.* New York, 1968.

———. "Political Experience and Enlightenment Ideas in Eighteenth-Century America," *American Historical Review* 67 (1962), pp. 339–51.

———. "Politics and Social Structure in Virginia," *Seventeenth-Century America: Essays in Colonial History,* pp. 90–115. James Morton Smith, ed. Chapel Hill, 1959.

Bargar, B. D. "Lord Dartmouth's Patronage, 1772–1775," *William and Mary Quarterly,* 3rd Sers. 15 (1958), pp. 191–200.

Barrow, Thomas C. "The American Revolution as a Colonial War for Independence," *William and Mary Quarterly,* 3rd Sers. 25 (1968), pp. 452–64.

———. *Trade and Empire: The British Customs Service in Colonial America, 1660–1775.* Cambridge, 1967.

Beard, Charles A. *An Economic Interpretation of the Constitution of the United States.* New York, 1913.

Becker, Carl L. *The History of Political Parties in the Province of New York, 1760–1776.* Madison, 1909.

Benton, William A. "Pennsylvania Revolutionary Officers and the Federal Constitution," *Pennsylvania History* 31 (1964), pp. 419–35.

———. *Whig-Loyalism: An Aspect of Political Ideology in the Ameran Revolutionary Era.* Rutherford, 1969.

Bonomi, Patricia U. *A Factious People: Politics and Society in Colonial New York.* New York, 1971.

Breen, T. H. *The Character of a Good Ruler: A Study of Puritan Political Ideas in New England, 1630–1730.* New Haven, 1970.

Brennan, Ellen C. *Plural Office-Holding in Massachusetts, 1760–1780: Its Relation to the "Separation" of Departments of Government.* Chapel Hill, 1945.

Bridenbaugh, Carl. *Cities in Revolt: Urban Life in America, 1743–1776.* New York, 1955.

———. *Seat of Empire: The Political Role of Eighteenth-Century Williamsburg.* Williamsburg, 1950.

Brown, Richard M. "The Anglo-American Political System, 1675–1775: A Behavioral Analysis," *Anglo-American Political Relations, 1675–1775,* pp. 14–28. Alison G. Olson and Richard M. Brown, eds. New Brunswick, 1970.

Brown, Robert E. *Middle-Class Democracy and the Revolution in Massachusetts, 1691–1780.* Ithaca, 1955.

———, and Brown, B. Katherine. *Virginia, 1705–1786: Democracy or Aristocracy?* East Lansing, 1964.

Brown, Wallace. *The King's Friends: The Composition and Motives of the American Loyalist Claimants.* Providence, 1965.

Buel, Richard, Jr. "Democracy and the American Revolution: A Frame of Reference," *William and Mary Quarterly,* 3rd Sers. 21 (1964), pp. 165–90.

Bushman, Richard L. *From Puritan to Yankee: Character and the Social Order of Connecticut, 1690–1765.* Cambridge, 1967.

Colbourn, H. Trevor. *The Lamp of Experience: Whig History and the Intellectual Origins of the American Revolution.* Chapel Hill, 1965.

Cook, Edward M., Jr. "Local Leadership and the Typology of New England Towns, 1700–1785," *Political Science Quarterly* 86 (1971), pp. 586–608.

———. "Social Behavior and Changing Values in Dedham, Massachusetts, 1700–1775," *William and Mary Quarterly,* 3rd Sers. 27 (1970), pp. 546–80.

Douglass, Elisha P. *Rebels and Democrats: The Struggle for Equal*

Rights and Majority Rule during the American Revolution. Chapel Hill, 1961.

Dunbar, Louise B. "The Royal Governors in the Middle and Southern Colonies on the Eve of the Revolution," *The Era of the American Revolution,* pp. 214–68. Richard B. Morris, ed. New York, 1939.

Eaton, Clement. "A Mirror of the Southern Colonial Lawyer: The Fee Books of Patrick Henry, Thomas Jefferson, and Waightstill Avery," *William and Mary Quarterly,* 3rd Sers. 8 (1951), pp. 520–34.

Elkins, Stanley M., and McKitrick, Eric. "The Founding Fathers: Young Men of the Revolution," *Political Science Quarterly* 76 (1961), pp. 181–216.

Frakes, George E. *Laboratory for Liberty: The South Carolina Legislative Committee System, 1719–1776.* Lexington, 1971.

Freiberg, Malcolm. "How to Become a Royal Governor: Thomas Hutchinson of Massachusetts," *Review of Politics* 21 (1959), pp. 646–56.

Friedman, Bernard. "The Shaping of a Radical Consciousness in Provincial New York," *Journal of American History* 56 (1970), pp. 781–801.

Grant, Charles S. *Democracy in the Connecticut Frontier Town of Kent.* New York, 1961.

Greene, Jack P. "Changing Interpretations of Early American Politics," *The Reinterpretation of Early American History: Essays in Honor of John Edwin Pomfret,* pp. 151–84. Ray A. Billington, ed. San Marino, 1966.

———. "Foundations of Political Power in the Virginia House of Burgesses, 1720–1776," *William and Mary Quarterly,* 3rd Sers. 16 (1959), pp. 485–506.

———. "Political Mimesis: A Consideration of the Historical and Cultural Roots of Legislative Behavior in the British Colonies in the Eighteenth Century," *American Historical Review* 75 (1969), pp. 337–67, including a "Comment" by Bernard Bailyn and a "Reply" by Greene.

———. *The Quest for Power: The Lower Houses of Assembly in the Southern Royal Colonies, 1689–1776.* Chapel Hill, 1963.

———. "The Role of the Lower Houses of Assembly in Eighteenth-Century Politics," *Journal of Southern History* 27 (1961), pp. 451–74.

———. "Search for Identity: An Interpretation of the Meaning of Selected Patterns of Social Response in Eighteenth-Century America," *Journal of Social History* 3 (1970), pp. 189–220.

Griffith, Lucille. *The Virginia House of Burgesses, 1750–1774.* rev. ed. University, Alabama, 1970.

Haffenden, Philip. "Colonial Appointments and Patronage under the Duke of Newcastle, 1723–1739," *English Historical Review* 78 (1963), pp. 417–35.

Hamilton, J. G. de Roulhac. "Southern Members of the Inns of Court," *North Carolina Historical Review* 10 (1933), pp. 273–86.

Harris, P. M. G. "The Social Origins of American Leaders: The Demographic Foundations," *Perspectives in American History,* Vol. III, pp. 159–344. Donald Fleming and Bernard Bailyn, eds. Cambridge, 1969.

Henretta, James A. "Economic Development and Social Structure in Colonial Boston," *William and Mary Quarterly,* 3rd Sers. 22 (1965), pp. 75–92.

———. *"Salutary Neglect": Colonial Administration under the Duke of Newcastle.* Princeton, 1972.

Hutson, James H. "An Investigation of the Inarticulate: Philadelphia's White Oaks," *William and Mary Quarterly,* 3rd Sers. 28 (1971), pp. 3–25.

Jameson, J. Franklin. *The American Revolution Considered as a Social Movement.* Princeton, 1926.

Jensen, Merrill. "The American People and the American Revolution," *Journal of American History* 57 (1970), pp. 5–35.

———. "The American Revolution and American Agriculture," *Agricultural History* 43 (1969), pp. 107–24.

———. "Democracy and the American Revolution," *Huntington Library Quarterly* 20 (1957), pp. 321–41.

———. *The Founding of a Nation: A History of the American Revolution, 1763–1776.* New York, 1968.

Kammen, Michael. *A Rope of Sand: The Colonial Agents, British Politics, and the American Revolution.* Ithaca, 1968.

———. *Deputyes and Libertyes: The Origins of Representative Government in Colonial America.* New York, 1969.

———. *Empire and Interest: The American Colonies and the Politics of Mercantilism.* Philadelphia, 1970.

Katz, Stanley N. *Newcastle's New York: Anglo-American Politics, 1732–1753.* Cambridge, 1968.

Kirby, John B. "Early American Politics—The Search for Ideology: An Historiographical Analysis and Critique of the Concept of Deference," *Journal of Politics* 32 (1970), pp. 808–38.

Klein, Milton M. "Democracy and Politics in Colonial New York," *New York History* 40 (1959), pp. 221–46.

Kulikoff, Allan. "The Progress of Inequality in Revolutionary Boston," *William and Mary Quarterly*, 3rd Sers. 28 (1971), pp. 375–412.

Labaree, Benjamin W. *Patriots and Partisans: The Merchants of Newburyport, 1764–1815*. Cambridge, 1962.

Labaree, Leonard W. *Conservatism in Early American History*. New York, 1948.

————. *Royal Government in America: A Study of the British Colonial System before 1783*. New Haven, 1930.

Land, Aubrey C. "Economic Base and Social Structure: The Northern Chesapeake in the Eighteenth Century," *Journal of Economic History* 25 (1965), pp. 639–54.

————. "Economic Behavior in a Planting Society: The Eighteenth-Century Chesapeake," *Journal of Southern History* 33 (1967), pp. 469–85.

Leder, Lawrence H. *Liberty and Authority: Early American Political Ideology, 1689–1763*. Chicago, 1968.

Lemisch, Jesse. "The American Revolution Seen from the Bottom Up," *Towards a New Past: Dissenting Essays in American History*, pp. 3–45. Barton J. Bernstein, ed. New York, 1967.

————. "Jack Tar in the Streets: Merchant Seamen in the Politics of Revolutionary America," *William and Mary Quarterly*, 3rd Sers. 25 (1968), pp. 371–407.

Lemon, James T., and Nash, Gary B. "The Distribution of Wealth in Eighteenth-Century America: A Century of Change in Chester County, Pennsylvania, 1693–1802," *Journal of Social History* 2 (1968), pp. 1–24.

Lincoln, Charles H. *The Revolutionary Movement in Pennsylvania, 1760–1776*. Philadelphia, 1901.

Lockridge, Kenneth A. *A New England Town: The First Hundred Years*. New York, 1970.

————, and Kreider, Alan. "The Evolution of Massachusetts Town Government, 1640 to 1740," *William and Mary Quarterly*, 3rd Sers. 23 (1966), pp. 549–74.

————. "Land, Population, and the Evolution of New England Society, 1630–1790," *Past and Present* 39 (1968), pp. 62–80.

Lokken, Roy N. "The Concept of Democracy in Colonial Political Thought," *William and Mary Quarterly*, 3rd Sers. 16 (1959), pp. 568–80.

Lovejoy, David S. *Rhode Island Politics and the American Revolution, 1760–1776*. Providence, 1958.

Lucas, Paul. "A Note on the Comparative Study of the Structure of

Politics in Mid-Eighteenth-Century Britain and Its American Colonies," *William and Mary Quarterly,* 3rd Sers. 28 (1971), pp. 301–9.

Lynd, Staughton. *Class Conflict, Slavery, and the United States Constitution: Ten Essays.* Indianapolis, 1967.

McAnear, Beverly. *The Income of the Colonial Governors of British North America.* New York, 1967.

McDonald, Forrest. *We the People: The Economic Origins of the Constitution.* Chicago, 1958.

Macmillan, Margaret B. *The War Governors in the American Revolution.* New York, 1943.

Maier, Pauline. *From Resistance to Revolution: Colonial Radicals and the Development of Opposition to Britain, 1765–1776.* New York, 1972.

————. "Popular Uprisings and Civil Authority in Eighteenth-Century America," *William and Mary Quarterly,* 3rd Sers. 27 (1970), pp. 3–35.

Main, Jackson T. "Government by the People: The American Revolution and the Democratization of the Legislatures," *William and Mary Quarterly,* 3rd Sers. 23 (1966), pp. 391–407.

————. "The One Hundred," *William and Mary Quarterly,* 3rd Sers. 11 (1954), pp. 354–84.

————. "Social Origins of a Political Elite: The Upper House in Revolutionary America," *Huntington Library Quarterly* 27 (1964), pp. 147–58.

————. *The Social Structure of Revolutionary America.* Princeton, 1965.

————. *The Upper House in Revolutionary America, 1763–1788.* Madison, 1967.

Martin, James Kirby. "A Model for the Coming American Revolution: The Birth and Death of the Wentworth Oligarchy in New Hampshire, 1741–1776," *Journal of Social History* 4 (1970), pp. 41–60.

————. "Men of Family Wealth and Personal Merit: The Changing Social Basis of Executive Leadership Selection in the American Revolution," *Societas—A Review of Social History* 2 (1972), pp. 43–70.

Merritt, Bruce G. "Loyalism and Conflict in Revolutionary Deerfield, Massachusetts," *Journal of American History* 57 (1970), pp. 277–89.

Morgan, Edmund S. "The American Revolution Considered as an Intellectual Movement," *Paths of American Thought,* pp. 11–33.

Arthur M. Schlesinger, Jr., and Morton White, eds. New York, 1963.

Morgan, Edmund S. "The Puritan Ethic and the American Revolution," *William and Mary Quarterly,* 3rd Sers. 24 (1967), pp. 3–43.

Morris, Richard B. *The American Revolution Reconsidered.* New York, 1967.

Murrin, John M. "The Legal Transformation: The Bench and Bar of Eighteenth-Century Massachusetts," *Essays in Politics and Social Development: Colonial America,* pp. 415–49. Stanley N. Katz, ed. Boston, 1971.

———. "The Myths of Colonial Democracy and Royal Decline in Eighteenth-Century America: A Review Essay," *Cithara* 5 (1965), pp. 53–69.

Namier, Lewis, *England in the Age of the American Revolution.* 2nd ed. New York, 1966.

———. *The Structure of Politics at the Accession of George III.* 2nd ed. New York, 1965.

Nash, Gary B. *Quakers and Politics: Pennsylvania, 1681–1726.* Princeton, 1968.

Nelson, William H. *The American Tory.* New York, 1961.

Owings, Donnell M. *His Lordship's Patronage: Offices of Profit in Colonial Maryland.* Baltimore, 1953.

Palmer, R. R. *The Age of the Democratic Revolution: A Political History of Europe and America, 1760–1800.* 2 vols. Princeton, 1959–1964.

Pares, Richard. *King George III and the Politicians.* Oxford, 1953.

Pocock, J. G. A., "Machiavelli, Harrington, and English Political Ideologies in the Eighteenth Century," *William and Mary Quarterly,* 3rd Sers. 22 (1965), pp. 549–83.

Pole, J. R. "Historians and the Problem of Early American Democracy," *American Historical Review* 67 (1962), pp. 626–46.

———. *Political Representation in England and the Origins of the American Republic.* London, 1966.

Rainbolt, John C. "The Alteration in the Relationship between Leadership and Constituents in Virginia, 1660 to 1720," *William and Mary Quarterly,* 3rd Sers. 27 (1970), pp. 411–34.

Robbins, Caroline. *The Eighteenth-Century Commonwealthman.* Cambridge, 1958.

Schutz, John A. "Succession Politics in Massachusetts, 1730–1741," *William and Mary Quarterly,* 3rd Sers. 15 (1958), pp. 508–20.

Sirmans, M. Eugene. *Colonial South Carolina: A Political History, 1663–1763.* Chapel Hill, 1966.

————. "The South Carolina Royal Council, 1720–1763," *William and Mary Quarterly,* 3rd Sers. 18 (1961), pp. 373–92.

Sosin, Jack M. *Agents and Merchants: British Colonial Policy and the Origins of the American Revolution, 1763–1775.* Lincoln, 1965.

Sweet, William W. "The Role of Anglicanism in the American Revolution," *Huntington Library Quarterly* 11 (1947), pp. 51–70.

Sydnor, Charles S. *Gentlemen Freeholders: Political Practices in Washington's Virginia.* Chapel Hill, 1952.

Thompson, Mack E. "The Ward-Hopkins Controversy and the American Revolution in Rhode Island: An Interpretation," *William and Mary Quarterly,* 3rd Sers. 16 (1959), pp. 363–75.

Walett, Francis G. "The Massachusetts Council, 1766–1774: The Transformation of a Conservative Institution," *William and Mary Quarterly,* 3rd Sers. 6 (1949), pp. 605–27.

Waters, John J., Jr. *The Otis Family in Provincial and Revolutionary Massachusetts.* Chapel Hill, 1968.

————, and Schutz, John A. "Patterns of Massachusetts Colonial Politics: The Writs of Assistance and the Rivalry between the Otis and Hutchinson Families," *William and Mary Quarterly,* 3rd Sers. 24 (1967), pp. 543–67.

Weir, Robert M. " 'The Harmony We Were Famous For': An Interpretation of Pre-Revolutionary South Carolina Politics," *William and Mary Quarterly,* 3rd Sers. 26 (1969), pp. 473–501.

Wickwire, Franklin B. *British Subministers and Colonial America, 1763–1783.* Princeton, 1966.

Williamson, Chilton. *American Suffrage from Property to Democracy, 1760–1860.* Princeton, 1960.

Wood, Gordon S. *The Creation of the American Republic, 1776–1787.* Chapel Hill, 1969.

————. "Rhetoric and Reality in the American Revolution," *William and Mary Quarterly,* 3rd Sers. 23 (1966), pp. 3–32.

Wright, Louis B. *The First Gentlemen of Virginia: Intellectual Qualities of the Early Colonial Ruling Class.* San Marino, 1940.

Zemsky, Robert M. *Merchants, Farmers, and River Gods: An Essay on Eighteenth-Century American Politics.* Boston, 1971.

————. "Power, Influence, and Status: Leadership Patterns in the Massachusetts Assembly, 1740–1755," *William and Mary Quarterly,* 3rd Sers. 26 (1969), pp. 502–20.

Zuckerman, Michael. *Peaceable Kingdoms: New England Towns in the Eighteenth Century.* New York, 1970.

Zuckerman, Michael. "The Social Context of Democracy in Massachusetts," *William and Mary Quarterly,* 3rd Sers. 25 (1968), pp. 523–44.

Finally, there were a number of studies which greatly abetted the
theoretical formulation of this investigation. Sidney Aronson's *Status and Kinship in the Higher Civil Service: Standards of Selection
in the Administrations of John Adams, Thomas Jefferson, and Andrew Jackson* (Cambridge, 1964), served as a model example of
collective biography. Harry Eckstein "On the Etiology of Internal
Wars," *History and Theory* 4 (1964), pp. 133–63, although addressed to European revolutions, made the critical distinction between "preconditions" and "precipitants" of rebellions. Eckstein,
too, suggests that European revolutions often should be assessed as
clashes among elite groups. Bernard Bailyn, "Politics and Social
Structure in Virginia," *Seventeenth-Century America: Essays in
Colonial History,* ed. James Morton Smith (Chapel Hill, 1959), pp.
90–115, discussed Nathaniel Bacon's attempted coup in Virginia
against Governor William Berkeley in terms of growing disequilibrium within the Virginia leadership elite. Indeed, the rebellions
within the American provinces during the late seventeenth century
all may be profitably analyzed within this context. Bailyn's "Communications and Trade: The Atlantic in the Seventeenth Century,"
Journal of Economic History 13 (1953), pp. 378–87, was suggestive of the distinction between merchants functioning in primary
and secondary orbits of trade. Ivo K. Feierabend, *et al.,* "Social
Change and Political Violence: Cross-National Patterns," *The History of Violence in America: A Report to the National Commission on the Causes and Prevention of Violence,* ed. Hugh D. Graham and Ted R. Gurr (New York, 1969), pp. 632–87,
demonstrated the need to perceive the impact of high levels of education upon expectations and the resulting tensions which emerge
in political systems when well-educated individuals find it next to
impossible to balance achievements with expectations. Samuel P.
Hays, "Political Parties and the Community-Society Continuum,"
The American Party Systems: Stages of Political Development, ed.
William N. Chambers and Walter D. Burnham (New York, 1967),
pp. 152–81, underscored the important relationship between lev-

els of officeholding, perceptions of political reality, and political behavior.

One subject that historians should pursue in the future is that of the comparative analysis of revolutions. Crane Brinton, *The Anatomy of Revolution* (New York, 1938), broke ground through a descriptive study of stages in four major modern revolutions. Indirectly, the work of Brinton has been carried forward by Hannah Arendt, *On Revolution* (New York, 1963), and by R. R. Palmer, *The Age of the Democratic Revolution: A Political History of Europe and America, 1760–1800* (2 vols., Princeton, 1959–1964). More systematic comparisons must be made, however, especially in terms of causation. Suggestive of new directions is Robert Forster and Jack P. Greene, eds., *Preconditions of Revolution in Early Modern Europe* (Baltimore, 1970), containing five theoretical and comparative essays by distinguished scholars of European social and political change. Of particular value are the selections by J. W. Smit on "The Netherlands Revolution," and by Lawrence Stone on "The English Revolution."

Index

ABOUT THE AUTHOR

James Kirby Martin is Assistant Provost for Administration and a member of the history faculty at Rutgers University. He was graduated summa cum laude *from Hiram College and holds the M.A. and Ph.D. degrees from the University of Wisconsin, where he held an N.D.E.A. Title IV fellowship from 1965 to 1968 and was a teaching assistant in 1968 and 1969. He has published articles in* Ohio History, Journal of Social History, *and* Societas—A Review of Social History, *and he is the editor of* Interpreting Colonial America: Selected Readings.

The text of this book was set in Times Roman Linofilm and printed by offset on Kenlyn Off-set supplied by Lindenmeyr Paper Corpora-tion, Long Island City, N.Y. Composed, printed and bound by Vail-Ballou Press, Inc., Binghamton, N.Y.

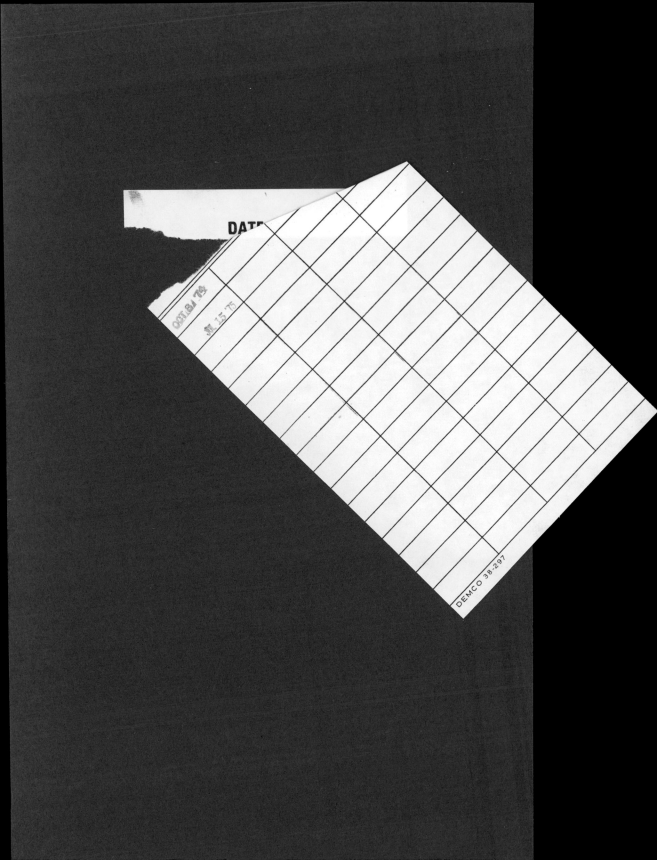